Dedicated to my loving wife,
constant companion and No. 1 driver Rosemary.

* * *

Acknowledgements

With thanks to:

Trevor Bottomley a supportive boss who gave me every encouragement at the start of my career and who ultimately inspired me to write this book.

In Botswana to Sandy and Elinah Grant for their help and advice about all matters local. To John Gaetsaloe and Patrick Van Rensberg for making time to meet again after 40 years. To Violet Mosele and all those we met in the Botswana Co-ops for their time and interest in my return visit.

In particular to my wife Rosemary for her encouragement on what has proven to be a long project and for her proof reading - although any remaining mistakes either factual or grammatical are entirely mine.

Bernard Le Bargy
March 2008

Back to the Bush

Bernard Le Bargy

Pen Press Publishing Ltd

First published in Great Britain by
Pen Press Publishers Ltd
25 Eastern Place
Brighton
BN2 1GJ

ISBN 978-1-906206-86-4

Printed and bound in UK by Cpod, Trowbridge, Wiltshire

A catalogue record of this book is available from
the British Library

Cover design Damian Le Bargy

Contents

Prologue

No sooner had I put the telephone down than I found myself leaping up the stairs two at a time and then clambering up the ladder that leads to the loft space in the roof.

Here I am now, in the half-light produced by a single 60-watt bulb, rummaging through the accumulated bits of long since discarded old furniture and assorted paraphernalia. I am looking for the brown tin box. Here it is. I clumsily fiddle with the metal catch until it springs open. Inside the box in neat piles are packages, each painstakingly labelled, dated and retained by a thick rubber band. Rosie periodically says, 'Bernard, you are such an anorak keeping that old junk in the loft.' Although not by nature a hoarder, and admittedly the contents rarely if ever see the light of day, they are important to me. Each package contains photographs, postcards, brochures and other memorabilia from journeys past. Today they are not the objects of my search.

I continue to delve through the contents of the box and at last, at the very bottom, a brown manila envelope. I open it and spread the contents – 20 or so photographs of different shapes and sizes – across the bare wooden floor. I pick up one particular photograph. It is of a young man. Clean-shaven, fresh faced and aged around 20. The hair cut short, a little too severely I am thinking. He is smartly dressed in shirt, tie and a double-breasted suit. Although taken outdoors, neither the backdrop, nor indeed his mode of dress, provide many clues as to when or where it might have been taken.

I turn the photograph over. Holding it to the dim light I can read, written in faint pencil and now barely legible, the words 'Gaberones, September 1966'. It is a picture of me.

Although I am alone in the house I shout out loud, 'I'm going back to Africa.'

Although the genuine euphoria of that moment soon passed, the decision was made.

It had all happened in a blur. Minutes before, I had answered my telephone. The caller introduced himself.

'Bernard, you probably don't know me but this is Derek Heffer.'

I'd never met him but his name was vaguely familiar and my brain must have gone into overdrive as I recalled that he had worked in Africa sometime after me.

'Derek, yes I do actually know who you are.'

We exchanged some small talk but in essence Derek's message was simple:

'Trevor wants you to call him; here is the number.'

Intrigued, but slightly embarrassed that I had lost contact with my old boss and mentor from all those years ago, I had immediately picked up the telephone again and dialled.

It had been something close to 40 years since we had spoken, yet as soon as he came on the line I had immediately recognised the distinctive tone and turn of phrase.

'Trevor, it's Bernard Le Bargy.'

'Bernard, how the devil are you?'

'I'm fine. I heard you wanted to talk to me.'

'Yes, I did put some feelers out. The jungle drums have obviously been working overtime. Look, I've written a book and you are in it.'

'I'm flattered, I think.'

'Don't worry, old chap, I've only said nice things about you. Look, as you are in the book I will send you a gratis copy.'

Only later, on reflection, did I appreciate that my reaction following those telephone calls was so out of character. But I was content. I took it as an omen.

As an inveterate traveller I have a little rule: 'Never go back'. It is quite irrational. The first time Rosie, my wife, and I visited New York as part of a touring holiday along the eastern seaboard of the United States, we decided that it being our first visit, and the city at that time having an unenviable reputation for street crime, we would stay 'out of town' and commute in for a little sightseeing. We checked into a hotel some miles to the north in the genteel sounding town of

Sleepy Hollow set beside the Hudson River. The next day we took a train into New York City, arriving at Grand Central Station in the middle of a warm summer morning. We had walked about 100 yards down Park Avenue, barely having had time to take breath at the sight of the awesome skyscrapers or to come to terms with the city hustle and bustle, when there was a tremendous kerfuffle. We were aware of people running and shouting and then suddenly, just feet away, was a policeman, gun drawn, aimed at the head of a man, arms and feet splayed against a wall. This small incident left me nervous and wary for the rest of my visit and consequently ill disposed towards New York.

That would have been that. Indeed, after that first visit I often asked the question 'why do so many people love New York?' I hated it and would have continued to do so because of my 'never go back' rule. Subsequently I have had to go back to New York several more times, not out of choice but on business trips over which I had no control. As a consequence I now feel more at one with the city. It's all so obvious really: it's about local knowledge. On each of those visits I have added to my familiarity with the city: the things to see, well at least those in Manhattan; where to stay; where to eat; the direction of the streets and avenues; and, importantly, which areas that it is best to avoid. What's more, there have been no more frightening incidents. Today I am quite well disposed towards the idea that New York is indeed one of the world's great cities.

So you can see that my 'never go back' rule is silly because visiting a place only once means you invariably get a very superficial and often distorted feel for the place. At least I recognise that my rule is a nonsense and do make exceptions. Venice, for example, which I think is special, both unique and fascinating. And Paris – I avoided it for years, but once I had been there I was smitten. Every trip produces something new to see and experience and right on my doorstep.

Yet despite knowing it to be nonsense, I still try and keep to my no going back rule because this planet of ours is so big, with so much to see. I have reached an age where I sense that for me time is running out and with so little time left in which to visit all the places I want to see, I feel I cannot afford to keep going back to the same places.

Not that I am foolish enough to think that my philosophy will suit everybody. Many prefer their own comfort zone and being able to relax in familiar surroundings. This need for the familiar has at least in part fuelled the boom in buying properties abroad and even the time-share market. A prime example of this was Roger, a former business colleague of mine, finance director of a major company and by the standards of the average person, extremely highly paid. When he was first married more than 20 years ago, and a struggling, not-yet-qualified accountant, he and his wife took their first summer holiday together and stayed at a small family hotel in Dorset. Every year since, and despite the arrival of a family and latterly his appointment to highly paid employment, he has returned to holiday at the same hotel during the same week in July. It takes all sorts.

They say rules are made to be broken and so much for my personal tenet of 'never go back'. Standing there in the loft, in an instant, without thinking, it is broken.

Trevor had taken that photograph as we said our goodbyes on the dusty airstrip at Gaberones all those years ago. Now as I gaze at myself as a young man, the thought occurs, what if Trevor has written my book? It is churlish of me, after all it was the first time we had spoken to each other since that long, long, long ago day.

At the end of our conversation Trevor had taken a note of my address and, true to his word, a small parcel arrived two days later containing a copy of his book and a charming note that reminded me of his kindness and generosity to me all those years ago. My fears were soon allayed – it wasn't my book, and of course it couldn't be. It was his biography and I featured quite appropriately as a bit-part player. Trevor is now into his eighties, so naturally the chapter that covered the year I had spent working with him in Bechuanaland was but a very small part of his story.

Reassured and reflective, I decided that instead of feeling any sense of disappointment somebody I knew had actually written about events we had shared, I let this be the inspiration to get on and write my book.

I had been developing the idea in my mind over the previous

year as I contemplated getting away from the stresses of big business – a desire compounded by the arrival of a new, and from my perspective, overbearing boss. I had spent six highly rewarding years working for the charming and charismatic Sir Colin Chandler. In just five years we had turned Vickers, a famous but ailing old British manufacturing company, from huge losses into profit. Even a sceptical City was impressed. Now Sir Colin had changed role, becoming company chairman, to be replaced as chief executive by the autocratic Belgian, Baron Buysse.

I have to put my hand up and say that I was in part responsible for my own predicament. In my role as personnel director I had helped recruit the man who was now my nemesis. What had I done to deserve this? Fluent and articulate in what was his third language, he had charmed his way into the job but he brought a management style redolent more of Genghis Khan than from the recommended texts of the Harvard Business Review. A large man with a florid complexion, he was never far from exploding into a million miniscule parts.

When he first arrived to take over his new role he explained that he was a chevalier, the Belgian equivalent of a knighthood; but with a duke, a lord and a sir already on the board this didn't really 'cut the mustard'. Nobody in the company was sufficiently impressed to start addressing him as other than Mister Buysse. However, we were to be confounded and within weeks of his arrival he announced that he was now a baron, a rare honour bestowed upon him by his personal friend, the King of the Belgians. Clearly he was not a man to be trifled with. He also introduced his 'aide de camp', a fellow Belgian who proved to be the most phenomenally highly paid 'gofer' I have ever met. Suddenly doors to strategy and decision making closed. It was a new and unhappy regime.

Worst of all was the bullying. Every executive took turns at suffering, but two colleagues, Tom and Ingar, were particularly harshly treated in a way that left the rest of the executive team cringing as their performance was surgically dissected in front of the rest of the senior management team. I kept my distance from the baron until, out of total frustration, he called me to his office one day to announce, 'I don't know what you do.' I took it as an essential part of my strategy to wind him up by not enlightening him.

It was not a happy time and before long I began thinking to the future, about taking early retirement, to travel and about writing my book. Thanks to the chairman and other supporters on the board, the baron hadn't got around to sacking me and I hadn't got around to telling him where to stick his job when, suddenly and unexpectedly, by some quirk of fate, the decision was taken out of our hands. The company had been taken over. Now we were both out of work. At least I had the satisfaction of knowing he was the first out of the door whilst I had several more months' tenure as the new owners asked for my help in integrating their new acquisition into their own businesses.

That job successfully completed, I found that I had time on my hands to plan and carry out my trip and to write my book, free at last from the pressures of executive responsibility: the travelling away from home, the ten-hour working days and daily four-hour commute. The excuses for not getting down to the task sounded ever weaker as the obstacles in my way were evaporating.

In the mid-sixties I had spent a character-forming year on voluntary service in Africa. During that year I had enjoyed exciting experiences and met some exceptional people in what was a very poor country that we described as the Under-developed or Third World. Although voluntary service was to become a well-trodden path for young people, at the time my fellow volunteers and me were trailblazers for a totally new idea in community service. To-day planet earth is a much smaller place and youngsters in their gap year or fresh out of university can literally travel around the world with nothing more than a backpack, a few pounds in their pockets and an air ticket purchased in some bucket shop for just a few pounds. Not forgetting, of course, the obligatory mobile phone to keep in touch with home and to provide the lifeline of tapping up the 'old man' for some more money if it runs out in some obscure far-flung part of the globe.

From what I had read, the country that had been my home for that year, now called Botswana, has developed into one of the few stable democracies on the African continent and has enjoyed unexpected economic prosperity. How and why? I wanted to answer those questions, but most of all, to find out what had happened to those people most influential all those years ago in shaping my own view of the world.

Chapter One

Going Back

Despite the good intentions nearly five years have passed since that telephone conversation with Trevor. At last here I am, looking down from my vantage point through the small cabin window of a noisy South African Airways turbo-prop, just 16,000 ft above the arid landscape at the end of a Southern African winter, casting my mind back four decades to when I first made this same journey from England. Memory is an amazing repository of one's past, but mine at least is a damn aggravating and at times unreliable organ. As hard as I try, I find that I can recall only fragments of that first trip, and then often small and inconsequential detail. Whatever the frustrations these gaps in recall present, I have to acknowledge that by any measure 40 years is one hell of a long time during which, quite typically, I have experienced courtship, marriage, fatherhood, divorce and the development of a new and hopefully enduring relationship. Not to mention the parallel universe of career with its promotions, new jobs and inevitable crises and disappointments.

However, now my journey of rediscovery has at last begun, I am confident that as it unfolds there will be memory joggers which will open deep recesses of my brain to long lost recollections of my time here in Africa in the mid-sixties.

Now I am concentrating I do recall a problem: me on board an aircraft for the first time in my life unsuccessfully trying to secure my safety belt and being helped by the businessman in the adjacent seat. As a young man I suffered terribly in embarrassing situations, blushing, from the neck up, a deep red, the colour of beetroot. This was one such occasion. Only a few weeks ago flying from Edinburgh to London I sat next to a clearly panic-stricken young girl of maybe 16 or 17 covered in the same confusion. In a role reversal I was able to offer assistance, reassuring; perhaps I hadn't been quite as stupid as I felt all those years ago.

On that first journey to Africa I flew from Heathrow in one of BOAC's (what is now British Airways) newly commissioned fleet of VC10s, little realising that by one of those little quirks of fate, some 30 years later I would reach the pinnacle of my working life by becoming the personnel director of the Vickers company, manufacturers of that then state-of-the-art airliner.

For sure, memory seems to suggest that legroom was more generous on that VC10 than on the modern aeroplane. Perhaps in that bygone age the airlines had yet to invent a class system in air travel? After all, flying in the sixties was still very much a rich man's luxury; we were at the very dawning of mass-market air travel for ordinary folk. When I came to check this out I discovered that early as 1952 BOAC had actually been the first airline to introduce Tourist Class, the now popular device to squeeze 150 seats in a space designed for 100. By the sixties BOAC had renamed this, using the rather North American sounding term, Skycoach. So I cannot be sure whether I travelled in Business Class or Skycoach. I was just happy to be travelling.

Today, despite the claims that we live in a classless society, in air travel the distinctions have never been clearer in respect of food and service, comfort and level of fares. The airlines still use fancy labels: Skycoach is now Economy but in my lexicon you fall into one of the categories 'cattle class', 'corporate expense account' or 'serious money'. One thing I do remember is that at the time I felt enormously privileged to have the chance to fly to such a far distant place at someone else's expense. I travelled with a genuine sense of 'you are a lucky boy; better make the best of the opportunity'.

Strangely, I am facing this journey with more trepidation than I felt all those years ago. Experience gives one the certain knowledge that travel generates huge amounts of stress and requires one to be ready to tackle uncertainty and the unexpected. When you're young you are imbued with the spirit of adventure and go with the flow, totally unaware of the potential pitfalls along the way. As I get older I get ever more certain that flights will be delayed, that we will encounter turbulence en route, there will be interminable queues at Immigration Control, connections will be missed and luggage lost.

Today was no exception. A four-hour wait at Johannesburg International Airport and moving between and around the terminal buildings laden with suitcases, we felt a little vulnerable. *We?* I had envisaged this as a solo trip and my wife, Rosemary, had encouraged my project to the extent of starting a fund for the trip with a £500 birthday present. That was over a year ago and perhaps I am showing signs of my age or perhaps she thinks she might be missing out, but sometime during the planning phase we started discussing this as a joint venture. From wanting to go it alone I completely changed my stance. I have become convinced that it is an experience we should share. And here we are, travelling together.

We start our descent into Gaberone and I am straining to see if there are any landmarks that are familiar, but already it is apparent that the city is unrecognisable from the one I left behind nearly 40 years ago. Where there had been an embryonic seat of government for the newly independent Botswana, set in virgin bush and populated by 3,000 or so people, most of them civil servants, now a city of a quarter of a million souls. I can see wide avenues filled with traffic, some high-rise buildings, but mostly what appear to be row after row of what I guess are low-cost houses. It's big, it's modern but even from where I am sitting I can see that it isn't pretty.

The non-stop flight from London to Johannesburg now takes around 11 hours. Back in the sixties it took considerably longer, not least because the plane stopped several times en route to re-fuel. In 1965 my plane called at Frankfurt, Rome, Nairobi and Salisbury before reaching its eventual destination. At Nairobi I remember leaving the aircraft and setting foot in Africa for the first time. Compared with what we expect today the term 'airport' would be something of an exaggeration; it comprised nothing more than a shed with a corrugated roof. Inside was unbearably hot – air-conditioning then a technology known only to the Americans. I hastily retreated back through the doorway, seeking the comfort of the shade and any wisp of breeze blowing across the parched landscape. Everything was brown and dry. As first impressions go, Africa wasn't up there with Sydney Harbour or the Manhattan Skyline, although to be honest at the time I had seen neither so wasn't in a position to judge. More relevant comparisons for me were Romford, Stratford and Bethnal Green, stations that I had passed on my way to catch the plane at Heathrow and by that measure this was all very strange.

Soon after taking off from Nairobi, as we continued our journey south, the pilot came on to the public address system, 'Ladies and gentlemen, we are flying over Mount Kilimanjaro. If you look out of the right-hand side of the aircraft you will see something quite spectacular.' I unbuckled my safety belt and clambered across to look through the window on the opposite side of the aircraft. There, thousands of feet below, the extraordinary sight of an active volcano spewing out smoke and molten lava. Even this recollection is overlaid by the enduring memory that the sighting was brief. Not entirely having come to terms with looking out of an aeroplane window flying five miles above the ground, I desperately wanted to see the volcano but was quickly overcome by an even stronger desire to quickly return to the relative security of my seat. In a very short time span we had moved from one deeply unimpressive to one unforgettable view of Africa.

Eventually my plane landed at Johannesburg's Jan Smuts Airport late in the afternoon. I had been given directions to find my way across the city to catch the overnight sleeper north. Although tired and apprehensive indelibly etched on the consciousness was for the first time facing the reality of apartheid, with signs 'Whites only' in English or 'Slegs blankes' in the unfamiliar Afrikaans. Suddenly in this strange and unfamiliar world I was overcome with the fear of taking the wrong entrance or corridor in case it was for 'blacks' or even for 'coloureds', having no comprehension as to the difference, and being scared as to the dire consequences from the 'regime' that I had just encountered for the first time in the shape of the formidably large and strange accented immigration officer. Are all Dutchmen 6 ft plus and built like the proverbial barn door? No. So how come their descendants who chose to emigrate to Southern Africa all appear to conform to this stereotype? Formalities completed, in this strangely bewildered state, I made my way from the airport to the railway station, although today I have no recall whatsoever as to how. My instructions were to board the overnight train to Bulawayo. Odd how parts of the same journey remain vivid, yet others are a complete blank.

Images from the remainder of my journey are clearer. The train compartment was designated First Class but had a distinct feel of Victorian austerity with dark panelling and a hard seat covered in leather. As I was to discover in the course of the next year trundling up and down this same line as it made its way through the eastern side of what was then the British Protectorate of Bechuanaland, this small confined space always had the benefit of feeling cool despite the outside temperature, which could easily reach 35°C, although not sufficiently cool to stop your underpants and shirt sticking glue-like to the skin. It was this experience, I am sure, that led in later life to my antipathy towards leather car seats despite the cost suggesting that they are a 'must have' luxury extra. The caution above the compartment door offered a chilling warning: 'Do not expectorate' and caused me much bemusement until some considerable time later when I was able to refer to a dictionary to discover it meant 'Do not spit'.

There were no other passengers in the compartment to quiz about the length of the journey or to tell me about the area through which we were travelling. I was alone save for the occasional visit by the conductor, with what I soon began to appreciate was a heavy Afrikaans accent, who provided a pillow and blanket for the night but with whom any form of serious communication seemed beyond my capacity, although I felt sure that he was of the opinion that the language he was speaking was English. It was typical of those iniquities of the apartheid system that at one end of the train the carriages designated First Class and Second Class were for use only by whites and were invariably all but empty. Towards the rear in Third Class and Fourth Class, travelling in acute discomfort, were hundreds of people with black skins invariably encumbered with battered suitcases, brown paper parcels crudely tied with string, or large bundles wrapped in sheets. In one train two quite different worlds.

Despite the fatigue of already being into my second day of travelling, through the night I dozed fitfully. A combination, I am sure, of excitement about the adventure upon which I was embarking, apprehension about entering the unknown, but in no small part down to the uncomfortable accommodation. Nevertheless, I must have eventually slipped into sleep for I was awoken by the shrill blast from the whistle of our steam locomotive. The train began to clank to a halt causing carriage to knock against carriage and I was aware of the hubbub of people outside. I sprang from my bed and peered cautiously around the blind that covered the compartment window. Only one week before I had been working in the cashier's office at the local Co-op in an English provincial town – now here I was in the heart of Southern Africa looking out at a warm early morning sun peeking above the horizon.

From the hustle and bustle it was evident that the daily arrival of the train from Johannesburg was a significant event; it was still only 6 a.m., yet the scene before me was one full of frenetic activity. Children played noisily, racing the locomotive as it finally ground to a halt; their mothers sat cross-legged in a long row along the rudimentary platform, selling their wares. I particularly recall the huge piles of watermelons, a fruit I had rarely seen in England. Other women were walking alongside the track, precariously balancing large bundles on their heads, the contents tied securely in colourful cloths. There were very few men in evidence and most of the waiting throng were black. We had huffed and puffed our way across the high veldt for 12 hours covering barely 200 miles to arrive here at Mafeking. It was 26 September 1965 and already my journey had taken 36 hours.

At the time little of what I saw had any context. All was to become clearer in the following weeks, as I quickly learnt about Africa. I was ignorant of the fact that the majority of the population here in this part of South Africa were black. Many years later, as apartheid moved into another phase, it was to become the semi-autonomous Homeland or Bantustan of Bophuthatswana. Whilst white, mainly Boer farmers occupied the best agricultural land; in this area were also tribal lands of Tswana speaking people, the same ethnic group that predominates in Bechuanaland. Nor did I appreciate that to eke a living most of the able bodied men, if not employed by white farmers as labourers, would travel to the gold mining area around Johannesburg for regular work, living for months at a time in hostels, sending home most of their meagre earnings to their families. This was the pattern not only here around Mafeking but in many rural areas across Southern Africa, the migrant labour being drawn not only from within South Africa itself but also from the neighbouring countries like Rhodesia, Basutoland and Bechuanaland, where I was headed. Cheap labour to fuel the only seriously developed economy in the whole of the Dark Continent.

Mafeking had a unique distinction. It had, until only weeks before, been the administrative centre, effectively the capital, of the British Protectorate of Bechuanaland, although it was situated in the neighbouring country, the Republic of South Africa. This was about to change; with decolonisation in Africa in an advanced stage, in one year Bechuanaland would become the independent Republic of Botswana. Already elections had been held and an interim government was in place. The country clearly needed its own capital. This was to be the new purpose-built city of Gaberones, my destination. The little I could see of Mafeking from my compartment window suggested that it was a one-horse town. I was later told that a small town in Afrikaans is a 'dorp'; mentally I quickly translated this to a 'dump' in English. The unattractive nature of what I could see of Mafeking prompted the thought, 'What the hell is Bechuanaland like if the British colonial authorities prefer to run the protectorate from this rather sad looking place?'

Apart from its recent history as the 'capital' of Bechuanaland, Mafeking's real claim to fame had come in the early part of the twentieth century, during the Boer War, the site of a famous siege. For seven months, until May 1900, a small British garrison had defended the town from the Boers until relieved by a force led by Colonel Bryan Mahon. The siege had produced a real life 'boys own' hero in the form of another British officer, Colonel Robert Baden-Powell. As officer in charge of the Mafeking garrison, he promoted the idea in the British Press of a heroic defence of the town and when Mafeking was eventually relieved the event led to an outbreak of joyous celebration back in England. Baden-Powell became a household name, a very successful campaign of self-promotion that proved invaluable in later years when he founded the Scout Movement.

Fast forwarding to planning my return trip and I thought that perhaps Mafeking deserved a closer look but I was faced with my first dilemma: organising my travel arrangements I discovered that the train running from Johannesburg to Bulawayo had been reduced to a twice-a-week service. Later research showed the service had been further reduced to once a week and the prospect of spending a week in Mafeking was not in the least an attractive proposition. Despite what I assumed was the introduction of new rolling stock, the total journey from Pretoria to Bulawayo still took a less than impressive 26 hours, the leg from Jo'burg to Gaberone a mere 11 hours.

Plan B. Perhaps I could travel to Mafeking on the train and then take a hire car up into Botswana. Then, as my departure date approached, I received news that the train no longer runs outside of Botswana. All that remains of this famous route is a very limited service within Botswana itself running between Lobatsi in the south and Francistown in the north, albeit with new rolling stock provided by the Chinese government.

Given these setbacks perhaps I should take a more practical approach, land in Jo'burg and take one of the frequent flights straight to Gaberone, a journey of just one hour. Pragmatism got the nod ahead of romanticism and as we make our approach at Gaberone International Airport I am confident this had been the right decision.

On that first trip the train had stopped at Mafeking for maybe an hour to take on water and coal for the steam locomotive. From here it continued its ponderous progress, crossing the border at

Ramatlabama into Bechuanaland, running up its eastern side heading almost due north. Soon I would discover another anachronism created by the apartheid system. As civil servants we frequently used the train, particularly given the poor condition of the roads within Bechuanaland. A travel warrant would be issued enabling us to travel Second Class on the train. However, if business required a visit to Mafeking, where a number of departments of the Bechuanaland government were still located, for my black colleagues this meant that shortly before the train crossed the border into South Africa they had to decamp from the relative comfort of Second Class to Third Class.

In 1965 Bechuanaland was into its fourth year of severe drought. This was immediately evident from the terrain as I journeyed north; for as far as you could see in any direction, a flat scrubland. Not desert in the sense of, say, the Sahara, with endless sand dunes, devoid of any form of vegetation, but nevertheless a desolate arid land dotted only with the occasional low tree and thorn bush, and no obvious grazing for the cattle that I knew formed the backbone of the country's economy. A combination of the drought and generations of over grazing meant that this once fertile land was now to all intents and purposes an extension of the Kalahari Desert that lies to the west and stretches for thousands of square miles across into neighbouring Namibia, then known as South West Africa. The annual rains, if there were to be any this year, were still months away.

My first journey to Gaberones was to take the remainder of the day. The train chugged along, stopping from time to time at small settlements along the way. The only town of note was Lobatsi. Here, as I was to discover later, was located the country's only abattoir, so significant for its cattle industry. It was also at Lobatsi that I spotted a tarmacadam road running parallel with the rail track but disappointingly this quickly petered out as we left the town behind. I only recently discovered that this short stretch of proper road was indeed an anachronism, having been laid as long ago as the nineteen-thirties for the visit of some minor British Royal so that they avoided getting too dusty on their short journey from the airstrip to the town.

After stopping at Gaberones, where I would alight, the train would continue its journey through a second night, crossing the border into the then rebellious colony of Rhodesia at Plumtree before arriving the following evening in Bulawayo.

Anyway my own marathon journey was reaching its end and I eventually arrived in Gaberones as dusk was falling at maybe six in the evening. I hauled my newly purchased grey suitcase, proudly adorned with name tags collected on my recent visit to the Soviet Union, from its perch on the rack above my head and clumsily clambered down the steps of the railway carriage onto the parched and dusty trackside. In the gathering gloom I could see that I was one of only a handful of alighting passengers. 'Bernard,' a friendly but distinctly North American voice called from down the track. I waved in acknowledgement and went to meet a middle-aged white man walking with the aid of a stick. He warmly greeted me and introduced himself as Paul Gott. Paul proved to be an amiable Canadian who worked in the Department of Co-operatives that was to be my employer for the next year. Much to my relief the first stage of my journey, now two days long, was at an end.

In contrast to my first journey here I suppose I should have marvelled at the very nature of my arrival back in Botswana: a short flight from Johannesburg before landing at the well appointed Seretse Khama International Airport containing all the attendant paraphernalia of modernity. But once through Immigration Control, suitcases safely recovered from the luggage carousel, instead of reflection I am anxious to complete this stage of our journey. Today there is no one to greet me so we hurry to the desk to collect our hire car. Another indicator of the scale of change here. Back in the sixties there were few registered vehicles and most of them were government owned trucks rather than private cars. It isn't the four-wheel drive I had ordered but the guy at the desk assures me that it will be suitable for all the places I tell him that we intend to visit. As we drive towards the city it is easy to believe that he is right. A tarmac surface, a dual carriageway and relatively light traffic. Rosie is at the wheel as she will be for much of our ensuing journey. She is a very proficient driver and unlike me, after years of driving cars with an automatic gearbox, has few problems with the gear changing.

But looking across at her from the passenger seat I am conscious that where I travel with a sense of destiny she is apprehensive about the journey ahead, not least because it lacks the detailed planning of many of our previous travels around the globe.

My attention wanders, absorbing the scene. The afternoon sun is high in a cloudless African sky as we approach the city. We reach a large roundabout junction with a main road. The signpost indicates 'North to Francistown', 'South to Lobatsi' and 'City Centre' straight across. This is the edge of Gaberone and beyond the roundabout the city is laid out before us. We navigate our way around the roundabout and take the second exit, along Nelson Mandela Drive. It is a wide thoroughfare. Set back on both sides are some low buildings, industrial units and sundry small business premises. It is nondescript and could be on the edge of a major conurbation almost anywhere except that it is hot and it is dusty.

Reassuringly, on the map the car hire company has provided, I identify exactly where we are and I instruct Rosie to turn left into Julius Nyerere Avenue at the junction with the brewery. Here are some vendors selling assorted products: cold drinks, bundles of firewood, another what look like carved decorations for the garden. After a short distance we take a right at the traffic lights, onto a six-lane dual carriageway road. The traffic is heavier now but relief is at hand; within a short distance the sign we have been looking for – we have arrived at the Sun International Hotel. Here I am back safely in Gaberone; it is 40 years to the day since I first arrived.

Chapter Two

Gaberone

Gaberones in 1965 comprised no more than a railway halt (station would be an exaggeration), a single general store, straight out of any Western film you have ever seen, and a small hotel containing the only bar in town. At the heart of the new capital, home of the provisional government, were four large office blocks set in a dusty open area around which was a development of new housing: smart bungalows for the expatriates and senior members; smaller, one-room accommodation for the junior ranks of the burgeoning Civil Service of this soon to be independent country. Tarred roads were at a premium although at least some were being constructed, unlike the rest of the country. And on the edge of town, at Notwane Field, a dirt runway, which represented base for the new Botswana Airways and its two ageing DC3 – better known around the world as the Dakota. In the coming months not much changed – there was to be the opening of the new co-operative store and completion of a modest construction project to build a national stadium to host the Independence celebrations.

The Gaberone I discovered on my return was very different. It had even managed a name change.

Town or city name changes are common in post-Independence Africa. The change in the Gaberones name is a minor one but worth mentioning now to avoid confusion. What we knew as Gaberones or Gabs became Gaberone shortly after Independence. Historically the site of a camp of Kgosi (or King) Gaberone, it was originally known as Gaberone's Camp by the British, but over time the word 'camp' and ultimately the apostrophe got omitted, hence the grammatically incorrect Gaberones. Independence presented the locals with the opportunity to properly name the city, hence Gaberone. You will excuse me if I recall that first visit using the name in use at the time.

My new boss was to be Trevor Bottomley, the registrar of co-operatives. Tall and gangly, a friendly and engaging Englishman with a gentle Wiltshire burr, at that time in his early forties. I had met Trevor shortly before my departure from England where he was on leave from his job in Africa. Through various contacts I received a message that Trevor thought that it would be good for us to get together before I left England and he kindly invited me to dinner to meet with him and his wife. He lived in East Leake, a small village very close to Stanford Hall where I had spent the previous year as a student; in fact unbeknown to me at the time I had regularly run past his bungalow on my early morning jogs whilst at the college.

Despite the difference in our ages we immediately established a good rapport and as a result of our meeting I felt very positive about my assignment and my ability to make a real contribution to establishing co-operatives in Bechuanaland. Trevor's wife Barbara was, like him, a lively and friendly person, a redhead who reminded me of a younger version of the famous Lancastrian singer and entertainer, Gracie Fields. At that time the Bottomleys' two children were at school in England.

When I arrived in Africa Trevor was still on leave in the UK, hence my being met at the station by Paul Gott. Trevor was due to return in a few days and meantime I became a house guest of the Gott's and settled into life in the Department of Co-operatives. I recall early visits out of town to nearby Thamaga and the large tribal village of Molepolole.

Paul Gott was working hard to establish a consumer co-operative in another tribal village, Mochudi, capital of the Bakgatla tribe, and he had arranged for me to spend a day there. Richard, a VSO volunteer, had been assigned the role of escort and duly arrived at our office in Gaberones to collect me in a pick-up truck. Younger than me by three years, the day spent with him tended to reinforce my perception that those three extra years of experience that I had were actually quite significant in terms of ability to really help in an emerging country like Botswana. Richard, who later became an eminent Harley Street based neuro-surgeon, was bright enough to recognise this himself and freely admitted that the experience he had gained on voluntary service far outweighed any real benefit that he was able to bring to the situation. In Mochudi Richard introduced me to his boss Sandy Grant, one of many interesting and dedicated people I was to meet in the coming year, a voluntary community worker totally committed to improving the lot of the people of this very poor country.

My understanding was that Sandy was a protégé of the authoress Lady Naomi Mitchison who had a house in Mochudi and who had been adopted by the local people and given the honorary title of 'mother of the tribe'. Lady Mitchison, already then in her late sixties, wrote extensively about her experiences in Africa in her later years. Although she came from a well-to-do aristocratic Scottish family, in her formative years she discovered her father was by inclination left-leaning politically and she herself became a convinced Socialist and subsequently married a Labour Member of Parliament. As such she was a natural supporter of the co-operative ideals and had developed a good relationship with Trevor during her regular visits from England to stay in Mochudi.

Forty years on and Sandy Grant is my main link with the past. He has remained in contact with Trevor and having been reintroduced through the medium of e-mail we have been in sporadic contact in the weeks leading up to my return to Botswana. Sandy is now a fully-fledged citizen of Botswana and from my research I establish that he has dabbled in various aspects of Botswana society since Independence including publishing a book using his own photographs illustrating 'the decorated houses of Botswana'. This is but one of his talents; he is also local historian, museum curator, author, writer and putative politician as well as an active campaigner on many local issues. In 2004 his services to the country had been recognised when he was awarded the country's highest civilian award, the Presidential Order of Honour.

Sandy's e-mails can be a little odd, sometimes ignoring straightforward questions I pose whilst happily addressing other more contentious matters. I am confused so I call Trevor to make sure that I am not an unwelcome invader into Sandy's life but Trevor assures me that there isn't a problem but that 'Sandy can appear enigmatic'. I am keen to meet him and don't have to wait long. On arrival I telephone and he agrees to come across to my hotel the following morning.

At the appointed hour we make our way down to the hotel reception to await Sandy's arrival. Ten minutes later, no sign of Sandy.

'What does he look like?' asks Rosie.

'Well I met him once 40 years ago but I think he is tall and fair.'

Then he appears and I go across and introduce myself. It is only later, on reflection, that I decide it was more likely by a process of probabilities that I had correctly deduced he was our man. Certainly he is shorter than I recall and his receding and greying hairline does not betray any obvious reason for the nickname Sandy.

We have coffee and a chat. Sandy is rather bemused when the muffin he has ordered arrives and I rather suspect that he had expected what the American's call an English muffin: toasted and served with lashings of butter. Instead, between updating us on the local gossip, he makes steady progress through the large sticky chocolate sponge cake that has been put in front of him. Sandy, we discover, is a cricket buff and is currently wrapped up in events in the old country where England are in the throes of wresting the Ashes from Australia. When we do get him talking about himself we establish that he is 68 years of age and has been in Botswana since 1963. He is the father of a 13-year-old son and has also inherited a rather troublesome stepson by his relatively recent marriage to Elinah.

Our first full day in Gaberone and Sandy has agreed to show us around the city. What has he in store to delight us in this modern metropolis? We are about to find out. Sandy drives a small pick-up truck that only seats two in the cab so we decide to take our hire car with Rosie at the wheel and Sandy in the front passenger seat as our guide. First stop: Sandy has taken us past the 30,000-seater national stadium along a dirt track to what proves to be the new national cricket ground. Sandy has established we have a common bond as cricket lovers. Not an obvious on the tourist circuit, the outfield is a little bumpy but is covered in grass, there is a scoreboard, neat pavilion and amazingly a modern looking set of floodlights. Overall, with Botswana having recently achieved affiliate status to the International Cricket Council, a well-appointed facility up to international standards. It transpires that Sandy's son plays cricket although a quick perusal of the membership list pinned to the notice board outside of the pavilion shows most of the local players are incomers from the Indian sub-continent.

Back to the car and following Sandy's directions we head off across the city eventually drawing to a halt in front of a rather austere building that looks like an East German architect from the pre-unification period had designed it: square and bland with windows that look too small for a structure of its size. Sandy hops out with the instruction to keep the engine running as we are illegally parked. He emerges minutes later with news that he has managed to settle a long overdue account with his dentist. Next off and Sandy instructs Rosie to follow signs to the dam but by the time we reach our next point of call I am mentally struggling with Trevor's description of Sandy as enigmatic; it wasn't quite the right word but I was beginning to sense what he meant: erratic, eccentric, vacillating, capricious. I eventually settle on 'mercurial'. We have arrived, not at the dam but at the adjacent garden centre. The dam – with its water levels perilously low due to the drought – and, we had read, a marina and water sports activities might have been interesting but we never get to see it. The garden centre is pleasant, rather akin the garden centres you find in England. That things are growing here in this climate is, I suppose, a minor miracle.

The 'tour' ends back in the city. Here Sandy takes us to a small complex of craft and clothing shops located in the middle of an industrial estate. All these businesses seem to exist primarily to meet the needs of the capital's small white community. He takes us to a shop selling a range of traditional African goods, crafts and clothing, where a personal friend is the proprietor, but after failing to buy his wife a birthday present here we end up enjoying a cappuccino at the adjacent café run by an Italian family.

Later we set out on our own exploration of the city. It is soon evident why Sandy had offered such an oddball selection of sightseeing. Our arrival at the National Museum doesn't auger well. Ours is the only car in the car park. In fact the museum isn't bad, but opened in 1968 it looks rather tired and the exhibits seem to end rather abruptly at the time the British arrived in the country.

Part of the museum complex is an exhibition hall where we find a display of locally crafted baskets. The quality of this work is excellent. Two young women from the museum staff are manning the sales counter but don't appear interested in the exhibits or us. In the gallery itself, sitting by what we discover are their own exhibits, we find some older women. They tell us that this is an annual national exhibition of basketwork although in practice it is a craft confined to some smaller tribes living in the north-west of the country a very long way from Gaberone. Traditionally the open, plate-shaped baskets have been used for carrying on the heads of women and also for the winnowing of sorghum grain after threshing. Closed baskets with lids are for storing grain or seed. They tell us that many of the patterns are traditional depicting key aspects of their lives. From the labels on the exhibits we see that they have names like 'Tears of the Giraffe', 'Back of the Python' and 'Flight of the Swallow'. All very evocative, that is until we come to a basket bearing the title 'Urine Trail of the Bull'.

The ladies have travelled from Etsha and are members of two small tribes, the Bayei and Hambukushu, that sometime in the past arrived in Botswana from Angola. In a sense this therefore is not an indigenous industry. The baskets themselves are made from sisal or mokola, a palm found only in certain parts of Botswana. Traditionally the baskets were a natural colour, that of the palm fibre, but now dyes are used. The dyes come from a range of sources, usually the roots and bark of trees but also from plants and the rather attractive pink from the husks of sorghum. The baskets are not cheap, even for visitors like ourselves, but not surprising when the ladies tell us that each basket takes two weeks to make.

From here we stroll up to the central shopping mall; it looks even more tired than the museum. I seem to recall that it was under construction when I was here and one of the first shops to open was in fact the co-operative. It is typical of sixties' architecture and the scene is one to be found in many small English towns today, even down to the youths wearing tracksuits and baseball caps lounging around in small groups. Most people are simply going about their business. There is a supermarket and various retail outlets selling clothing, shoes and white goods. Noticeable is the proliferation of loan shops. Later we learn that this relatively new phenomenon amongst the burgeoning urban population has an unpleasant yet familiar ring. Borrowers surrender their credit card and pin number to the loan company, and then on payday the company uses the card, withdrawing the due repayment from an ATM, together of course with interest at some usurious rate.

At the north end of the mall we dodge a seemingly endless stream of traffic to cross Khama Crescent into the government enclave, home to all the ministry buildings. I take a few photographs of the parliament and the nearby statue of the first president, Sir Seretse Khama. On our map we see that State House, the presidential palace, is nearby and thinking this might be worth a look we walk in that direction, but find that it is totally hidden from public view behind a high wall.

Trevor had asked me to take a photograph of his old home. Sandy is convinced it has been bulldozed to make way for the South African High Commission but I think I have found it. I am outside this bungalow and try and recall from all that time ago the driveway, the porch, the entrance hall and the large living room at the front of the house. It kind of fits except that the property now has a double garage and is surrounded by a wall and security fence. These additions have changed the whole character of the place. I am standing in front of somebody's house with a security camera peering down at me so I decide against taking a picture and we move on and return to the hotel.

After dinner we return to our room and contemplate an early night to catch up on our sleep. It has been a long day and we are still tired after the journey from the UK but despite the fatigue my mind is still buzzing. I find myself thinking back over the day's events. Meeting with Sandy, the city and Trevor's house. I am sure now it was Trevor's house. Instead of falling readily into sleep I can't help thinking of Trevor's house when I had first arrived all those years ago and the finer detail of those first few days in his company.

I understood from Trevor when we met in England that he wanted me to work in an area north of Gaberones in the Bamangwato tribal reserve; however, before taking up my post I was to spend some time in the new capital getting acclimatised. Trevor arrived a few days after me from his leave in England and he was insistent that I would move from the Gott's and stay with him at what was then his new and pleasantly appointed government owned bungalow. I would then travel north to my new home at a place called Radisele.

Barbara had not returned from England with Trevor, which meant that we were left in the capable hands of their maid, Lucy. Lucy, whilst devoted to the Bottomleys, was a lady with a strong opinion about right and wrong and how things should be around her territory, and Trevor was constantly battling her for supremacy whilst madam in the form of Barbara was away. I later discovered that when Barbara was in residence Lucy melted away as a 'seen and not heard' member of the household. Evidence, as I was to discover, that in Botswana it was the women who got things done whilst the men spent their time talking about it. The only other permanent resident of the bungalow was Zander, a yappy dachshund that the Bottomleys had brought with them from their last posting in Basutoland.

Time at the Bottomley household was well spent. This was to be a year rich in new experiences, a year in which I was to rapidly mature as a person and a period that shaped my personal political philosophy. To start the learning process there were three important new things I discovered in those first few days: Nelson Mandela, the Economist and Scrabble.

Mandela was the subject of an article in a magazine I found in Trevor's house. He was at that time into the first year of his life sentence serving hard labour on Robben Island but the article retold the story of his exploits as the Black Pimpernel on the run from the South African police in the period before the Rivonia Treason trial at which he delivered his now famous speech on being sentenced to life with hard labour. From that time Mandela became a particular hero figure for me, long before he became a household name around the world; it also generated a personal interest in South Africa and its abominable apartheid regime.

The Economist, with its extensive coverage of world politics and economics, was a revelation for someone brought up in a house where the Daily Mail formed the major source of news. No wonder at that point I was largely apolitical, if anything a prospective Tory voter with imperialist leanings. Not that the Economist was or has ever been a radical journal, but it was just a fantastic source of enlightenment about a world of which I was barely aware. All that was soon to change.

Scrabble was another great find, an essential skill to be first learned and then honed for future visits to Gaberones where Trevor and myself regularly joined battle for supremacy over Jon Harlow, an Oxbridge type who held a senior role in the colonial administration. Competing in this company was to further raise my own self-esteem, suffering as I did at the time from a bit of an inferiority complex over my own educational background. Overall the first days in Africa proved to be a pretty good experience.

But in a sense these were frivolous diversions from my real purpose and very readily Trevor began my education into things African. Firstly he imparted the important basic information about the country that was to be my home for the next year. Botswana, or Bechuanaland as it then was, is a large country covering over 500,000 km², bigger than France and well over twice the area covered by the British Isles. Yet at the time the population was barely more than 500,000, mostly cattle farmers occupying a strip of land rarely more than 50 miles wide down the eastern side of the country between the South African province of Transvaal to the east and the Kalahari Desert to the west; a ribbon of land stretching some 400 miles from the border with South Africa at Ramatlabama in the south up to Plumtree on the border with Zimbabwe, then still Rhodesia, to the north.

Given the huge size of the British Empire one wondered why such a backwater as this had been brought under the Union flag, it appearing to have neither obvious strategic or economic importance. Way back in 1885 three Tswana chiefs, Khama, Bathoen and Sebele, famously visited London where they met Queen Victoria and requested that Britain help defend Bechuanaland against the Boers. However, it was another ten years and only after deposits of gold had been discovered around Francistown that the British government, and even then somewhat reluctantly, eventually acceded to this request, creating the British Protectorate of Bechuanaland. As part of this deal the Ngwato chief, Khama the Third, ceded a strip of land in the north-east of the country to the British. Called the Tuli Block, it is still largely occupied by white farmers.

Perhaps because of its reluctance to become the colonial power in the ensuing 70 years, the British had provided Bechuanaland with an administrative structure but little investment. Trevor explained that unlike in some other parts of Africa like Kenya, where the movement towards Independence had been painful and often bloody, here when the first political parties had been created in the early sixties they had been encouraged by the British, and in elections early in 1965 a provisional government had been elected under Seretse Khama, of whom I was soon to learn more.

Trevor began by explaining the tribal system and the importance of cattle not only for the economic future of the country but its social importance as a determinant of status in Tswana society. All of this data was so relevant to me at the time and I marvelled as knowledge was imparted and this new world began to make sense to me and my project took on real meaning.

Apart from the indigenous people – the Basarwa, better known as the Kalahari bushmen – the majority of the population here can trace their ancestors to tribes that arrived in the area from what is now South Africa during the nineteenth century ahead of the advancing Boer settlers. These tribes have a common bond in terms of language – Setswana – and culture, being primarily pastoral farmers. The largest Batswana tribe is the Ngwato. Thus Bangwato are the people of the Ngwato tribe. The Ngwato settled in the area around Palapye and Serowe. The other main Tswana groups, the Bakwena, settled around Molepolole, and the Bangwaketse around Kanye. Minority tribal groups from different ethnic roots and language can be found in the Maun and Francistown areas, having over time migrated from Namibia, Angola, Zimbabwe and in some cases even further north from central Africa. The largest of these groups are the Bakalanga who live around Francistown.

Traditionally land tenure in Botswana is tribal and the tribe communally owns most land although the chief grants rights to build and occupy. In a Tswana village the people typically live in a circular hut, a rondavel, made from mud and cow dung bricks and contained within a walled yard or 'lolwapa'. The house of the chief is the focal point of the village and the chief, or kgosi, has traditionally wielded a huge influence on tribal affairs. Usually close to the chief's house is the kgotla, or tribal court, where the chief, supported by his Council of Elders, gathers to discuss important issues and rule on cases requiring judicial judgements. Status determines where one lives and vice versa. Thus because the chief has enormous influence it is a measure of one's status how close you live to him, and his relatives will be found in wards around the chief's home.

Unlike some other parts of Africa, Tswana villages are characterised by their size, being very large with populations – even in former times when the population overall was much smaller – of 30,000 or more. Given that the area around each family dwelling can be significant a Tswana village can cover a huge area.

In addition to its home in the village each family is allocated 'lands' by the chief. These lands are what we would call a smallholding and are usually located between 30 and 50 miles west of the village. Here family members go after the summer rains in

February and March to plant subsistence crops and vegetables for their family. Even further west are likely to be cattle posts where cattle are taken during the dry season when grass close to the village has been fully grazed. Typically at the cattle post a borehole will have been sunk to obtain water. Here cattle will be tended by children as young as eight or ten. This was the Bechuanaland I found in 1965. On my return I discovered that today, despite increasing urbanisation, this pattern of tribal life still remains broadly in place although with universal primary education now the norm, older children or the very old often tend the cattle.

Despite the lengthy orientation programme provided before I travelled to Africa, I have to confess that in terms of clothing and equipment I was ill prepared for the hot and dry climate that I was to experience. Arriving at the end of September it was just entering the African summer and already daily temperatures were around 30°C. Although my new grey suitcase, especially purchased for the journey, was full, this was largely due to a wide range of textbooks on law, accountancy and economics rather than a reflection of an extensive tropical wardrobe. I had, correctly as it proved, anticipated that in the absence of much else to do by way of entertainment, this would be the opportunity to continue my studies by correspondence. Clothing suitable for this tropical climate, however, was at a premium.

In mid-sixties Britain although I never owned a scooter or motorcycle I definitely erred towards the 'mod' rather than 'rocker' mode of dress: smart suits rather than leathers. I therefore spent a substantial part of my modest salary on personally designed suits. I would make a drawing of my latest creation and have the garment made up for me by a local tailor. I particularly recall two 'stand out in a crowd' creations: one in plum with clover leaf lapels, and a lime green ensemble, the jacket sporting what at the time I thought was a rather nifty centre pleat. Both were in mohair, a material that was regarded as extremely trendy. My favourite, slightly less garish in colour, was in navy blue with a three-button jacket cut high and shaped at the waist in the Italian style very popular at the time. But the real 'tour de force' that set this outfit apart was the matching blue leather and suede shoes acquired for a small fortune in some

Carnaby Street boutique, which I much preferred as the footwear of choice compared to must-have of the period, the Cuban-heeled Chelsea boots that offered elevation but at some crazy angle that made you feel like some Soho tart balancing precariously on her 3 inch high stiletto heels. For Africa I selected another of my 'creations', a relatively conservative double-breasted suit in light grey. It wasn't to see much service in the coming year.

Totally absent from my wardrobe were shorts. Having been forced by my mother to wear short trousers until I had reached the ripe old age of 12, exposing my knees was something of an anathema and to be honest at that stage of my life I doubt whether I had actually ever owned any shorts.

At breakfast on my first morning at Trevor's bungalow he had drawn attention to my totally inappropriate attire. When I confessed that my wardrobe did not include shorts he offered me a spare pair of his. Being a rather taller man and of middle age they could be described as 'unfashionable' and on me they hung rather low even by the standards of the time and required a safety pin at the waist to ensure a reasonably snug fit. At least they were more fit for purpose than the clothing I had brought with me. I quickly decided that shorts were indeed a necessity in this climate and that my knees were likely to remain exposed for the next year. I therefore dug deep into my modest allowance and supplemented Trevor's loan pair with another pair purchased from the local store. Memorably and totally in keeping with my unconventional taste in suits, they were a rather natty light blue pair in a silky material. My wardrobe, now complete, offered a splendid contrast between my newly acquired, seductively cut to mid-thigh 'silk' shorts, and the on, or to be more accurate below-the-knee khakis that Trevor had kindly lent to me.

Not a pretty sight I daresay but the reminder brought a smile to my face as at last I slipped into contented sleep.

Chapter Three

Getting to the Beginning

I could kid you along and say that Africa was in my blood, that it was my destiny to help those less fortunate than me; but in truth my decision to become a long-term volunteer was entirely unplanned and in some measure opportunistic, although in the event life changing. Indeed instead of Bechuanaland it could actually have been Fiji or Jamaica or Mauritius. Frankly, wherever in the world I had been offered I would have said yes. Perhaps more readily if it had been any of those more exotic sounding places than my eventual destination, Bechuanaland.

So how was it that in short order humble clerk at the local Co-op is transported to a then remote part of Africa as a highly regarded expert? What I do know is that I am something of a restless spirit and in part this transformation I attribute to some kind of 'travel gene' inherited from my father. He died when I was only seven so most of what I know of him is limited personal recollection and family anecdotes. He was born in 1892 and joined the Army as a very young man. As a soldier he travelled widely and was involved in many obscure campaigns in support of the British Empire, most long since forgotten. I recall as a boy the tin boxes full of his medals covering military operations and skirmishes around the world in which the British Army had found itself entangled, one from Afghanistan and dated 1910, awarded when he was even younger than I was on my journey to Africa. Later he had gone through the First World

War and beyond as a soldier. A few years in Civvy Street during the thirties left him restive and even before the formal outbreak of war in 1939, he had volunteered again, although by that time he was already nearly 50. In all honesty I don't know exactly what he did during the war except that his last mission was involvement in the building of Mulberry Harbour and the subsequent Normandy Landings and that the war had taken its toll on his health.

I am not sure he was ever well in those immediate post-war years after he was demobbed; he certainly found it hard to settle back into civilian life and during my early years up until his death we lived in many places. My earliest childhood recollections are of Clacton-on-Sea during the horrendously cold winter of 1947 where my father worked in a hotel. I am not sure of his job; he was a plumber by trade so I guess it was some sort of handyman role. The plates and cutlery bearing the hotel name adorned our dining table for the next 20 years. We then moved to London's East End where the old man was caretaker of a church on the East India Dock Road and we lived in an adjacent terraced house that presumably came with the job. Poplar was already one of the capital's most deprived areas and Hitler's bombers hadn't done much to improve the scenery. It was here amidst a torrent of tears that I started school. Fortunately shortly afterwards we moved again, to the leafy lanes of Rickmansworth in Hertfordshire, where we lived in the lodge at the entrance to a rather grand stockbroker pile where my parents worked, Mum as housemaid and Dad as odd job man, in the big house. From there we moved on to Paignton in Devon, to a small private school set in beautiful grounds where Dad was the caretaker and my mother the cook and where I enjoyed a free education amongst the fee paying kids. This was all too short-lived. Father was on the move again. I remember one episode. He was going for a job interview. We travelled by train, alighting at Shepshed where the old man asked my mother the address of his interview to discover that we were in entirely the wrong place. The next move was not long coming, this time to Cornwall.

My mother acted as companion to an old lady in a small village called Millbrook across the Sound from Plymouth. I guess the old man was by now not at all well and unable to work. I have few specific memories although I recall sufficient to know he was a stern disciplinarian from the old school of fatherhood and I more than once felt his firm hand or bamboo cane, of which he had a collection, across my nether region. On one occasion I remember him on his knees encouraging me to box. I landed one, bloodying his nose, and was fearful of taking a beating but he surprised me by congratulating me on the blow.

My father was taken to hospital in Plymouth sometime in December 1951 and died on Boxing Day of septicaemia and pneumonia. Shortly after that my mother and I moved to Colchester to live close to my mother's older sister, and that is where I spent the rest of my childhood. My world was to shrink but it did little to inhibit my wanderlust.

As a kid I never had a proper holiday, having to be content with visits to uncles and aunts living in the urban wastelands of Woolwich and Orpington. But even then, clearly lingering deep down I had inherited some of the old man's restless spirit, for my operating boundaries in my early teenage years were not confined like many of my contemporaries to our housing estate or even to the town of Colchester. With pals like 'Prickle' Thorne and Len Thake, we spent our school holidays riding our bicycles literally to the very edges of the county of Essex. When that became too boring or exhausting we would take to the A12, hitch-hike to London for train-spotting or watch cricket or football at one the great sporting venues, Lords and the Oval, and pretty well every major football ground in the capital. The big adventures though were the train-spotting visits. Not content with standing on the end of the platform at Paddington or Kings Cross, we would surreptitiously enter the engine sheds always located close by the major railway terminals, at Old Oak Common for Paddington, Camden for Euston or Willesden for Kings Cross. Here, between those towering steaming monster locomotives, we would avidly record their numbers. In today's world a health and safety hazard that would be totally unacceptable, then apart from occasionally being chased by some over-zealous railway employee we invariably were able to quietly go about our work undisturbed.

Even then I had a fascination for travel and had developed a wide knowledge of places based on hours of poring over maps of the world so I could recite the countries and capitals in every part of the globe. Mr Cook, my fourth year geography teacher, had discovered my talent in this department and whenever he fancied an easy time he would hand me a long pointer and a position in the front of the class from where I could point at various places on a blank outline map of the world that was fixed to the classroom wall. I do recall that although there was usually someone in the class capable of correctly identifying a city or country, Tierra del Fuego was guaranteed to stump even the well informed.

Then, before I knew it, I was 16 and a school leaver. Ambitions to become a journalist thwarted, I found employment as a clerk with the local Co-op. Four years' diligent study by correspondence, what today is called 'distance learning', followed. Then I won a scholarship to study accountancy at the Co-operative College in Loughborough. Two years at the college would give me my diploma and save another eight to ten years' study at home. It was an exciting prospect.

The college occupied Stanford Hall and its estate in the heart of rural Leicestershire. The Hall was a superb old English country house once owned by Sir Julian Cahn who, an avid cricket fan, was famous in the years between the two world wars for hosting country house cricket matches in the grounds, attracting many of the great cricketers of the era, both from England and abroad. The rich and famous of the time, as his weekend houseguests, formed a small and very select audience watching the feats of these great cricketers. Cahn, a self-made millionaire and cricketer of modest talents, indulged himself by playing for his own 11, batting in a revolutionary design pair of inflatable pads. This an idea so far ahead of its time that it still has yet to catch on in cricketing circles.

The college had only about 100 full time students divided roughly between four small faculties. Management: lads who were training to run Co-op shops. Social Science: a strange bunch. They included lads like Paddy, whose dad was a well known Trade Union leader; he had left school without the requisite A levels and wanted a qualification to get into university. Others, like Dennis, a 30-something journalist from Sunderland, who introduced me to the imaginary world of Tolkien, were simply taking time out from their careers to reassess their lives. Most though seemed to be or want to be social workers, a profession that at the time I didn't really understand. Duggie, a Londoner, had a hair-lip, a limp and an intense concern about the problems of the world. And there was Bob, a doppelganger for Hank B Marvin of the Shadows, until the Beatles, the biggest thing in British pop music, who spoke in a slow measured way in a deep gravelly voice that seemed to catch people's attention. I was so smitten by his manner that I found myself spending a whole Christmas vacation replicating the effect, disconcerting friends and family into the bargain. Then there were some 30 'overseas' students, primarily from developing countries. Again usually mature students, an Indian in his fifties and a genuine Nigerian tribal chief. Finally there were us – the accountants. We naturally viewed ourselves as the elite, and in practical terms it was true that if successful we were most likely to have a career route to the top of what was in those days a massive retail business in the UK.

In retrospect it was a truly cosmopolitan bunch. We all lived in the Hall or in the adjacent purpose built accommodation block. Life was pleasant if a little more frugal than the lifestyle enjoyed by the late Sir Julian. Being resident under the same roof and given our small number it was more public school than university. Although the staff tried to create an adult ambience there was nevertheless a long list of house rules and collective duties like washing-up performed on a rota basis, although au pairs from various European countries did many of the menial cleaning tasks around the house and provided a welcome distraction considering the student body was predominantly male. There were only two female students in that year. In the newish accommodation block students had their own study/bedroom but I drew the short straw and had to share a room in a wing of the main hall, which in the old days had probably been part of the servants' quarters. My roommate was a lad called Alan. We all had sponsorship from our local Co-op or organisations within the Co-operative Movement. Alan, I recall, came from the oddly named Ten Acres and Stirchley Co-operative Society, the location of which would have remained a mystery to me save for his strong Brummie accent.

We ate communally in a dining room with superb views across rural Leicestershire – real hunting country. It was sometime in the spring of 1965 that the college principal, who rather pretentiously on college letterheads was announced as Lieutenant Colonel R L Marshall OBE, asked during his customary daily luncheon announcement if any students were interested in the opportunity to work overseas on a volunteer basis to help Third World countries. I was sitting next to my friend, Keith Mayle. We exchanged glances. 'What do you think?' Keith was as intrigued as me and as soon as lunch was over we hurried to the college secretary's office to arrange to see the principal to find out more.

Although the whole voluntary service overseas idea was in its infancy, the newly elected Labour government was keen to promote the concept. There was a wide public interest in the idea. Conscription had ended in the late fifties and a public debate continued to rage about the merits of National Service and of a new generation of young people that lacked the disciplines instilled by serving for two years in Her Majesty's Armed Forces. Voluntary service appeared to offer a new way for young people no longer subject to conscription to make a contribution to help others, a rite of passage to good citizenship. The American version, the Peace Corps, almost certainly had an even more overtly political agenda, a way of creating American spheres of influence in these newly emerging countries.

Seeking an interview with the college principal was not an everyday event and a few days later as Keith and I approached his office it was with a certain amount of apprehension. Although 'Chuck' Marshall used his military rank on official documents, I always felt it rather pretentious and uncharacteristic of the man. It was rumoured that he was the youngest officer in the British Army to have achieved the rank of Lieutenant Colonel. It was in the Education Corps indicating that he was first and foremost an educationalist. The Co-operative Movement had been very fortunate to attract a man of his calibre into the job. If we didn't use his nickname 'Chuck' he was alternatively known as 'RLM' and I feel sure that when we went to speak to his secretary to arrange the meeting we would have politely enquired as to when RLM was available. I have to confess that at the time neither I, nor any of my fellow students, would have considered calling the college principal by his first name, Robert, or Bob, to his face, even less likely by his nickname. Indeed Mr Marshall was an imposing figure. He was physically solid, not particularly tall but broad chested. He had that quiet cultured Scottish accent I always associate with Edinburgh. He was your archetypal canny Scot, an imposingly erudite man of high intellect. He had, what over the years I have come to appreciate more fully, a rare quality: the ability to see you as you really are and not as you might want to be seen. He was one of the few people I have ever met with this insight and the effect could be unnerving. I was of course young and naïve and easy prey but I can still recall being caught out in a way that, with others, I feel I would have successfully blagged my way out of a potentially embarrassing situation.

My first meeting with RLM was at a panel interview for a scholarship place at the college. He asked what I had read recently and I truthfully replied, 'A book on psychology.' At the time understanding Freud was like trying to understand Egyptian hieroglyphics so I was barely prepared for his supplementary, 'And what have you learnt?' I got a place so perhaps he recognised some potential behind my blushes and fluster. Later when at college I used to hitchhike to and from home in Colchester and keep the expenses paid to me for the rail fare. On one occasion I was thumbing a lift only a few miles from the college when who should draw alongside but RLM in his bloody great Rover saloon.

'Where have you come from?' he enquired.

'Loughborough Station,' I lied to save further embarrassing cross-examination.

'The four o'clock train must have arrived very early,' he intoned.

I muttered a hesitant response. Cunning old bugger, I thought. As usual he's onto my game.

What was already apparent at the time from the early experiences of sponsoring organisations like Voluntary Service

Overseas or VSO that had started in 1958 was that 'cadet volunteers', who were school leavers taking a gap year before going to university, despite their best endeavours, were only able to make a limited contribution in the Third World. These young people of 18 or 19 often lacked in maturity but more importantly they lacked any specific professional skills. Most tended to be employed overseas as teachers. Sure, they tended to be bright and committed young people who could bring to bear their own recent educational experience but this rather tended to ignore the fact that teaching is in itself a profession requiring months if not years of specialist training.

The Ministry of Overseas Development in the UK was keen on the volunteer concept but recognising the limitations of the VSO model wanted to attract more mature people with specific skills, people who could offer real and lasting value to developing countries: agriculturalists, agronomists, and hydrologists. The Ministry approach to Bob Marshall was very much in this vein; specifically they wanted his help in getting young people with practical knowledge of co-operatives to go to Africa and other parts of the world to assist in developing the burgeoning co-operative sector in the economies of these new countries.

With around a third of the 100 or so students at the college from overseas in my year, from diverse countries such as Argentina, Malaya, Nigeria, Turkey, India and Fiji, with the biggest number from developing countries, I am sure that Bob Marshall saw great kudos for the college and its programmes if it was seen to support the government in this endeavour, and an opportunity for the college to reinforce its reputation as the world centre for co-operative education. As a result he gave us every encouragement to apply.

When the meeting took place with RLM in his imposing dark oak-panelled office, he made it very clear that he desperately wanted to be able to support the overseas volunteers initiative. My agenda was I wanted another year at Stanford Hall to complete my studies. The alternative was years more of study by correspondence. Admittedly another influence was that I was rather smitten with the college lifestyle. I figured that if I went along with the voluntary service idea he could bring influence to bear to get me another scholarship when I returned. Nevertheless I recall that for me the decision required some agonising. On one hand I wanted to complete my studies as soon as possible, on the other hand the idea of foreign travel was undoubtedly attractive. RLM was persuasive, indicating that with the tag of 'the co-op's first overseas volunteers' on our application forms, re-entry to the college after a year's break might be more likely than either of us getting a scholarship for the following year. Although we were young and by modern standards rather naïve 20-year olds, I think we got the drift of his argument.

At the end of the meeting with RLM he gave Keith and I some time to consider whether we wanted to pursue our interest in volunteering. I had to make a judgement call. There was some element of risk because it would be another year before I would know about the second scholarship, and by then I would be in some far corner of the globe; but I had made my mind up, I wanted to volunteer and was delighted when Keith told me that he had reached the same decision. We quickly conveyed our decision to RLM. He was quite evidently pleased and assured us that it was a decision that we would not regret.

Nearly 40 years on. It was a party to celebrate RLM's 90th birthday. Just 70 of perhaps 3,000 students that passed through the doors of Stanford Hall in his 30 years of stewardship had turned up. I looked around the room for at least one familiar face albeit weathered by the intervening 30-odd years. A figure approached and shook me firmly by the hand. He said he recognised the face but couldn't put a name to it. At close quarters it was obvious that he had spent the early afternoon in a local hostelry waiting for the event to start, sufficient imbibing to have impaired his judgement. Exchanging dates when we had attended Stanford Hall proved my first instinct correct. I didn't know him, or him me.

So, where were you Willie Tucker, small and round and plump, eminently sensible and bound for high office? Where Graham 'Muckle' Fisher, nicknamed because of his propensity to use words from the Scottish Borders' dialect that even his fellow Scots didn't understand. My old roommate, who would creep back from the staff quarters at two in the morning from shagging the French au pair, Luci. So French, and lovely – shame about the early signs of a moustache. Where George Wildman who I had shared a taxi with from the station on that first day back, me the second year student fresh back from my African adventure. Yet it was George, so young and immature, the Black Country lad so cocky and full of himself who did all the talking. Where Tom and Drew, the Glasgow Catholic and Protestant thrown together in this closed community and able for the first time to make contact at a personal level across the religious divide between their two communities. Were we not the infamous 'Clique' who dominated our year? 'One for all and all for one'. Where were you Clive Brooks, Exeter lad, tall and blonde. And you Jeff Gardner, older but after a few bevvies not wiser; remember the time you rolled over your Reliant Robin returning home late one night from the Three Horseshoes? Surely Jeff, you who went on to become a lecturer at the college are going to be here. Or you Keith. My old mate from the first year and from your year in Africa. Not sure whether you wanted to be part of 'The Clique' but a mate for life surely, dear Keith, who I haven't heard from in 30 years.

And here is the great man, the distinctive hooked nose and square shoulders but now ever so frail. Those penetrating soft blue eyes under hooded brows now just a watery hue. He gives a speech. The style is the same, it has symmetry, but the delivery is halting and he reads from his script.

Afterwards I go and say my goodbyes. 'Bernard Le Bargy,' I intone, knowing his superbly retentive memory. I shake a limp hand and look into those eyes for the spark of recognition. I can add '1964 to 1967, student president, editor of the student magazine, the first ever co-operative volunteer overseas' but I don't; I can see the name rings no bells and nor would the supplementary information. I look at Beryl, his loyal wife and constant companion for more than 50 years. She knows what I am thinking and squeezes my hand in a farewell gesture.

I have travelled up with Trevor. He asks that we make a detour to Stanford Hall from where we had both graduated, albeit quite a few years apart. I draw up at the North Gate. It is closed. The property developers who are the new owners have a notice posted. We are not welcome. All we can do is forlornly peer through the firmly closed gate and up the long drive to the house. It is early autumn, the trees are still full – yellow, gold and red – but they obscure any final view of the Hall itself. Nostalgia: its crap. Never go back.

Although the British government supported the volunteer idea, unlike the Americans with its Peace Corps, it did not want British volunteers to be seen as agents of the government. For HMG this was a particularly sensitive issue as they were conscious that volunteer workers should not be seen as an insidious method of retaining the influence of the former colonial power but, transparently, young people wanting to help those less well off than themselves in an entirely non-political and therefore non-governmental way. A solution to this dilemma was to use sponsoring organisations independent of government and free to seek placements and to select suitable candidates dealing directly with the host organisation in the receiving country. This was the role of VSO, already well established in the UK, and of International Voluntary Service or IVS, an organisation new to the idea of long-term voluntary service.

I was to be one of the first long-term volunteers sponsored by this Swiss based organisation better known internationally as Service Civil Internationale. A pacifist, Pierre Ceresole, had founded SCI in 1920. The original Ceresole concept, which is retained even today in much of the work of SCI, was to establish what he called 'work camps' manned by volunteer workers to assist with community projects, often following some local natural disaster. The first work camp organised by Ceresole in 1920 was in a small French village devastated by the First World War. Flood relief projects in communities seriously affected by the economic Depression in the late twenties and assistance to displaced civilians in the Spanish Civil War in the thirties were further examples of the SCI programmes across Europe in the years up to the start of the Second World War. SCI wanted to alleviate human misery resulting from war and natural disasters but Ceresole also had a broader vision. Not only was SCI a pacifist organisation but also increasingly an international one, Ceresole believed that if people drawn from different nationalities could work side-by-side they would realise the futility of war and conflict. By the outbreak of the 1939-45 war the SCI reputation was well enough established for the British government to recognise that conscientious objectors could serve as volunteers with SCI as an alternative to service in the Armed Forces. Only later the British branch of SCI was renamed International Voluntary Service (IVS).

In the early sixties interesting developments were taking place within voluntary service organisations. The SCI work camps were typically organised for a short duration, days or weeks, manned by people giving up their leisure time and holidays to work on the projects, usually outside of their own country but certainly alongside people from many other countries. Now a new phenomenon was emerging. In 1961 in his inaugural address the new United States president John F Kennedy challenged the youth of America with the now famous words 'ask not what your country can do for you, but what can you do for your country'. Within six weeks in a blaze of publicity he launched the Peace Corps. In the UK his words struck a chord. VSO had already been formed under a similar premise that bright young people might be prepared to give some of their time to help the peoples of the emerging new countries of the world in the period of de-colonisation. For IVS change was also afoot with the appointment of an energetic young new General Secretary, Frank Judd.

The really 'big idea' of these newly formed organisations was 'long-term' voluntary work, not simply giving the occasional weekend or two weeks of a summer vacation to voluntary activity but a year or even two, and not in Europe where SCI in particular had based its activities but in the newly independent countries of Africa and beyond, the so-called Emerging, Developing or Third World. Frank Judd, for one, saw the value of this type of voluntary work and SCI with its non-political and international credentials as a perfect vehicle through which the idea could be developed. Frank, who later became an MP and a junior minister in the Labour government, was to retain his interest in overseas development throughout his career. After losing his parliamentary seat he returned to the voluntary sector first as director of VSO and then of Oxfam. He now sits in the House of Lords as Lord Judd.

It was some weeks after our initial meeting with RLM that we were summoned to his office. He told us that a number of countries had requested volunteers with co-operative experience and that provided we were accepted by the sponsoring organisation we would indeed become the very first co-operative volunteers. There was no doubt that he was very happy with the prospect. So it was that Keith and I formally completed our application forms, forwarded them to International Voluntary Service and awaited developments.

Not surprisingly at the time the idea of voluntary service came into view my opportunities to travel abroad had been extremely limited, the sum total of my international travel being just two trips. The first a visit to Boulogne, of which I have little recall but which my friend Mick insists we took on a day trip leaving from Clacton Pier sometime in the summer of 1962. The second, a week in Rimini on Italy's Adriatic coast in the summer of 1964 that was rather more memorable. Being early pathfinders for what is now routinely known as 'sand, sun, sex and sangria' holidays in Ibiza or some other Mediterranean resort, we finished with too much of some and not enough of the other, but then that is another story. In those far-off days it wasn't a case of Luton Airport and a two-hour charter flight to the sun but a long and tedious journey across Europe by train. The trip to Rimini was spiced by a day trip by boat to Venice and a helicopter ride to the minute mountain principality of San Marino. Memorable experiences that were sufficient to whet my appetite for further travel.

I cannot remember the exact order of events or timeframe but seem to recall that interviews followed and quite quickly both Keith and I were told that subject to passing the rigorous orientation process we would, by the time autumn arrived in England, be on assignment in Africa: me to the British Protectorate of Bechuanaland; Keith to the Kingdom of Swaziland. At least with my interest in geography I didn't need to refer to an atlas to know that we would be relatively close neighbours in Southern Africa, although the approximate location on the globe was about the sum total of my knowledge of either country.

The summer of 1965 was to prove hectic. Apart from the excitement of voluntary service and preparing for the important end-of-term exams, I had been a prime mover in organising a student study tour to visit co-operatives in the Soviet Union and other parts of the Eastern Bloc. The whole trip had become rather complicated. Fifteen students had signed up for the adventure but when it got now to planning the itinerary there were two schools of thought. Some wanted to reach the Soviet Union by driving through Sweden up into the Arctic Circle then down through Finland to what was then Leningrad. The rest wanted to take a more direct route through Eastern Europe to Moscow. Eventually both groups got their way, amicably agreeing to a split. Five bought a Land Rover and travelled to Russia through Scandinavia. Ten of us, me included, signed up for the more direct route and pooling our funds we were able to purchase a second hand mini-bus for £80.

To support the trip we sought sponsorship in the form of food and supplies from various co-operatives in the UK. As their contribution the Nottingham co-operative, closest to the college, offered to service our vehicle in preparation for the 5,000-mile journey to Moscow and back. A couple of our party drove the mini-bus over to the Nottingham co-op vehicle workshop. Later that afternoon I took a call from the transport manager. 'In my opinion not only will your vehicle not get to Moscow I cannot guarantee that it will even get down the M1.' Our trip was in crisis. Opinion was divided between those who wanted to ignore the advice and those who wanted to abort the trip. Then salvation, the transport manager rang again. Nottingham co-operative was about to purchase a mini-bus. The board of directors had agreed that in return for acknowledgement of their sponsorship in any Press publicity that we gained they would loan us their new vehicle for our venture. We were overwhelmed with joy at this turn of fortune. I was instructed to sell our minibus and an advertisement was placed in the local newspaper.

On the day of publication I received a telephone call with an expression of interest in purchasing our bus. The caller asked a number of questions about the vehicle and a rendezvous at the college was agreed. The potential purchaser arrived together with a colleague in a large and flashy motor. Although I wouldn't describe myself as streetwise in those far-off days I instinctively knew they were a couple of wide boys. On reflection they were very obviously second hand car dealers, down to the trilby hats, large rings and camel hair coats. They gave the bus very close scrutiny and offered me £70, which I immediately refused. I had mentally decided that we should not suffer any loss on our purchase. They assured me that I wouldn't get a better offer but I was adamant and they left. Most of my soon-to-be travelling companions had been away playing football for the college team. When they returned and heard the news they were outraged, particularly one lad, Paddy, and the air was full of expletives. I was unmoved and assured them that we could do better. By the next morning we had received no further telephone calls in response to the advertisement and I began to wonder whether my confidence was misplaced.

Then that afternoon as I was walking to a class in the Hall a rather breathless fellow student ran up to me. 'There is a call for you on the lobby telephone.' It was the car dealer, would I accept £100 for the mini-bus? I said I'd had a lot of interest in the vehicle but if they brought £100 in cash across to the college later that afternoon they had a deal. They duly returned and paid me in crispy £10 banknotes. These were virtually unheard of in those days, coming in the form of a large white sheet about twice the size of their modern counterpart. Even me who had spent the previous year as a bank cashier at the local Co-op had rarely seen these notes. This episode was perhaps another portent for the future, as at that time I little realised I would spend much of my working life as a negotiator, albeit in industrial relations rather than commerce. Anyway in the eyes of my colleagues I had very quickly gone from villain to hero.

We were now well set with a new vehicle and extra funds for our journey. On the 25 June last day of term, we left the college, a party of ten students including my good friend Keith, travelling across Europe in a bright red spanking new bus to Berlin, Warsaw, Minsk, Moscow, Kiev and Prague before returning to England a month later. Further evidence of my burgeoning wanderlust?

By now my schedule was getting more hectic. The day after arriving back in the UK I was required to attend the first stage of our orientation programme together with Keith and about 50 other young people, a course run by IVS in London.

The purpose of the course was to let us know what we might be letting ourselves in for by volunteering and to give IVS a further chance to sift out candidates unlikely to hack it as volunteer workers in the Third World. There was a little propaganda about IVS, our sponsoring organisation, and Frank Judd played a prominent role on the course selling the idea that we were representatives of both IVS and our country. There were practical tips about surviving in a strange environment cut off from the normal luxuries and I guess at another level a lot of observation of people's behaviours and abilities to work together cohesively or to exist without support as many postings were to be to quite isolated parts of our host countries. At the end of this week of lectures about being an effective volunteer we were told whether we had passed muster. Nobody was really sure what was expected of us. In the event we were individually told whether we had been successful. The only person not selected came as a shock when we were subsequently told that only one candidate – an amazingly self confident and opinionated 'Sloany' type – was rejected. She quietly slipped away, presumably suitably chastened.

For the rest of us the 'reward' for passing this stage in the selection process was to be lined up for a cocktail of jabs for protection against an array of tropical diseases. Again the memory is hazy but I do recall standing in line and catching sight of the needle being injected into the arm of the person in front and being shocked to see the instrument of torture consisted of not one but six needles. My arm still faintly bears the circular pattern. I was subsequently required to visit the London Hospital for Tropical Diseases for the yellow fever injection – even more painful; I then went to the local hospital for a blood test. It was here that I discovered that I am squeamish at the sight of my own blood. The nurse left me holding a swab on my arm over the vein from which the sample had been removed and left me to rest for a few moments. It was at this time that I caught sight of the phial containing my sample. At that moment it was easy to relate to the Tony Hancock sketch 'The Blood Donor' because frankly it seemed rather a lot of blood simply for testing purposes. Suddenly the room began spinning and when the nurse returned minutes later I was lying in a crumpled heap on the floor sporting a rather large lump on my temple having bumped my head on the opposite wall as I tumbled forward in a dead faint. In today's litigious world she may have shown more concern.

Our course in London ended on Friday and on Saturday afternoon, having barely had time to go home to collect a change of underwear, we assembled again, this time at Victoria Station in London to catch the overnight sleeper to France. I recall changing trains in Paris as we headed south towards the remote and then rather poor Department of Ariege, close to the border with Spain and a few kilometres from the tiny principality of Andorra. Here we were to spend ten days in a typical SCI work camp, which involved lots of heavy labouring work building a drainage system in a small remote village.

Our group returned to London leaving me just enough time to get home to Colchester to collect another change of clothes before making that brief visit to Nottinghamshire to see Trevor, my new boss, in Bechuanaland.

Two days later it was Sunday and I was back in London starting on a community project for IVS. This was helping to decorate the house of an old age pensioner. The precise location sticks in the memory because first thing on the Monday morning the team leader thrust a paintbrush into my hand. For the first time in my life I was to be a painter. My task was to paint the bedroom window frame. The reason for my strong recall of this situation was that the window looked out across the Caledonian Road to the main gate of the Holloway Women's Prison. The work group comprised me and five other volunteers from various parts of Europe. We painted and decorated by day, ate by candlelight, talked through the evenings and slept on the floor in our sleeping bags at night. To celebrate the successful conclusion of our project the team leader took us on a boat trip down the Thames. Before we said our farewells to one another the team leader pulled me to one side and told me that all was well, I had passed this the final test of my suitability to be an overseas volunteer.

By now it was late August; I was fully indoctrinated, orientated and assimilated and ready for action. All that was left was to await the call to travel to Africa.

As flights were provided free under a sponsorship deal from BOAC, what today is British Airways, we had to be on standby to travel whenever a free seat became available. We didn't have a telephone at home but two weeks later a registered package arrived. It contained details of my travel arrangements and flight ticket. And so it was that on 21 September 1965 I set out upon my journey to Africa. In the previous few weeks I had become quite a seasoned traveller although this was to be my first time on an aeroplane.

Chapter Four

What's it all About?

At this juncture, a few words to describe a co-operative and why this form of business was seen as apposite to the developing world.

Readers will be familiar with the local Co-op still to be found in most UK towns and cities in the form of supermarkets, your friendly milkman or even the funeral director but the co-operatives widely found today in many developing countries owe more to the original co-operative ideas formulated in Britain in the nineteenth century. The principles of co-operation can be traced back to the very heart of the industrial revolution. Robert Owen, a successful industrialist, believed that the working environment influenced ordinary working people's attitude to work. Improve their environment and contentment would follow. To support his ideas he experimented during the eighteen-twenties with a number of totally self-sufficient communities, ideas latterly embraced in starkly contrasting political ideologies such as the Soviet collectives and Israeli kibbutz.

Although his communities all failed, Owen had sowed the seed of an idea that others who followed were to propagate. The significant translation of these ideas into something workable and practical came in the Lancashire mill town of Rochdale in 1844. A group of 40 weavers and their families formed a co-operative society aimed at providing the members with a range of staples at reasonable prices. This was really a members' buying group. Mill workers paid for shares to create sufficient capital to enable a small store to be established and unadulterated products, like flour and sugar, to be bought and then re-sold to the members at a reasonable price.

From this humble beginning a massive co-operative movement grew in Britain through the latter half of the 19th and well into the 20th centuries with co-operative stores in almost every town and large villages supported by farms and factories producing and manufacturing the goods sold in those stores. Latterly a decline set in with the retail revolution in the UK towards the end of the last century. However, the principles of the original Rochdale pioneers are contained in the co-operatives in the developing world and are built on the twin pillars of the Victorian ideal of self-help and the socialist idea of collectivism. When applied in a developing country the overriding premise is one that poor people with limited financial resources can, by working together and pooling their limited resources, form wealth creation opportunities.

Co-operatives take many forms from savings and loan organisations, which are really simple forms of banks which encourage the idea of saving but which offer those with initiative the chance to borrow to buy, say, seeds to grow a cash rather than a subsistence crop to marketing co-operatives where a group of farmers combine to get their product to market and retailing with which we are more familiar in the UK.

On his return to Bechuanaland, Trevor brought exciting news. Whilst in England he had been in negotiation with Oxfam who were running what they called their 'Freedom from Hunger' campaign and Trevor had secured funding of £7,000, a substantial amount in those days, thanks to Oxfam's fundraising efforts in the Suffolk town of Stowmarket. With this funding Trevor set me the task of establishing the first cattle marketing co-operative in Bechuanaland in the Bamangwato reserve.

The significance of the project was not immediately apparent to me but should be viewed in context: a poor country with gross average annual income at that time of £30 per head; an economy that was 90% dependent upon export of cattle to generate its modest GDP; a country into its fourth year of drought, a year during which it was estimated that 400,000 cattle representing one third of the national herd were to die, and a year in which some 350,000 out of the total population of 540,000 would rely on food supplies provided by international aid agencies.

As the days passed and I absorbed information about the country, its culture and the significance of cattle, I became increasingly excited. I think I can state with some degree of modesty that I was to be involved with what was a radical venture.

In the sixties the Bechuanaland cattle industry was effectively controlled by a small number of white South African traders, at the time we called them speculators, which says something about the nature of their business. Although 'speculator' implies some element of risk, as I will describe, in reality these people took relatively little risk in return for a generally handsome profit. Most of them were farmers owning large ranches along either side of the border between Bechuanaland and the Transvaal. The biggest of these ranches I recall being owned by a man called Trotman. Although the indigenous Tswana population were by nature cattle herders what they lacked was access to market. Typically they would want to sell one or two cows. But how could the small and often illiterate farmer get his cattle from the lands to the country's only abattoir in Lobatsi? The white traders ran a cartel and offered the only physical means by which the local populace could sell their cattle to the market. We estimated from the prices they were paying local farmers that the traders were making profits of 50-100% on each cow purchased.

This is how the system worked: Periodically a white trader would travel from his farm in the Tuli Block or cross the border from the Transvaal and enter one of the larger villages. Here through the headman (the village chieftain) he would let it be known that the purpose of his visit was to buy cattle. He would have a target of, say, 50 or 100 cattle. Farmers would bring their cattle to the trader. To rig the market the trick was to ensure supply exceeded demand. The speculator wanted many more than his target number of cattle to be brought to the selling place. This ensured that it was a buyer's market and he could select the best and purchase at the lowest possible price. The speculator would then organise transport of the cattle to the slaughterhouse. This invariably meant having the cattle taken by drovers to the closest railhead where the speculator would have organised rail trucks for their transportation to Lobatsi. Alternatively, where proximity to his own ranch allowed, he would pay some villagers to drive the cattle to his own property where he would fatten the animals on high protein feeds before slaughter as a method of adding value to his purchase. Whilst the exploitation of the poor local farmers was something we were seeking to overcome, at the same time we wanted the indigenous farmers to learn from the farming practices the speculators used.

What was clear was that these traders would not welcome any competition, particularly in the form of co-operatives run by the local people. The potential impact on their business was obvious: more competition equals lower profit margins. Entry into this market would not be easy. On the plus side was the fact that the newly elected provisional government naturally wanted the Tswana people to take control of their own economy and through the prime minister and president-elect Seretse Khama and his dynamic deputy prime minister Quett Masire, the co-operative idea had support at the highest levels in the new administration.

The Department of Co-operatives was very new and still one of the smallest in the government. We were therefore very fortunate that the minister responsible for the Department was Quett Masire, co-founder, with Seretse Khama of the ruling Botswana Democratic Party, which had gained a big majority in the country's recent first democratic election. Co-operatives were part of Masire's portfolio aimed at future development of the economy in the post-colonial period. Masire was just 40 at the time. Born in Kanye into the Bangwaketse tribe he was the ideal foil to Seretse who in contrast came from a rather regal background and the largest tribe, the Bamangwato. Coming from a small tribe and from more humble origins, Masire was the embodiment of what could be achieved in a democratic society where everyone was equal. Masire later became vice president and minister of finance and is attributed with being the architect of the successful transition in the Botswana economy during the years after Independence when large mineral deposits were discovered in the country. Subsequently Masire was to succeed Sir Seretse Khama as president, a post he held from Seretse's death in 1980 to his own retirement in 1998. Having such a heavyweight political master meant that the Department certainly 'punched above its weight' in the political sense.

Manning the Department was just a small handful of people with of course Trevor at its head. Trevor had worked in the co-ops in England primarily as an educationalist before taking his first overseas posting in Basutoland as deputy registrar of co-operatives. This was his first job as number one. His number two was Paul Gott who had been the first person I had met on my arrival in Gaberones. Paul, as I have said, was a Canadian who acted as Trevor's deputy and who had many years' experience working with the Eskimos in Northern Canada establishing savings and loan co-operatives. Paul sadly was in the early stages of a degenerative disease, MS I seem to recall, that required him to walk with the aid of a stick and generally tended to slow him down. The office administration was run by a British expatriate, Ray Pepperall, who had been seconded from another ministry to help establish the new Department. He knew little about co-operatives but had the merit of understanding the 'how to work the system' after many years in the British Army and extensive administrative experience accumulated in various parts of Africa. Then there was John Gaetsaloe, a bright and studious looking young co-operative officer eager to learn about the co-operative principles, who was to later graduate from the Co-operative College in England. In contrast senior co-operative officer Geoffrey Oteng, stocky and chubby faced, inclined to rush into action without thinking through the consequences of his actions. And there was Eli, the messenger, holder of the most junior job in the Department. Rather slow but anxious to please, who at least had the good sense to laugh at my inane jokes. Later I recall Grace joining the Department as Trevor's secretary. Bubbly and well rounded, she weighed in at around 15 st of perpetual effervescence. In addition we had three or four field officers with whom I had little contact as they were out-based covering different geographical regions in the south of the country.

Finally there was the newly appointed Tshoagong who was to be my working partner in the Bamangwato but who at this juncture I had yet to meet.

About a week after Trevor's return Tshoagong entered as a key figure in my new life but before that meeting I was introduced to another person who was to be influential in my stay in Bechuanaland, Vernon Gibberd.

At Trevor's request Vernon travelled down from Radisele and he and I were to spend two intensive days working on what in modern day parlance was a business plan for the cattle marketing co-operative. Vernon made a positive first impression; a naturally open and friendly man but also an imposing figure, tall and handsome, and unlike me quite obviously at one with his environment, being dressed, even here in the very heart of government, in shorts and open-necked shirt nicely set off by a pair of large hobnail boots that I was soon to realise were very much his trademark.

During this two-day stint I discovered that Vernon was a Cambridge University graduate with a degree in agriculture, in his mid-twenties and married to a Dutch girl who was about to give birth to their first child. He told me that Trevor had arranged for him and his wife, Tineke, to be my hosts at the Bamangwato Development Association, or BDA, based close to the small village of Radisele some 200 miles north of Gaberones.

Vernon explained that the BDA was an experimental farm community founded by Guy Clutton-Brock, another of that strange breed of 'British friends of Africa'. Clutton-Brock had started St Faith's Mission Farm in neighbouring Rhodesia where he provided his black workers with education and gave them wide responsibility in running the community. Ideas anathema to the whites that dominated all aspects of that country's economy. Clutton-Brock had established the BDA using the same model with the support of the Bamangwato tribal elders in 1959. Subsequently Clutton-Brock left the BDA to return to Rhodesia leaving its management to another expatriate, Arthur Stanley, who in turn had been succeeded in 1963 by Vernon. Vernon, I discovered, was passionate about rural development and a devotee of the Clutton-Brock philosophy. They were both Quakers and Vernon actually spent his gap year after leaving school working at St Faith's Mission Farm.

Vernon revealed that together at Radisele the Gibberds and myself would be the only white people for about 40 miles in any direction.

At the time, of course, little of what Vernon had told me made much sense.

After two productive days' work we presented our ideas to Trevor and having received his wholehearted support Vernon took his leave, assuring me of a warm welcome and comfortable accommodation at Radisele. We parted with agreement that I should travel north within a few days of our meeting.

Having met with Vernon, and now with a plan of action, I was anxious to get started. However, first I had to meet my new colleague and working partner. Trevor had told me, 'You will be working with Phalatse Tshoagong who I have recently appointed to the post of co-operative officer in the Bamangwato. He is a former teacher but very committed to his new role. You two will get along fine.' Despite an inauspicious start to our relationship these were to prove prophetic words.

One morning, shortly after the meetings with Vernon, I was sitting at my desk when I became aware of a figure standing over my me. Looking up, I saw the beaming countenance of a black man maybe in his mid-forties. Although of average height and build he was possessed of a strong presence. Apart from the broad smile, he sported a handsome moustache and his tight curly hair showed the first flecks of grey. 'Hello Bernard, I'm Tshoagong. Trevor tells me we are to be partners,' he said, thrusting out a firm hand in my direction. At that time it was a conventional European handshake. He had not yet had the opportunity to teach me the African handshake, firstly palm to palm and then a second movement as thumbs entwine. All part of my education yet to come.

Returning all these years later I felt that I should see if any legacy remains of what Trevor and I and our colleagues at the time were trying to put in place. After many failed attempts to contact the Botswana government direct I had tried some international agencies and individuals who I knew had in times past worked in the country. All to no avail. I was despairing but then had a thought, 'What about my old college? I had looked at the website and amazingly on its news page was a picture of the current principal, Mervyn Wilson, with the heads of several co-operative colleges from various parts of Africa, one of them from Botswana. The man from Botswana, I read, had the rather unlikely name of Modukanele Modukanele. I contacted Mervyn who kindly gave me Mr Modukanele's e-mail address and I wrote him a message explaining my mission. Once again like all my previous efforts there was no reply. I contacted Mervyn's office to check that I had the right address and was advised, 'Just keep trying, we have had the same problems.'

Hey, it worked. I re-sent my e-mail and this time in response Mr Modukanele Modukanele wrote back a friendly reply. Yes, both he and his boss, the commissioner of co-operatives, would be delighted to meet with me. Through further exchanges of e-mail it was agreed that I would meet the commissioner on my arrival in Botswana and Mo, due to his absence on business in Lesotho, at the end of my trip.

The afternoon of our first full day in Gaberone and having enjoyed the morning tour with Sandy I am looking forward to the opportunity to revisit the Department of Co-operatives. A car is to be sent to my hotel to collect me and take me to meet the commissioner. Spot on time, quite an achievement by African standards, a rotund figure appeared in the hotel foyer approaching Sandy, who was just leaving, and asked if he was Mr Bernard. Sandy replied, 'No but I know a man who is,' pointing to me. This roly-poly figure came across and introduced himself, but still struggling to tune into English spoken with the local dialect, a problem that had thwarted me when I telephoned from England to try to obtain the commissioner's name, it didn't register. I later discovered he was Lesetswe and his job was that of auditor. He appeared far too jolly for such a role.

In the government limo we drove through the heart of the city to the administrative enclave passing some hugely impressive architectural monoliths, far too grand to be other than the offices of petroleum or insurance companies. At least that is what I thought until Lesetswe proudly declared that they were new buildings to be occupied by the ministries of finance and health respectively. I wondered how many hospitals could have been built for the cost of the latter.

Shortly we drew up outside a more modest three-storey building. Clambering out of the back of the car I was overcome with a sense of déjà vu. This was one of the four original office buildings constructed in 1965 and there, not 100 yards away, the block containing Trevor's old office. These offices at Independence housed the whole administration for the country but were now both dwarfed and outnumbered by their more modern counterparts. I later learned the Civil Service has grown numerically more than ten-fold since 1966.

The co-ops are in the middle of an important strategic change. In the 40 years since Independence they have been part of the Ministry of Agriculture. Recently the Department has been transferred to the Ministry of Trade and Industry. These are the offices of that ministry where the commissioner has been attending a meeting this morning with the minister. The Department, however, is still housed in its old offices within the Ministry of Agriculture.

Lesetswe takes me to a first floor office. Here I am introduced to the commissioner. Her name is Violet Mosele. My first thought is 'butterfly'. Everything so perfect yet at the same time so delicate. Her greying hair is swept back into a bun and she is dressed immaculately in a business suit. She extends her arm towards me in welcome. I take her hand. It is surprisingly long and almost pitifully thin, I am fearful that I might crush her fingers with my handshake. Violet is not what I expected. Newly appointed to this role I for some reason expected someone younger and when she sits behind a large desk on an enormous leather executive chair, I am sure normally occupied by an overweight permanent secretary, she looks out of place. But first impressions can be misleading; she proves bright, intelligent and resolute. I am totally charmed by her.

This is no sinecure; Violet appears to be the latest in a long line of civil servants who have held this post in recent years. None it can be said from my research with any degree of success. Lesetswe and two of Violet's heads of department, Ngae and Elizabeth, join us. Ngae is bespectacled and rather sour-faced and rarely engaged by our subsequent conversation whilst Elizabeth is younger, animated, and enthusiastic. However, I cannot look at her without becoming morbidly fascinated by her choice of an unusual orange hue of lipstick generously applied.

I had read that the Co-operative Bank had been liquidated and various co-ops had gone bust in recent years so I was not expecting a good news story. Violet told me that as she was new to her role she could talk dispassionately about the problems faced by the co-operatives, that I soon appreciate are many and varied. Consumer co-ops running shops seem to be hardest hit and for the very same reasons as the co-ops in the UK, they have fallen behind the competition: relative size equating to superior buying power, more effective distribution chain, lower prices, easier access to capital, better trained management resources. Since Botswana is now relatively prosperous it has become a more attractive market for a number of South African retail chains that have simply had to extend their branch network across the border. They bring modern style premises and a wide range of cheap goods.

I am of course interested in the cattle marketing co-ops and they tell me that some have survived but so have the speculators. The co-ops are handling only around 10% of the cattle sold into the country's abattoirs. For historical reasons, due to problems of sustaining these co-operatives during periods of drought, a new form of co-op multi-purpose has been created to provide a wide range of services that a village community feels that it needs.

What we used to call thrift and loan co-ops are now called SACCOS, which stands for Savings and Credit Co-operative Society, and these appear to be prospering in parts of the country. Violet is upbeat about future prospects for the co-operative sector but I wonder if Ngae shares that optimism.

We spend an hour or so 'chewing the cud' before I sense that I have occupied enough executive time of these senior civil servants. Before leaving, however, I thank Violet and her colleagues for their time and recalling how significant my year in this country was in influencing my own personal development, I tell them that I want to make a small presentation. I have brought with me a framed print depicting a scene from the beach at Frinton-on-Sea, close to where I live in England. It is a sea view, which I thought was oddly apt given that Botswana is so far from the sea but also having ample quantities of sand.

Before leaving I ask Violet whether arrangements can be made for me to visit some co-operatives when I travel north to my old stamping grounds. I had particularly wanted to return to a small and remote village called Matsiloje where we had set up a co-op back in 1965 but was firmly advised that the co-operative there had 'gone bust'.

Violet responds positively to my request and Ngae is assigned the task of both returning me to my hotel and setting up my visits. In the car she tells me that after nearly 30 years in the Department she is taking early retirement. I wonder if she had been passed over in favour of Violet and that is the reason for her rather negative demeanour. Given her length of service in the Department I ask if she knew of any of my old colleagues. I mention Tshoagong but she hasn't heard of him but tells me that John Gaetsaloe had for a time been the commissioner of co-operatives but has now retired and is living in Mochudi whilst Geoffrey Oteng had become an MP for the governing Botswana Democratic Party. I resolve to try and contact John on my return to Gaberone.

Later Ngae telephones me at the hotel and says that when I am in the north I should call the regional manager for the Department of Co-operatives based in Francistown. She says he will be expecting my call, his name is Botho and she gives me a telephone number.

Chapter Five

Trevor Bottomley

Having re-established contact with Trevor and with my mind made on the decision to return to Botswana, I was keen to meet my old boss. From our brief telephone conversation we had established a mutual desire to discover what had happened to each other during those intervening years but in Trevor I saw someone who might have some relatively recent intelligence on what I might find in Botswana and with whom I might be able to make contact.

After receiving my copy of Trevor's book *Happy Highways* it was only a few days later that I called to congratulate him on an entertaining read and set up a rendezvous.

On this first occasion we agreed to meet for lunch in a Hertfordshire pub suitably located somewhere between our respective homes. On my arrival Trevor was already ensconced in a conversation with the publican, a modest half of bitter in hand. As I entered he turned and warmly greeted me and almost instantaneously we were absorbed in conversation about our time in Bechuanaland and how our lives had progressed in the intervening years.

We were to meet again several times before my return to Africa and Trevor, apart from now being an old man well into his eighties, has changed little but for a slightly more pronounced stoop and a thinning head of hair. I have always been grateful to Trevor for the way that he treated me in Africa. From the outset he regarded me as a professional with a valuable skillset that he wanted to deploy to enhance the credibility of the Department of Co-operatives. This had the effect of fundamentally heightening my self-perception and raising my self-esteem, not only during my time in Africa but throughout my working life, yet at the time I was inexperienced both in terms of being given and being able to cope with responsibility and, as an 'expert' on co-operatives barely qualified for the job. Apart from him regarding me as an equal I have always enjoyed Trevor's company lacking as he does any sense of malice or malevolence towards others. Not a person who is so naïve that he cannot see bad in others but someone recognising that whilst other people can be unscrupulous, it is preferable to see the good things first and give the benefit of the doubt. A philosophy these days viewed as rather old-fashioned, being in Trevor's case based upon the principles of Christian Socialism.

Trevor remains a truly charming man. Delightful company and an accomplished raconteur, recalling often minor incidents with a light and humorous touch. My more recent boss, Sir Colin Chandler, was another great storyteller. It is an art form in which, lacking such accomplished skills myself, I greatly admire, no matter how many times I have heard a tale. On that first reunion meeting I was therefore a little taken aback when hardly had we gotten into serious conversation when Trevor remarked, 'Do you remember that yarn of yours about crocodiles somewhere down in the Karoo?' But that is another story, more of which later.

Trevor had, apart from Army service during the Second World War, spent all of his working life in the co-operatives. Like me initially working in retailing then winning a scholarship and subsequently graduating from the college at Stanford Hall. He had returned to the college in the fifties in a staff role. Indeed despite the generational difference in age our backgrounds were remarkably similar.

Trevor had left school at 14 and like me his first job had been at the local Co-op, in his case in the small market town of Trowbridge in Wiltshire. Any career progression was halted when the war intervened and Trevor enlisted in the RAF doing service in far-off India.

When he was demobbed in 1946 like many young men from

working class backgrounds, Trevor contemplated returning to full-time education to obtain the university degree. Not only was the war won but also within UK society a fundamental change was happening; the old class system was falling apart. There was no clearer evidence for this change than in the general election, with a huge majority for a Labour government with a radical agenda of reform and at the expense of Winston Churchill who had guided the country through harrowing times to its ultimate victory. Like many of his working class contemporaries Trevor realised that access to higher education should be based on merit and not subject to the limitations of his secondary education in pre-war Britain. A place was secured at Southampton University to study engineering and he approached his old employer, the Trowbridge Co-op, for financial support. This request was carefully considered but they came up with the alternative proposition: a scholarship to the Co-operative College. An offer that Trevor gratefully accepted and where, like me nearly 20 years later, he fell under the benign influence of Bob Marshall. So much so that after completing his studies Bob Marshall encouraged him to take an educational role with the organisation responsible for running the college, the Co-operative Union. A path I myself was to follow in the late sixties before my career took me in a completely different direction. Trevor later worked directly for Bob Marshall based at Stanford Hall where he spent most of the fifties before the opportunity arose to work in Basutoland and of course later, in Bechuanaland.

It was in 1961 that he was persuaded to take that first overseas role, as assistant registrar of co-operatives working for his old friend Bert Youngjohns in what was then Basutoland, now Lesotho. He moved to Bechuanaland in 1964 in the newly created role of registrar of co-operatives. It was of course in this role that I met and worked with Trevor. Sadly after my return to the UK in 1966 we lost contact.

Only now, meeting Trevor again after all these years, did I appreciate that he had not remained in Botswana for very long after I left. He told me that towards the end of his contract in early 1967 he had been summoned to the presidential suite where the president of the newly independent Botswana, Seretse Khama, made a determined effort to persuade him to stay. Trevor said whilst he was flattered, both he and Barbara had spent many long hours discussing the future and had decided to return to the UK. By now their children, Ann and Steven, were into their secondary education and the couple were anxious to give them a stable home environment. So it was that Trevor and his family returned to England, although Trevor was jobless.

Perhaps because of his unemployed state and his need to fulfil his role as breadwinner in something of a career change, Trevor left the Co-op and found himself a job as a lecturer in economics at a college of further education in Hertfordshire.

Trevor related to me his arrival in his new job. His status was described as 'supernumerary' meaning that he was without any assigned teaching duties, the principal having taken advantage of a temporary budget surplus to build in some extra resource contingency against future pressures to reduce numbers. Trevor had secured a job, a reasonable salary, but no meaningful work. In terms of job satisfaction it was not a success. He was bored.

Later in the seventies, once his children had completed their full-time education, Trevor was to return to his foreign travels taking long-term assignments in Laos and Jamaica before eventually retiring in 1986. Sadly Barbara died from cancer in the very year that Trevor retired.

Trevor told me that he had returned briefly to Botswana on a fact finding mission for one of the international agencies in the early nineties and had maintained one very useful contact in that country, someone who was to prove very helpful in planning my return – Sandy Grant.

Chapter Six

Oodi

Sandy had invited us to visit his home for Sunday lunch. Sunday arrives and late morning we set off for Sandy's house in a place called Oodi, about ten miles outside of Gaberone halfway between the capital and the important tribal village of Mochudi. The village of Oodi is situated beneath a prominent hill that can be clearly seen from miles away. Sandy is concerned that we will get lost trying to find his house so we are to travel north on the main road until we see a sign to Oodi and here he will meet us. We arrive on schedule and there, sure enough, is Sandy in his pick-up truck. With a wave from the open window of his cab he indicates that we should follow him. We are leaving the main road behind and heading towards Oodi Hill when after about three miles Sandy makes a turning to the left onto a rough unmade road and through a ford. This comes as something of a shock as finding surface water here in this part of Botswana is very unusual, particularly at this time of year and given news that the reservoir in nearby Gaberone is at an all time low. Soon we are in the outskirts of the village and shortly we arrive at Sandy's house.

It is a small modern bungalow set in a garden of about half an acre, although a huge outcrop of granite rock dominates the site. In the garden are two brightly painted rondavel. I have read about the tradition of painting huts but have never actually seen them. Later, Sandy, who we discover is an accomplished photographer, tells us that he and his wife have accumulated photographs of these painted huts over many years of travelling around Botswana and are joint authors of a lavishly illustrated coffee table book on the subject.

We are welcomed into the house by Sandy and introduced to his African wife Elinah, and briefly to his stepson who has the unlikely name of Zippo. If we listen to Sandy's account of the lad's behaviour he is well named but on short acquaintance he seems quite normal and it is impossible to make a judgement on the cause of Sandy's apparent parental problems. Elinah is an attractive well-rounded lady, much younger than Sandy, I'd guess in her forties. At first she is a little withdrawn but soon warms to Rosie's very open and friendly demeanour. Sandy's son by this marriage, we are told, is away at boarding school across the border in South Africa.

We take pre-lunch drinks on the stoep. Sandy points out the adjoining plot currently containing one solid looking building that resembles a large shed. This, he tells us, represents a speculative property venture on his part to build a technical college on the site.

On the warm breeze is the distinctive sound of choral music. Sandy explains that there is an open-air church close by. It appears to us to be both loud and intrusive but Sandy suggests that the music and chanting we can hear is nothing compared to a funeral around these parts. He says that the noise generated is both louder and longer, usually stretching through the night. Whilst religion is important here it is no longer the Catholic and Anglican churches that hold sway but obscure sects, some influenced by American missionaries, others purely local and combining elements of both Christian and traditional beliefs. Botswana has a long history of contact with the Christian faith from as long ago as the eighteen-forties through the London Missionary Society. One of their early missionaries was Dr David Livingstone who lived here for many years before his own passion for travel famously took him further north.

The conversation over a light lunch covers many topics and is helpful in filling some of the gaps in our understanding of Botswana. Sandy is a font of knowledge and there are not many Botswana pies that he hasn't had his finger in. He has a wealth of stories and given our itinerary relates one about some inexperienced tourists in the bush – on safari without a local guide and convinced they knew all about life in the bush having read all the good survival literature. Textbook style they established camp, erecting their tents in a circle and lighting a fire in the centre. In the middle of the night one of the party became aware of an intruder. It was a lion. Petrified, he managed to alert his fellow travellers who, taking extreme care, evacuate their tents and make their way to their vehicles, scrambling into what they thought was safety and firmly slamming the doors shut behind them – only to watch in horror as the lion knocked over a can of petrol they had used to get the fire started. Within seconds the tents and equipment had gone up in smoke although by then the lion, in fright, had taken off into the bush.

The conversation moves in a different direction. I glance across to Rosie and with the merest movement of her eyebrow she communicates that like me she senses some tension between Sandy and Elinah. The problem relates to the Phuthadikobo Museum in Mochudi, founded by Sandy and very much his baby for nearly 30 years. Technically in semi-retirement, Sandy is just one of a number of trustees with Elinah officially the curator. The museum, it appears, is in serious financial difficulties and within weeks funds will be exhausted, the staff will have to be paid off and the museum closed. The fate of the artefacts remains uncertain. Already the site has suffered from some acts of vandalism and Sandy is fearful that the whole venture will collapse and the historical collection that he has assiduously gathered over 30 years will be destroyed.

It is easy to sympathise with Sandy's position but his solution is to bombard ministers and senior civil servants with telephone calls, letters and e-mails until they submit to his will, in this case for them to drastically increase the government grant. This tendency towards trying to bully people in the government to provide the museum with more funds now seems to be backfiring and it looks like he may be running out of credit with those in power. His campaigning style that appears to have enjoyed some success in the past has clearly also made some enemies along the way, perhaps to the point where nobody wanted to listen to him anymore.

The real problem, however, is that these two people, both so committed to this particular cause and living under the same roof, are unable to talk to each other about the best way to tackle the problem.

Elinah has gone strangely silent as Sandy continues his tirade against the bureaucrats in Gaberone. Rosie encourages her to express her opinion sensing that Sandy's approach does not really meet with her approval. Suddenly very emotional, she blurts out, 'I can't talk to him about how I feel.' Rosie offers encouragement, 'Both you and Sandy want the same thing, to save the museum, but to work out the best way to achieve this you have to be prepared to say what you really think.' Gradually it emerges that Elinah wants to build bridges with people in government and feels that Sandy is in danger of exacerbating a situation where the goodwill towards him has all but disappeared. Elinah nevertheless takes a fatalistic view and believes everything will be all right in the end. We try to apply some of our professional counselling skills to reconcile these viewpoints to achieve a degree of domestic harmony and hopefully a positive outcome to the overriding problem. All in all it had been an interesting afternoon and we take our leave with a promise that we will come back at the end of our trip to visit the museum.

Oodi is not only home to the Grants but also to an interesting, and in Botswana, a unique co-operative: the Lentswe La Oodi Producers Co-operative Society. I have always personally believed in co-operative ventures where the workers actually make and sell their product, whatever that might be; in this case we have read that the output are woven wallhangings.

So it is that a few days later we find ourselves once again leaving Gaberone. We make our way out of the city and along the Francistown road. We take the turning where we had our rendezvous with Sandy and continue towards Oodi but instead of taking the track on the edge of the village through the ford to Sandy's house we continue heading in the direction of the hill assuming that, as this road was signposted Oodi, it will lead us into the centre of the village, our guidebook stating quite clearly that the village is set beneath the hill. However, as we approach the hill the road veers to the left and the tarmac surface becomes one of loose stones. At this point we grasp the fact that we are skirting Oodi. The village already lies away to our left and we realise that if we continue along this road we will soon leave Oodi behind and find ourselves in Mochudi. We need to take a left turn into the centre of the village. There are a number of alternatives and I choose what I think looks like the main road, and for the first, but certainly not the last time during our time in Botswana, I forget how large and sprawling a Tswana village can be. There are small modest brick built houses but mainly rondavel within the traditional yard but just when you need them nobody on the street. We are in danger of being lost.

We come to a T-junction and in the absence of anyone to ask the way I guess that it is a left turn, which according to my mental map of the village layout would take us in the general direction of Sandy's house. Sandy, I recall, said the co-operative was only a few minutes from his house. Rosie is not convinced but follows my instructions with some hesitation but shortly I am vindicated when we see a sign to the co-operative and soon we spot some buildings along a rough track some way away from the road.

The co-op is contained within a compound surrounded by a two-strand wire fence. There are two separate buildings. Outside of one a number of ladies sit working. We park the car and make our way across towards them. We soon realise that they are hand weaving rugs or carpets on large wooden frames. The ladies appear happy to explain what they are doing and one of the women, quite plump and jolly, puts down her work and offers to show us around.

Our guide says that she was one of the original weavers and is now a supervisor. She explains that the rather exotic sounding name of the co-op refers to the 'rocky hills of Oodi' that dominate the approach village and that the co-op has been running some 30 years. It was started back in 1973 thanks to the enterprise of a Swedish couple, Ulla and Peter Gowenius, who came to Oodi and taught some of the ladies in the village how to spin, dye and weave. The very basic equipment still in use in the workshop was imported from Sweden at that time and is beginning to show its age, as indeed are many of the weavers.

The supervisor leads us inside the large wooden building where there is an array of spinning machines, although most are clearly quite literally gathering dust. Out of perhaps a dozen machines only three or four are still in use. A young girl, whose age I would guess is around 20, is operating one of these. All the other ladies we have seen are at least 40 and most much older When we mention this the supervisor tells us that the co-op that once supported more than 50 workers now has only 20-odd people, who of course are not only workers but also the owners of the enterprise. She says that the men who looked after the maintenance of the machines have all left because of the poor pay whilst other women have either died or left for better paid work in Gaberone. We take some photographs in the spinning hall and chat with the young woman and her colleagues. They seemed delighted that we are interested in what they are doing. As she leads us out of a rear door the supervisor tells us that the co-op produces a range of products: the wall hangings that we had been told about but also handbags, tablemats, tablecloths bedspreads and cushion covers. Here behind the workshop there is a row of vats. This is where the wool, hand spun by the ladies on the wooden spinning wheels, is dyed by boiling in large pots over a fire.

At this juncture a white man appears. He tells us that he is a Norwegian now living in Botswana and he tries to give the ladies business advice. 'Marketing,' he says, 'that is their big problem.' It is hard to disagree because there must be a market for these products even though they have a certain rustic air.

The supervisor tells us that there are examples of all the products in the showroom contained within the second building we saw on our arrival so we say goodbye and take our leave of the workshop and the weavers and wander across the yard to the office-come-shop. Inside it is dark and a musty smell hangs heavily in the air. To our left behind an old desk a small bespectacled lady is performing office tasks, slowly and methodically working her way through what appears to be a pile of invoices. Another woman, rather more typically African with heavy breasts and a large backside, is busying herself tidying up the stock. As I look around I realise that it is something of an Aladdin's cave with a wide array of products although most impressive are the woven tapestries designed by the ladies and depicting local village life. Thinking about the Norwegian gentleman's comments I wonder whether another problem is stock control. Too many unsold products.

We chat to the ladies and I ask whether the designs on the tapestries are traditional scenes but the smaller woman says, 'No, there are drawings to follow but the more experienced weavers literally make up the designs as they go along from their memories and personal experiences.' Before leaving we make a modest purchase, the larger wall hangings regrettably being far too large to carry in a suitcase throughout the rest of our trip.

It is sad that the co-op is struggling to survive because this is surely exactly the sort of community project that is needed. It can generate proper jobs; income for the village economy and encourage learning of new skills.

Chapter Seven

Radisele and the Road North

Before we travelled to Botswana, in one of his e-mails Sandy had politely declined my invitation to come across to our hotel in Gaberone and join us for dinner, claiming, 'The roads are far too dangerous.' Not sure if this was due to street crime or driving standards I asked for clarification. He replied, 'Friends have insisted that the worst drivers in the world are to be found in Belgium. My opinion differs; I would argue that those here are vastly worse. A view that I have heard is that this essentially first generation of drivers have little idea about speed, distance, control and so on. If correct, which seems likely, that well describes the situation here. The problem generally is: overtaking equals power – which is usually when disaster occurs. And night driving is best avoided.

I did not pursue the matter but felt I might be a good judge of local driving standards, recalling my own experiences driving in Bechuanaland in the sixties.

On the day before I was due to travel north for the first time, Tshoagong came to meet me in Gaberones, travelling down in the Bedford truck that was to be our main mode of transport in the coming months and what was to be the cause of one of my most embarrassing moments.

Nearly 40 years and many, many thousands of miles later, I admit that I am far from being the best driver in the world. At the time I left England for Africa my experience behind the wheel was limited to 20 driving lessons taken whilst at college, and a failed driving test that as an experience in itself was bound to leave me scarred for life. The examiner foolishly applying the dual brake to stop me crossing a junction on a red traffic light initially unnerved me. This probably explains how on the instruction 'take the next turning on the left' I reacted too quickly and found myself on the driveway in front of a large and imposing Victorian mansion somewhere in the middle of Loughborough. So it was that arriving from the UK without a driving licence I was informed by Paul Gott that I would need to obtain a licence locally, but this would be a pure formality. When I expressed serious doubts about having the requisite driving skills for the conditions he pooh-poohed my objections and encouraged me to become acquainted with local driving conditions by giving me permission to drive his Morris Traveller around Gaberones.

When Tshoagong arrived at the office that morning he informed me that as we were heading to Radisele the following day he had decided that I should do so with a Bechuanaland driving licence and had therefore taken in hand arrangements for me to take my driving test at noon that very day. He, like Paul, assured me that this was a formality and not to worry. Despite the advice I did worry, particularly when he dropped what was, from my perspective, a totally unexpected bombshell: the driving test would of course be in his government Bedford truck. Fortunately I did not have long to wait. It was classic chicken and egg. Not having a licence meant I couldn't actually drive the vehicle on the road so I was left to a short practice drive up and down outside the Ministry building. This was not encouraging. Needless to say for someone whose driving experience comprised a few hours driving a Mini through the lanes of rural Leicestershire with the occasional foray into the quiet market town of Loughborough, the sheer size, the ruggedness of the vehicle, judging the dimensions when reversing and manhandling a temperamental gearbox were each in themselves new experiences not likely to be absorbed in minutes. The omens were not good.

Tshoagong drove me to the government test centre, which was the yard of the PWD, the Public Works Department. The yard was an area of maybe 100 x 100 yards within which the bush had been cleared and then enclosed by a wire fence. Inside this compound was a simple concrete building, the workshop where government vehicles were brought for maintenance and repair. The area in front of the building had been marked out with a series of cones. At the front of the PWD workshop there was a concrete ramp onto which vehicles could be driven for inspection. Being around lunchtime the vehicle mechanics and apprentices in their smart blue dungarees were lolling around the yard. The driving tester was a gnarled old expatriate who doubled up as the workshop foreman. He explained that I was required to perform a number of manoeuvres driving around then reversing between the cones. I was then to drive onto the ramp, stop on the upward slope, holding the vehicle still by using the clutch rather than the brake. Then on the tester's instruction I was to drive up and across the flat top and down the other side. Needless to say the whole episode was a disaster, stalling the engine, crunching the gears and eventually nearly toppling the vehicle off the ramp – sideways. For the tester it was an all too easy yet clearly embarrassing decision, failing a white man – the first time it had ever happened. At least I had made history. For the apprentices I had provided some great lunchtime entertainment judging by their laughter at the spectacle.

Having admitted my own limitations as a driver I have to say that since that embarrassing experience I have nevertheless driven many thousands of miles both in the UK and in different parts of the world and seen many examples of appalling driving even worse than my own, but after that first morning driving around Gaberone with Sandy I was beginning to see his point. Lane discipline appeared non-existent and the Batswana drivers' approach to circumnavigating that great British invention, the roundabout – a complete nightmare for the unprepared visitor. Naturally I left the driving to Rosie, little realising at the time that I was imposing upon her a huge amount of stress.

Seeming to confirm Sandy's view the following day, the banner headline in the Daily News, the local newspaper, read 'Botswana Leads in Road Deaths' with the introduction 'Botswana is ranked among countries with the highest number of road accident deaths throughout the world'. The article, quoting a senior civil servant, went on to compare the record of Botswana with its closest neighbour: 'The number of deaths are even more than double those of South Africa'. Given the relative size and population of the two countries it was a frightening statistic.

That very evening we took a post-dinner stroll and were confronted by a scene of utter mayhem. A substantial crowd of excited onlookers had gathered around what on closer inspection proved to be an almighty pile-up blocking the entrance to our hotel involving a saloon car and pick-up truck, both of which were total write-offs. Already in attendance were medical rescue and auto recovery vehicles. Only later when a pukka ambulance arrived did we realise that these were accident chasers. Sure testament to the number of accidents there were on a regular basis on the streets of the city. One of the vehicles involved in the accident had lost a wheel, which now lay some 100 yards down the road where somebody had marked its location with a triangle. Eventually a lone policeman in a squad car arrived on the scene. He began to take measurements. When he went down the road to inspect the wheel it had mysteriously disappeared.

After our days in Gaberone getting acclimatised, meeting people and readying ourselves for the journey north back to some of my old haunts it is time to venture forth and Rosie and I set out from Gaberone on the long drive to Francistown, some 270 miles. Although about two thirds of the way up we will pass by Radisele I have decided that I will not try and find the BDA site and my old home, if indeed either still exist, until our return journey.

With all this accumulated negative information about the dangers of driving in Botswana it is therefore with some trepidation that we begin our journey. Having mutually agreed that we are not in a hurry we pledge to drive at an absolute maximum of 100 kph throughout our trip, well within the permitted maximum of 120 kph. (An undertaking I can honestly say that we met.)

After piling our bags into the boot of the hire car we exited the Sun Hotel. Driving onto a dual carriageway means that we initially head left down Julius Nyerere Avenue before taking a life threatening 360° turn around the roundabout at the junction with Notwane before heading back in the direction of the airport. At the edge of the city we met the ring road and instead of continuing straight towards the airport we turned north onto the Francistown road. We have of course been this way before on our visits to Oodi but soon we passed the Oodi sign and at last, we sense, we are truly on our way.

The road north for the first 20 miles or so is a superb four-lane highway. Then, soon after passing the sign to Mochudi, it narrows to a two-lane road with no central reservation but is as straight as far as the eye could see. A seemingly endless road ahead, either side is dotted with thorn bushes and occasional low acacia trees. Every so often some goats or a cow graze – a scene exactly as I recalled. Since my first trip with Tshoagong the only major change is that the actual road had been improved immeasurably. The word 'improved' hardly seems to do justice to the degree of change yet as we make our way on this new super-highway it is easy to recall that first journey with Tshoagong as for much of the way, still clearly visible alongside the new tarmac road, runs the old sand road on which Tshoagong and I spent so much of our time.

On this, the country's major highway, traffic is still relatively light. Save for the occasional car or truck, the most common vehicle we see are buses all bearing a sign in the window stating simply: 'Gabs', and with barely any traffic it is difficult to foresee any impending danger. Yet every few miles we pass old wrecks by the roadside and even more frequently tyre marks indicating where braking vehicles have either collided or left the road and driven into the bush.

After an hour or so we see a plume of smoke on the horizon. We drive on and on for 20 miles, never quite reaching the source until quite suddenly, coming over the brow of a hill, we spot ahead a bus ablaze by the roadside, a gaggle of passengers huddled together at a safe distance from the wreck. Despite our speculation about approaching a serious accident in this case it proves to be not a crash scene but a definite case of overheating. I judge that the petrol tank has long since exploded, nevertheless taking no chances I hurriedly accelerate past the shell of what until recently had been a luxury long distance coach.

The roads prove to be only one aspect of communication that has changed out of all recognition over the past 40 years. In the sixties we relied on a rather inadequate radio system; what telephone links that did exist were at best tenuous, crackly to the degree of being inaudible and frequently out of order. As I was soon to discover they did not extend as far as the BDA. But think about it: hundreds upon hundreds of miles of overhead cables to link relatively small numbers of telephones when with today's technology a better result can be achieved by constructing a comparably small number of masts. Yes, the mobile telephone has had a major impact even here in the African bush. As we drive north this marvel of modern technology is amply demonstrated. My mobile telephone rings. It is a call from a car dealership in England; my new car has arrived. When do I want to collect it? The salesman is totally oblivious to the fact that I am several thousands of miles away in the very heart of Africa.

Back in 1965 after the driving test debacle I had rather shamefacedly returned to Tshoagong who was less than amused, I suspect, being embarrassed by association. He made a sucking sound through his front teeth which I was to learn was his trademark reaction when he was annoyed and he thrust a set of L-plates into my hands with the rather curt instruction that I was to return within a month and pass. Our relationship had got off to a poor start. So it was on 12 October 1965 I headed to my new home.

That first journey north was an early opportunity to better get to know Tshoagong who was to be my colleague and almost constant companion for the next eight months. Important given the stuttering start to our relationship. By the end of that first journey I felt that we had already developed an excellent rapport and I was totally confident that ours would prove to be a successful partnership.

Phalatse Tshoagong was designated as a co-operative officer and had been given responsibility for establishing co-operatives in the Bamangwato tribal area. During that first journey together I discovered he was a refugee from South Africa. His profession was that of a teacher and he had been married with three children but was now divorced. Tshoagong told me that he had only recently moved to Botswana and now lived in Pilikwe, a village some ten miles from Radisele behind the Tswapong Hills. He had already remarried and he and his new wife had just had their first child. His wife, who I later met, proved to be a pretty but very shy local girl barely half his age.

Through my working life I have always preferred the use of first names with colleagues, whether they senior or junior to me in the organisational hierarchy. In the sixties colonial environment everyone knew Tshoagong by his surname. Looking back it seems odd. I recall that junior members of the Department were known by their first name and Tshoagong always called me Bernie. I am sure sometime early in our relationship we must have discussed this subject because we talked about most things.

Through Tshoagong I was to develop a better understanding of Africa; of village and tribal life; of apartheid and, greatly influenced by this relationship I would develop my own liberal set of values on matters of race and politics. Although I had spent the previous year at college with people from many different countries and cultures this was the first real relationship that I had formed with a black person. The chemistry in a personal relationship is important and despite the differences in our race, upbringing and age we quickly formed a strong bond of friendship. To help us succeed in our task we also had complementary skills. Me, knowledge of co-operatives; of bookkeeping and how to take minutes and keep records. For his part Tshoagong, although not a native of Botswana, knew the people and the area and spoke the local dialect. His background meant that he had a worldliness that many of the locals lacked and a liberal outlook on life. Combined this made us a formidable partnership and the relationship was to prove both productive in terms of work achievement and one valued by me at a personal level. I am confident that Tshoagong felt the same way.

In the weeks that followed I was to regularly make the same trip from Gaberones to Radisele and back. If Tshoagong and I were travelling together we would use the Bedford truck but if I were travelling alone this would be by train, a journey of some six hours. Travelling north the train halted at Radisele, although apart from a small store on the nearby main road it was not obvious that such a place existed. Those were far-off days but my recollection was that from the railway line the BDA lay some two miles to the east along a dusty and little-used track. A fact soon to be tested on my return these many years later. Back then if I was lucky Vernon might come down in the Land Rover to collect me, but as the train arrived at sometime after midnight this was really too much to ask on a regular basis and I would hope for a clear sky and full moon or grope my way up the track at dead of night with only the sound of crickets for company.

By road that same journey from Gaberones was just as long and tedious as I was soon to discover on that first journey with Tshoagong. Although the main north-south road that ran through the country linked South Africa and Rhodesia and passed through the major Bechuanaland towns of Lobatsi, Gaberones and Francistown, at that time there were few signs that it was an important transnational highway. Apart from the two miles of tarmac I had seen in Lobatsi the whole 400 miles of road from border to border comprised a rough unmade surface. Even on this the main highway Tshoagong and I were frequently forced to stop as we lost traction in the deep soft sand blown by the prevailing wind from the Kalahari Desert to the west. Then the tedious job of digging ourselves out.

Meeting a vehicle travelling in the opposite direction was always a nightmare. A cloud of billowing dust signalled its approach from miles away. As the two vehicles approached each other, with windows firmly wound shut, it required the driver to slow and pull over towards the deeper sand, which formed the verge. A hazardous manoeuvre slowing but never stopping as the vehicles passed within inches. It was critical to maintain some traction even though visibility through the cloud of dust was almost zero. Then the after effect, despite the closed window of the truck cab you found yourself covered by a fine film of sand which by journey's end left you yellow and in desperate need of a shower. This being a luxury enjoyed only if travelling south to Gaberones. At Radisele, as I was to discover, we had to be content to pour a bucket of cold water drawn from our communal borehole and have a flannel wash.

Later in the day, finally ensconced in our hotel in Francistown, I reflected on how different the day's drive had been from the travails of the old days. Yet having said that, the towns of Mahalapye and Palapye apart, the scenery had been exactly as I recalled.

It had been a long day behind the wheel but for perspective I was anxious get Rosie's reflections so asked for her thoughts about the country on this our first day outside of Gaberone, and wondered how her first impressions compared with my own all those years ago. Here are Rosie's thoughts:

'Although many times you have described to me what the bush is like it is far more barren than I ever envisaged. So dry. Those poor starving animals, thin and emaciated with their ribs showing through. Again, just like you had told me. I was still surprised by people appearing from nowhere in areas where there seems to be nothing but endless bush and absolutely no signs of any habitation. I was struck when we passed over some quite long bridges, like those at Tati and Shashe, to see the riverbeds below completely dry. Being on the main road we of course did not pass through many villages but we still saw plenty of traditional rondavels, yet once we had travelled through large towns like Mahalapye and Palapye for me it was evident that soon the traditional homes will be lost. Concrete blocks and tin roofs seem much more popular than mud bricks and thatch.

I couldn't help but notice how the colour of the sand is constantly changing. This was very evident north of Mahalapye where they were excavating for a new road. The colours change all of the time from pale yellows to deep orange. We speculated that rather then being caused by some geological phenomenon this may in fact be influenced by water and how far it is below the surface at different points.

Talking of strange phenomena we also experienced the wind funnels or mini-tornadoes that whip up huge swirls of sand high into the air as they make their way through the bush.

The road itself was at the same time both interesting and tedious. Nothing like the road conditions you had described to me. The road was excellent and we could easily have driven much faster. Having said that there were so many wrecks along the way it was incredible, including the blazing bus by the roadside that the passengers had obviously rapidly evacuated, and our more cautious driving was probably sensible. Sometimes, looking in my rear-view mirror, it was scary seeing a fast approaching vehicle and knowing that this idiot driver was going to blast past me and have to violently cut across into my path to avoid a head-on crash. And, despite the crazy drivers, what a waste of time with all those police speed traps and checkpoints on a road with so little traffic.

Finally what were those concrete chambers every kilometre or so all the way up from Gaberone?'

The answer to that latter conundrum we subsequently gleaned from various sources. It appears that some years ago there was a plan to pump water from the north where it is relatively plentiful to the dry south. A pipeline was laid along the line of the north-south road and pumping equipment installed along the way. Unfortunately the pipes used were made of plastic and not fit for purpose; considerable leakage occurred undermining the whole project. Later it was discovered that a government minister responsible for awarding contracts had a financial interest in the company supplying the piping.

In planning my return to Botswana I was surprised to find Radisele marked on maps because as I have said in the sixties it wasn't, in my recollection, really a place in the sense of being a town or even a village of any consequence. It was a halt on the railway line, a place where the train would stop to enable the steam locomotive to take on water. More importantly for me of course was that it was nearby my new home at the Bamangwato Development Association, the farm funded by British charities and run by Vernon Gibberd.

Although when I had met Vernon in Gaberones he had told me about Radisele on that first journey north with Tshoagong, I had little inkling as to the nature of my new home. After all I had spent my first three weeks in Gaberones living in the comfort of Trevor's bungalow and working in a modern office complex. I had made forays out to some of the tribal villages so wasn't totally unaware of typical living conditions in the country but as I was to subsequently discover when meeting and talking with my fellow volunteers over the coming months, none of them were living in quite such a remote location nor in the primitive conditions I was to encounter at Radisele.

For Rosie and I it had been a relatively easy drive north and after passing Radisele we had been able to press on the remaining 100 miles or so to reach Francistown in a day's drive from Gaberone. For Tshoagong and I it was a shorter but altogether more challenging journey. We eventually arrived at Radisele in mid-afternoon, crossed the railway track and headed up the dusty track towards the BDA. There was no signpost but suddenly, set in the same flat scrubby bush that we had travelled through for the whole of our drive north, I was aware that we were approaching some kind of settlement.

First, there in the bush in front of us was a rondavel, then another and another. A rondavel is the traditional hut found in most parts of Africa – round in shape and constructed with mud bricks and topped with a thatched roof. The settlement comprised maybe six or eight such huts. Taking in the scene I realised that the first hut was quite large and sturdy and stood out because unlike the traditional huts it had been whitewashed. There was another more modest traditional hut next door. This I was to discover was not occupied and was to remain empty for some months, but was later to become the temporary home of an interesting occupant – but more of that in due course.

After passing these two huts the track opened up into a clearing around which there was a semi-circle on the left of several more huts. On the right was a large low rectangular building made from bricks and with a corrugated roof, which I rightly assumed housed the farm office of the BDA. My recall is that it comprised two separate offices, one of which was to become the head office of the Bamangwato cattle marketing co-operative. In the centre of this circle of buildings was a well.

On our arrival Tshoagong stopped the truck outside the office block and before we had time to clamber down from the cab Vernon emerged, as ever in cheery mood, to extend his welcome. With a nonchalant gesture he indicated that I was to take residence in the first hut, the whitewashed hut at the far end of the settlement, at the same time explaining that the farm manager Jimmy and his extended family occupied the other huts closest to the office. But before taking my belongings to what was to be my home for the next eight months he led me along a short path to the far end of the settlement. Here, half hidden by the bush were two more rondavels built in traditional style. These he proudly announced were the Gibberds' home, the first hut being their bedroom, the second their living quarters: kitchen, dining room and lounge combined. It was here that Vernon introduced me to his wife Tineke – Dutch, tall, angular, bespectacled. Her very plainness struck me in contrast to Vernon's spectacularly handsome features.

Where Vernon had a permanently friendly and amiable disposition Tineke's welcome was friendly but restrained. I was always less comfortable in her company and looking back with the benefit of hindsight I feel that she probably and understandably resented my intrusion into the life that she and Vernon had chosen in this remote African bush location. In addition, as I was soon to discover, she was at the time in the first stages of pregnancy and subsequently returned to Europe for the birth of what was their first child.

Introductions completed, Vernon led me back through the settlement to the white rondavel to view my new accommodation. It proved to be spartan but surprisingly large and had the advantage over the traditional Tswana rondavel insofar as it was built around a raised concrete floor and I always felt secure here against any unwanted intrusions by snakes or unpleasant creepy-crawlies. With its high roof the hut was always cool relative to the high temperatures outside. There was no running water; this was obtained from a tap set beside the well in the centre of the settlement, which in turn was drawn from a borehole sunk deep below the surface. My own personal toilet, set some 20 yards away from my hut, was the traditional thunder box – a small square construction, rather like a sentry box used by the military, surrounding a deep hole. Needless to say in a climate where temperatures could easily reach 35°C it could get unbearably hot and smelly and definitely not a place to sit contemplating the meaning of life.

As I was to eat with the Gibberds when at home, my hut had no cooking facilities and the simple furniture comprised a bed and a small bedside chest of drawers. Living out of a suitcase took on a new meaning. Lighting was by candle. For what amounted to £1 a week it was agreed that Maria, a married woman from the nearby village, would come and clean the hut and do my washing.

Chapter Eight

Swaneng

I quickly got work underway to establish our new co-operative business venture. On my second day at Radisele, Tshoagong and I visited the three nearby villages – Seleka, Ramokgonani and Pilikwe – to begin the process of sounding out the tribal elders about our ideas for a cattle marketing co-operative.

Then a few days later I travelled with Tshoagong to an important meeting in the tribal capital of Serowe, where together with Trevor Bottomley, we were to meet Chief Leapeetswe Khama and the district commissioner. Importantly for me in Serowe was the Swaneng Hill Secondary School, our first port of call. Visiting Swaneng was for me at that time an exciting prospect.

Serowe lies some 40 miles to the west of Palapye set amongst a range of low undulating hills and is the tribal village of the Ngwato people. Swaneng School was located on the eastern outskirts before reaching the village proper. It was where Tshoagong and I were to stay overnight.

As we approached Serowe from the direction of Palapye, the school buildings, set around one of the first hills that rise from the plain that is a feature of the landscape here, were the first thing that we saw. The school, founded by Patrick Van Rensburg in 1963, has a unique place in modern Botswana history. However, for me at that time the visit to the school was significant in that it offered a chance to meet some of my fellow IVS volunteers for the first time since we had gone our separate ways at Victoria Station following the end of our work camp in France. In that first year of full-time volunteers to the developing world, IVS had sent eight of us to Bechuanaland. Apart from myself there were two nurses, Carmel and Judy, based in Gaberones, and five teachers working at Swaneng School.

I have happy memories of Swaneng, a refuge from my isolated existence in Radisele. Unlike most other volunteers who either worked in Gaberones or in schools and communities together with other volunteers, I was very much alone at Radisele and devoid of creature comforts. Swaneng offered relative luxury in their guest accommodation, facilities like electricity, a hot shower and good food. The school even boasted an open-air cinema where I recall watching the epic movie 'Quo Vadis' one balmy night under the stars. But the most important element of Swaneng for the volunteers based there was that they had each other for mutual support. This was to be the important ingredient for me, both now and on subsequent visits: the good companionship simply being amongst a group of bright young people of my own age. My diary from the time shows that my visits were frequent.

The founder, headmaster and chief fund-raiser for the whole Swaneng enterprise was the South African exile Patrick Van Rensburg. A large man sporting a heavy beard, Pat was in appearance every inch the archetypal Boer but the actual person was something quite different – quiet, understated with a gentle sense of humour supported by a grittiness that enabled him to pursue his dream despite many setbacks along the way. Pat had been in the South African diplomatic service in the fifties but increasingly disillusioned by the apartheid policy of his government he had resigned, returning to South Africa where he became an active member of the Liberal Party. Not an extremist by any conventional measure, he was clearly regarded by the National Party government in power in Pretoria as someone with dangerous ideas and after having his passport confiscated he fled to the sanctuary of Botswana where he began his hugely innovative educational programmes.

Pat's vision for Botswana was that whilst there was clearly a need for a universal system of education and an end to illiteracy, the education system had to meet the immediate needs of the country by teaching a range of practical skills like carpentry and building. A skill set relevant to the needs of the country rather than a purely academic education that in practice in those days meant a choice between a job in the Civil Service and no job at all. From his ideas emerged what Pat called the Brigades Movement, seeking a fusion of the traditional craft and developed world technical skills.

As a visitor to Swaneng, one of many transients drawn magnet-like to this hive of energy, activity and innovation, this might have been the extent of my relationship with Pat. A guest of Swaneng School and an admirer of him and his efforts to develop the education system in this backward country, where the British colonial government's preparations for the country's independence were quite frankly negligible. However, as another string to his bow Pat also had the distinction of forming at Swaneng the first registered co-operative in Bechuanaland, a consumer co-operative managed by him and his staff for the students at the school. Pat had an intuitive sense of the value of co-operatives but little knowledge of the co-operative ideals and even less experience about how to run one successfully. My visits to Swaneng therefore always included personal time with him to discuss problems of bookkeeping or stock control and more intense discussion on the historical and philosophical basis of the co-operative ideology, and the more time I spent with him the more I was impressed by his vigour, commitment and downright cussedness in the face of adversity.

Supporting Pat, the staff at Swaneng comprised two groups. Mature people like Donald and his Indian wife Susheela, and Peter, the water diviner and his wife Diane. These were professional teachers who chose to be there because they had been attracted by the ideas of Patrick Van Rensburg. People who had made a long-term commitment to the Swaneng project. The second group were the young volunteers like myself, almost all at that time from Britain, volunteer workers who had arrived at Swaneng almost by chance and beforehand would have had little or no knowledge of Patrick and his ideas and who would stay for one, or in some cases two years before returning to the UK to continue their studies or their careers.

The full-time staff had their own family rondavels set on the hill overlooking the school whilst Pat, together with his charming young English wife Liz and their young son Tom, lived in a house at the top of the hill. For the volunteer teachers life was more communal and they spent most of their spare time in a staff room dubbed 'the mess', a large single-storey building with table and chairs for eating or working and large comfortable armchairs for relaxing.

The mess provided the focal point of activity at Swaneng and was the scene of constant comings and goings and the source of huge amounts of energy. Apart from being both the physical and spiritual centre of their world, for the volunteers there were frequent visitors both from within the school and outside. From Patrick bouncing this idea or that around before disappearing off at great speed, and from Donald who clearly enjoyed the energy generated by the younger members of staff but who could also retreat to the sanctuary of his own home and family whenever he liked. Most of the other full-timers were more occasional visitors. The constant stream of outsiders included people like myself. Other regulars, as I was to discover, were the chief himself, Leapeetswe Khama, and his younger brother Segkoma.

The conversation in the mess was at a mind stretchingly high intellectual level; even today I recall the heated discussion on the taxing subject of why men roll up the emptying toothpaste tube from the bottom whilst women simply press the middle of the tube. But whoever might pass through here as teacher, helper or transient visitor the focal point for everything that happened within the boundaries of Swaneng was the remarkable Patrick Van Rensburg himself.

Chapter Nine

Patrick Van Rensburg

Back in the sixties I had developed a huge regard for Patrick Van Rensburg and he was undoubtedly one of the most remarkable of all the people I was privileged to meet during my time in Africa. Not that he was a man without his faults. The Pat I recall was very much a unique but at times incredibly frustrating personality, constantly going off at tangents to pursue his latest idea, leaving mayhem and confusion in his wake but engendering in turn huge amounts of enthusiasm and goodwill amongst his disciples. Naturally on my return to Botswana I was anxious to make contact with him.

From my research I had read that after Independence, Pat had become a Botswana citizen. During those post-Independence years he was to work closely with the new Botswana government, in addition to Swaneng starting another two new schools, but that relationship was to become increasingly fractious.

Although I knew that Pat must by now be well into his seventies, I had read that he had established and was now running an organisation called the Foundation for Education with Production. Sure enough, this organisation was listed in the Gaberone telephone directory. I called. A young woman answered the telephone, I guessed his secretary or personal assistant. She told me that Pat was not available so I explained the purpose of my call and asked whether he would agree to meet with me. She suggested I call again the following day. I called back. The young woman answered again. 'I am sorry but Pat is still not available in person to speak with you but he has left a message. Yes, in principle he would be delighted to meet but he has some pending legal business to conduct in Johannesburg and is reluctant to commit to a meeting at present as he is expecting to have to travel to South Africa at short notice any time in the next few days. Would you call him in around a week's time?'

A week later and I call again. No reply. It is a Sunday so perhaps he is not in the office today. I have an acute dislike of rejection. Perhaps he was just trying to put me off. Rosie has a more positive take. 'If he said he will see you and he knows the reason you want to meet him I'm sure he meant it.' I look up the telephone directory. There is an out of town number under 'Van Rensburg, P'. I call. There is someone on the other end. It proves to be Patrick's youngest son speaking from the family home in Serowe. I explain my predicament. He tells me that his father is indeed in Gaberone in his flat-come-office and has probably gone out for some shopping. I should keep trying the Gaberone number. I call again. On this third occasion Pat answers in person and not only agrees to a meeting but suggests that he come across to my hotel that very afternoon.

It proves to be a fascinating encounter and Pat is able to fill many of the gaps in my knowledge of Botswana over the intervening 40-year period.

When Pat arrives in the hotel foyer I immediately recognise him. Now 74 years old he has naturally aged and part of that ageing process is that he seems physically much smaller than I had remembered. Still, with a full head of now white hair and the trademark beard, the facial lines cut deep, sure evidence of his years in the African sun. When I go across to greet him I am looking for the signs of recognition but to be honest I am not sure that he remembers me as such; he certainly gives no indication, perhaps I no longer conform to the mental picture he has of me. In fairness it had been a long time and my appearance has changed; certainly in the sixties I did not sport my moustache and unlike him my hair is thinner than in those days. Perhaps he had visualised someone from the past and I didn't somehow match the picture that his mind had conjured. On the other hand he is absolutely as I recall, not only the facial features but also his deceptively quiet voice and measured tones. Both considered and sincere.

The initial exchanges seem quite formal reinforcing my concern that he has no recall of me. Anyhow it didn't seem to matter because despite that initial awkwardness we quickly establish some common ground and when he specifically asks me to send salutations to both Trevor and Jon Harlow, which I naturally agree to pass on when I return to England, I sense that our conversation is truly up and running.

So after that slightly hesitant start we quickly establish a rapport and within minutes I find myself in a fascinating conversation in which Pat very openly responds to my prompting about things that have happened to him and his projects.

Talking with Pat I realise that whilst I broadly understood his background, the Afrikaaner liberal, and his philosophical differences with the National Party government, there are an awful lot of gaps in my knowledge about how he first came to be in Serowe and my questions come at a fast and furious rate.

I am intrigued by the idea that Pat has business in South Africa knowing that back in the sixties after his escape from house arrest he had been banned from his homeland and I wonder when the ban was lifted. Pat proves the perfect interviewee and takes me back to the very beginning to answer my question.

'Of course my problems with the South African authorities started when I resigned from my diplomatic post whilst I was based in the Congo. The decision of a young fairly junior civil servant to leave a government post would of course in normal circumstances not create any ripples except that in my case I specifically cited my disagreement with the government's apartheid policy. It made me a marked man. When I returned to South Africa I joined the opposition Liberal Party and became an active anti-apartheid campaigner. By no measure was the South African Liberal Party an extremist organisation, indeed as the name implies it had much in common with your own Liberal Party in the UK. Anyway I got involved in a lot of political activity and was a keen advocate of the idea of countries overseas boycotting South African goods as a way of forcing the government to confront the efficacy of its apartheid policy. I visited the UK where I sought support for this idea and when I returned home I was put under house arrest by the South African authorities.'

Unbeknown to them at this time Pat was already writing and later published his seminal critique of apartheid.

Pat told us that in 1962, on the very day that this book titled *Guilty Land* was published in the UK, he fled from his homeland by crossing into neighbouring Swaziland en route to England. The ban preventing him from returning to South Africa was to remain in place for almost 30 years from that day. Like many other South African dissidents at the time, both black and white, he regarded himself as 'in exile' in the UK for as long as it took for apartheid to be ended, little realising how long that would take.

Soon after arriving in England Pat met his future wife Liz. But Pat couldn't settle down to life in England and little more than a year on and hankering for a return to Africa, he and his new bride travelled back through Europe and Africa eventually finding themselves in Serowe in Bechuanaland, the closest he could get to his homeland free of the risk of long-term incarceration.

Initially taking jobs as primary school teachers in the village, Pat and Liz were befriended by Leapeetswe Khama who had recently returned from attending university in Dublin. Leapeetswe had been made the acting chief of the Bamangwato and as a well-travelled and well-educated young man he was anxious for improvements in the education system recognising that Bechuanaland was ill-prepared for statehood. It was this relationship between the tribal chief and the Van Rensburgs that spawned the idea for Swaneng School. A vision emerged: Leapeetswe made tribal land available and Pat, through his contacts abroad, raised funds and support enabling the new school to open its doors to its first pupils in 1963.

Pat concluded this part of his story by telling us that the banning order preventing his entry into South Africa remained in place until 1990 when the then President, P W De Klerk, as part of the process towards dismantling apartheid, offered a general amnesty to political prisoners and opponents of the separate development policy.

As a little aside Pat went on to tell us that for many years he had an almost unique distinction of being a banned person not only from South Africa but also Rhodesia and Namibia. The Rhodesian banning came as a shock when he was formally ejected from the country after one of his many journeys abroad seeking funding for his activities at Swaneng School. As a consequence thereafter for many years his only legal method of exiting Botswana was to cross the river at Kasane in Northern Botswana into Zambia at one of the shortest borders between two countries in the world.

The story of his ban from entering Rhodesia is in itself a fascinating reminder of the birth pangs of democracy that Southern Africa suffered during the second half of the twentieth century.

In the sixties Pat had travelled north from Swaneng across the border into Rhodesia, then still a British colony, to meet Garfield Todd, the liberal-minded former Southern Rhodesian prime minister. The two men had much in common with similar liberal credentials. During his time in power in the fifties, Todd had taken various actions to improve the lot of the black population in Rhodesia including reform of the education system. His fellow whites were not convinced, Todd was ousted and the white-only government moved further to the right under successive leaders Edgar Whitehead and Winston Field until finally the white supremacist government under Ian Smith unilaterally declared independence from Britain in 1965. Todd was subsequently arrested and later held under house arrest on his farm near Bulawayo. It was here, during his visit to see Garfield Todd that Pat noted a train on the track passing through the middle of the Todd farm laden with goods that he knew were subject to UN sanctions imposed on the Smith regime. On his return to Bechuanaland Pat reported details of what he had seen to an official in the British government. However, instead of this leading to a tightening of sanctions the fact that he had provided this intelligence must have come to the attention of a Smith sympathiser somewhere in Her Majesty's Government who in turn tipped off the illegal regime in Salisbury. The outcome was a banning order preventing Pat from entering Rhodesia again.

I knew that once established, Swaneng School had been dependent for its teaching resources on an almost endless stream of supporters from the UK and other parts of the world spending time at the school. As I have indicated many of these were volunteers, others professional teachers, paid, albeit modest salaries, supported by various charities and Pat's international fundraising efforts. When I asked Pat about some of my fellow volunteers from the mid-sixties it was apparent that over time there had been so many volunteers, most staying one or two years, that it was difficult for Pat to remember who was there and when. He was better able to talk about his main lieutenants: Peter Fewster, who worked closely with Pat in developing the Brigades; he also spoke fondly of Martin Kibblewhite, who it appears is now a wealthy architect but still in contact with Pat, and Robert Oakeshott who became headmaster of Shashe School when Pat had gone into expansionist mode. When I enquired about Donald Curtis, who I regarded as a rather cool character with a wicked sense of humour, Pat said that he and his family had returned to the UK in the late sixties. Donald was back in Botswana relatively recently to undertake a short-term project.

I had a vague idea about Pat's eventual disengagement from Swaneng and asked him to relate how things had changed following Independence. Pat told us, 'By the end of the sixties I was trying to balance my time between many projects. With Swaneng School now well established I began to implement my plan to open further schools; eventually two were started, one at Shashe and another at Mahalapye. With the increasing work pressures I realised that I had to vacate the headship at Swaneng and the day-to-day running of the school. I appointed Sheila Bagnall, one of my senior staff, to fill this post.'

Sheila was an experienced teacher and also someone with good political connections in the UK and in Africa who had come to the school in 1966, in fact almost to the day I left the country, so someone I never met.

'Sheila had come to Swaneng to be its first science teacher and with her vast teaching experience I had also appointed her vice principal so she was the obvious candidate to take on the headship.'

The bottom line seemed to be that although Pat had eventually relinquished his role as principal to Sheila in 1970 their relationship was already in decline. Sheila Bagnall kept a diary, a version of which in book form, edited by Sandy Grant, was published in 2001 under the title of *Letters from Botswana*. This offers an insight into the decline in the relationship between Pat and Sheila from Sheila's perspective but more interestingly illustrates the phenomenal scale of activities in which Pat was then engaged.

'After appointing Sheila to run Swaneng I was always uneasy but in 1972 things really went awry at the school with a student riot; you may have heard about this. Anyway things got very unpleasant and for weeks we had the local equivalent of Special Forces on site.'

'Yes,' I replied, 'I have heard about the riots but the idea of schoolchildren rioting to that extent is hard to reconcile.'

'I understand your point and in part this illustrates how bad things had got but you may have forgotten that students at Swaneng in those days were not typical of secondary school children elsewhere in the world. For a start they did not neatly fall into the age range of 11 to 18; many, you may recall, were older, often young men in their twenties.'

Pat was right to remind me about the intake of students into Swaneng in those early years. Typically in a village there would be a primary school and schoolteacher, not necessarily properly trained. The curriculum would provide some basic education in maths and English to Grade 6. At the time secondary education in Bechuanaland was virtually non-existent there being literally a handful of secondary schools in the whole country. Swaneng therefore provided an almost unique opportunity to gain a proper education and attracted, as students, many who had long since left the education system, some even in their twenties. A class therefore typically contained a wide range of ages and levels of education. Indeed because of the fee structure it was often young people who had work who could afford to attend. This mixture of children and young adults of course brought its problems in terms of expectations but also a volatile mix of social problems. The catalyst for the riots, led by a group of older students, was poor quality of food, most students being boarders. Whether this was cause or effect is difficult to determine after all this time but what was clear was that events became extremely unpleasant.

Even today Pat clearly regrets his decision to appoint Sheila Bagnall because he feels that events should never have been allowed to develop in the way they did; in the circumstances Sheila felt obliged to resign and at that point the Education Department of the government took over full control of Swaneng School. After nearly ten years it was the end of an era at Swaneng School.

By this time Pat had his hands full with the building and subsequent opening of his new schools at Shashe River and Mahalapye. Although Sheila's appointment to the headship at Swaneng had proved something of a disaster from Pat's perspective, it was also clear from his comments that after Independence the amount of political interference in the running of schools increased markedly and ultimately led to his total withdrawal from the formal education structure. When the inevitable happened and both of his schools at Shashe and Mahalapye too fell under government aegis, Pat decided to leave secondary education to the government and concentrate his endeavours on developing the Brigades Movement.

Co-ops, as I have said, are close to Pat's heart because they are absolutely about self-help. He imparts another piece of bad news. His co-operative at Swaneng, the first registered in the old Bechuanaland, no longer exists, having been sold to Chinese traders as a way of paying off its debts. He clearly expressed his disgust.

Back to the Brigades. They always formed an integral part of the Van Rensburg vision of education in post-Independence Botswana and in the seventies – with Pat now able to dedicate all of his energies to them – they burgeoned, covering many trades; not only farming but car mechanics, brewing, printing, tanning and many more.

The Brigades had an important role in the post-Independence history of Botswana and there remains evidence around the country that they still form an important part of the economy, albeit they are now run by a government agency.

It was obvious that Pat has an abiding sense of disappointment that government has hijacked his ideas. However true, there is no doubt that his efforts have made a huge contribution to the development of this country and I sought to give him some reassurance. Nevertheless the same disenchantment that overcame Pat in respect of secondary education has been repeated with the Brigades.

By the eighties, with a mixture of government meddling and antipathy towards the Brigades, Pat turned his attention further afield. I have mentioned his earlier visit to Garfield Todd in Rhodesia and he told us that when that country eventually achieved independence as Zimbabwe in 1981, the new president Robert Mugabe invited Pat to move north to help develop Brigades in that country. Pat feels that despite the turbulent recent history of Zimbabwe the legacy of the Brigades is stronger there than in Botswana. Despite this new venture Pat has maintained a house in Serowe but now heads up an international organisation aimed at further promoting the Brigades' concept in developing countries from an office-come-flat in Gaberone.

By now it was early evening. We had sat chatting and drinking for several hours. As our conversation moved towards a close one of the saddest aspects of the meeting was when Pat revealed his own personal circumstances. He told us that once the two boys had grown up Liz had sadly left Botswana to return to live in England. His eldest son Tom, who I recall as a toddler in the sixties, now teaches at a university in Ireland. His youngest son Mothusi-Joe, who I had spoken to earlier on the telephone, remains in Botswana living in the family house in Serowe and working with his father on various business ventures. Liz now lives in Penzance remaining on good, if rather distant terms, with Pat and his activities in Africa.

It was a low point on which to end our conversation. Pat now appeared a rather sad and disillusioned figure, nevertheless it was still a great pleasure to meet him once again. After 40 years there was nothing to change my opinion of him as a sincere, courageous and significant contributor to his adopted country. Sure, the energy level has reduced over time but he remains as committed as he ever was to his ideas that remain as relevant today as they were 40 years ago. If I have any reservations it is a little sadness that he came across as a man tinged with some bitterness, feeling that his ideas had been hijacked, diluted and even corrupted by politicians, whereas in reality I think he will leave a powerful legacy. At least his groundbreaking work has gained international recognition. In 1981 he was awarded the 'Right Livelihood Award', dubbed the 'Alternative Nobel Prize'.

Later that evening I am reflecting on our meeting with Pat, remembering that Rosie of course had never met him before. She remarked, 'I can see why you hold him in such high esteem; although his manner is understated he has that rare quality – gravitas.' Thanks, Rosie, I couldn't have put it better myself.

Chapter Ten

Serowe

The district commissioner (DC) was an important figure in British colonial history, the representative of HMG and administrator for a given geographical area. A model widely used wherever the British ruled. Although Bechuanaland had its first free and democratic elections in 1965 and had achieved a degree of self-government with a firm commitment to full independence in 1966 the traditional British colonial structure of administration was still firmly in place. The DCs retained and could, at will, exercise extensive powers. In my experience Bechuanaland was lucky to have DCs who genuinely wanted to facilitate a smooth transition of power to the incoming government. Although the DC as the representative of the colonial power wielded much influence in Bechuanaland, underpinning the formal structure was the ability of the DC to work with the tribal hierarchy. However powerful he was in theory, the DC needed the tacit support of the chief if we were to be able to operate effectively. I am sure this was generally true throughout Africa during the colonial period. Therefore although the DC would support our endeavours to start the cattle marketing co-operative it was important that we had Chief Leapeetswe as an ally if our venture was to succeed.

On that first evening at Swaneng, before our important meeting in Serowe, both Tshoagong and I were gingerly absorbing ourselves into this new, strange but highly convivial atmosphere when framed in the doorway we were aware of a very large figure of a man. It proved to be none other than the chief himself, Leapeetswe Khama. Cousin of Seretse Khama, the recently elected prime minister of the soon to be independent Botswana, and paramount chief of the Bamangwato tribe. He was not quite what I had expected of a tribal chief. Firstly, his age, I guessed in his twenties, perhaps a little older than me. Apart from his youth the second feature of note about Leapeetswe was his size. An enormously large and apparently well-fed figure, he stood out in a country where most of the population survived on a subsistence diet of maize or sorghum, he was a big person whichever way you measured him. My first impression was of an extremely affable and engaging man who clearly enjoyed the company of the young teachers at Swaneng, not least the female variety. In this barren and poor country he was the closest I was likely to come to meeting a 'playboy'.

Back in 1965 my first experience of Serowe village was on the morning after arriving at Swaneng for the first time. Trevor had arrived at Swaneng late that evening and was in a positive frame of mind about the cattle marketing co-operative now that we had funds from the UK. Nevertheless it was with some trepidation that Tshoagong and I drove in the Bedford down into the village. Despite our best efforts at Swaneng the previous evening to engage Leapeetswe, he had been in social rather than business mode so we were unsure what form his support might take. Patrick, a great co-op supporter who as I have said before had already started the first registered co-op in Bechuanaland, drove Trevor in the school truck and we headed in convoy for the DC's office in the centre of the village.

The support of the chief was an absolute necessity in persuading the very traditional Batswana people to accept change. The tribal structure was still very evident even though this was now a democracy. The meeting in the DC's office went well and Leapeetswe pledged his support for the co-operative venture; so positive indeed was his response that he suggested that Trevor return in about a month to address a meeting of the whole tribe that he would convene at the kgotla, the tribal meeting place. However, although Leapeetswe's support was forthcoming he spoke at length about the problems we would face in persuading his people to change their traditional thinking about farming, even with his support. The very same problem that so frustrated Vernon. Not least of these problems was that in Tswana society a man's standing is measured by the number of head of cattle he owns, notwithstanding the quality, value or condition of the beasts. The meeting concluded with Leapeetswe suggesting that before the meeting with the tribe, Tshoagong and I travel around the Bamangwato area as widely as we could to explain the principles of the co-operative.

In the days that followed Tshoagong and I followed up as instructed and we began addressing a series of public meetings about the co-operative throughout the Bamangwato tribal area. No easy task. It covers some 8,500 square miles. In one week alone we held 14 meetings in Serowe, each attended by perhaps 100 or more people. This was an intense period of activity but at least it ensured a week enjoying the hospitality of my friends at Swaneng. Fourteen may sound a lot of meetings in one village but the term village is a misnomer in the sense that the tribal capital was even then a large sprawling community with a population at the time of around 40,000 people.

A month later, thanks to Patrick's generosity, we gathered at Swaneng again in preparation for the mass gathering at the kgotla the following morning. That evening in the mess Leapeetswe was a notable absentee. His younger brother Segkoma arrived, but he showed little interest in tribal affairs. Therefore despite Leapeetswe's words of support at our earlier meeting with him it was with a sense of apprehension that we once again made our way back to the village that morning. Patrick, perhaps wisely given his 'finger in so many pies' in and around Serowe, decided not to come so Tshoagong, Trevor and I squeezed into the cab of the Bedford and headed off towards the centre of the village.

At the kgotla a table had been set up in front of what proved to be a large crowd of 500 or more men. Testament indeed to the efficiency of the 'bush telegraph' in a country virtually totally devoid of any form of modern communications. Eventually the chief, the district commissioner and the registrar of co-operatives took their seats. Befitting our station Tshoagong and I were mere bystanders as the meeting began.

After a short speech of welcome from Leapeetswe it was the turn of Trevor to address the meeting on the merits of a cattle marketing co-operative. This in itself was unusual and represented something of a risk for Leapeetswe, as strangers are traditionally not allowed to speak at the kgotla. Trevor was followed by a short speech in support from the DC. Tshoagong whispered to me that things were not going well. This was change and these people, even if it is change for the good, do not like change. Then Leapeetswe stood and addressed the meeting at great length in Setswana, somewhat theatrically closing in English by declaring that he would be the first person to enrol as a member. We frankly could not ask for more.

There were lots of questions to Trevor about representation, the significance of which I did not fully understand at the time. Part of this was due to a lack of understanding about the whole idea of democracy. Only months before the country had held its first democratic elections for the provisional government that would rule after Independence. One outcome was that although the co-operative covered the Bamangwato tribal area it would have two committees, one in the east and one in the west. Only later did I appreciate the tribal politics. Pilikwe to the east of the railway line was the family home of Tshekedi Khama, Leapeetswe's father and former regent whilst Seretse and his side of the Khama family were based here in Serowe to the west. I will return shortly to this family affair. What the meeting clearly illustrated was the sheer sway and influence that Leapeetswe held over this meeting, being evidence that the tribal system still prevailed in the minds of the majority.

We had kick-started the whole Bamangwato cattle marketing co-operative project and Tshoagong and I headed back to Radisele in high spirits.

Rosie and I took a detour to visit Serowe. It was an odd experience insofar as I never once had any sense of having been there before. Today as we approached from the direction of Palapye it was clear to me that the village had grown but I still expected one of the first sights would be Swaneng School. Not so.

In the old days it was a large village of traditional houses. Today it comprises mainly modern buildings including a partly constructed hospital behind which an estate of what I could only describe as 'executive' houses. Before going into the town proper we were to visit the Khama Rhino Sanctuary about ten miles to the west and soon after entering the outskirts of the town we took a right turn onto what had the appearance of being a new road and was signposted Orapa, which I knew from my research was where De Beers had a large diamond mine. Diamonds were something we didn't have in the colonial times, deposits having been found since Independence, a find that has helped transform this pitifully poor country to one of the richest nations on the African continent.

The Khama Rhino Sanctuary is a classic type of development that could not have been even considered in the sixties. It combines elements of protecting an endangered species, eco-tourism and community involvement. The reserve is a substantial 4,300 hectares and has been in existence since 1992. Seretse's son Ian, the Ngwato chief, is patron of the project, which has a breeding programme for the endangered white rhino. We took a guided tour but failed to see any of the 18 rhino but plentiful are zebra, giraffe and the varieties of deer seen throughout Southern Africa: eland, springbok, impala, kudu, gemsbok. It was a pleasing diversion.

On our way back into town by chance we came across the 'Red House'. Once Leapeetswe's home, it now contains the Khama III Memorial Museum. We decide to take a look. Not surprisingly a substantial part of the museum collection is devoted to the Khamas. The family that has so dominated the Ngwato tribe for more than 100 years since Khama the Great visited Queen Victoria in England in 1885 to seek British protection from the advances of the Boers into the region. Recounting the recent history of the Khama dynasty through pictorial records proves helpful to Rosie's understanding of Seretse's significance in Botswana history, not least the intimate family photographs of Seretse, Ruth, his English wife, and their young family. She finds one image particularly poignant, a photo of Seretse's aeroplane being turned away from landing at Mahalapye where a distraught Ruth, with their baby son in her arms, waits to welcome him home from his long exile in England.

On the wall of the museum a Khama family tree is displayed but it does not show dates of death only birth dates. I ask the attendant how long she had been in her job. 'Fifteen years,' she replies. 'So you can tell me what has happened to Leapeetswe and his brother Segkoma.' She said they were both deceased and that Leapeetswe had donated the Red House to become the Khama Museum shortly before his death.

Later when I asked Pat Van Rensburg the same question he sadly confirmed that Leapeetswe had indeed died, he seemed to think around 1980, but that Segkoma is still alive and in good health. Odd that in the very heart of the village of the Khamas we should have been given this misinformation, but a sign of changing times. In the old days everyone in the village would have known the chief and his brother. Today even the Khama museum employee seems uncertain who they are.

Leaving the museum we drove into the centre of the village with me looking for anything to jog my memory. The centre contained a modern but recently burnt out shopping mall and a more traditional market. We found two schools, but neither was Swaneng. There were no signs of the kgotla.

As we left Serowe to return towards Palapye we stopped for petrol and at once I recognised the name of Dennis's Garage. Founded in 1941 in the old days it was one of the landmarks in Serowe. I recognised the name alright, but little else; today it is a modern service station and Toyota dealership. I asked the pump attendant if Swaneng School was still here and he pointed down the road that we intended to take out of the town.

I was expecting the school to be on the left. Shortly we passed a modern school building on the right. It must have been Swaneng because soon we were out of town and heading towards Palapye where we were staying. I had come and seen and remembered nothing, it was like I had never been here before. Rosie wanted us to turn back and search for Swaneng. I said no. This was the point. Forty years was a long time. Much had changed, savour the bits that remain in the memory.

In my subsequent meeting with Pat Van Rensburg, he confirmed, 'The school is still there alright, but you would have entered and left the town on the new road. The school was of course on the now little used old road.'

Chapter Eleven

Leapeetswe and the Khama Dynasty

The Leapeetswe Khama that I met first met in 1965 was always extremely good fun and fine company. He had at this point recently returned from attending university in Dublin to assume the chieftainship. Judging by his roly-poly stature and liking for a convivial drink his further education in Europe had clearly also involved enjoying the odd beer in the student bar.

On a more serious note, to fully understand his role in the tribe and the considerable amount of 'baggage' he had inherited in trying to perform this task it is necessary to delve further into his family history, not least the position of his cousin Seretse, who only months before had been elected prime minister in the country's first democratic election.

Seretse Khama became the tribal chief of the Bangwato in 1925 at the age of four. This followed the death of his father Segkoma, who had ruled over the tribe for just two years after acceding to the chieftainship following the death of Khama III, Seretse's grandfather, also known as Khama the Great; he had ruled over the Ngwato for nearly 50 years from 1875 to 1923. To avoid instability in the tribal hierarchy with the chief being a young child, Seretse's uncle, Tshekedi, was appointed regent.

Tshekedi proved an able and popular leader who, if anything, enhanced his reputation by at times finding himself at odds with the colonial authorities. By the end of the Second World War although

Seretse was now old enough to assume the chieftainship instead he was sent to England to study law. After completing his degree at Oxford he continued his legal studies for the Bar at the Inner Temple in London where he met and subsequently married a white woman, Ruth Williams. Ruth, then still in her early twenties, had left school during the war and amongst other things had become an ambulance driver in the Air Force. When she met Seretse she was working as a clerk in the City with a Lloyds underwriters. It was now that this relationship became something of a 'cause celebre'.

Some 50 years later it is difficult to appreciate how the marriage of the chief of a tribe in some obscure African country could create such a huge furore in Britain and almost lead to the downfall of the government. Yet that was what happened in the following weeks and months as the events in the two countries began to unfold.

Back in Bechuanaland Tshekedi was furious at his nephew who he accused of a breach in tribal law; Seretse was expected to marry a 'Tswana royal' as part of the tradition of maintaining and enhancing family alliances within the tribal structure. Shortly after his marriage to Ruth in 1948, Seretse returned to Serowe and addressed the kgotla of tribal leaders and elders to explain his actions before returning to England. Although opinion amongst the Bamangwato people was divided, after the initial excitement it appeared that the majority acknowledged the right of their chief to choose his wife and in June 1949 Seretse and Ruth returned to Serowe. Here the uncle and nephew once again addressed a mass meeting at the kgotla. With opinion moving in his favour, Seretse asked those who supported him to stand. It was a personal triumph as the body of the body rose almost as one to acclaim him as chief, leaving Tshekedi to contemplate his own future in voluntary exile.

However, the matter was far from over. Back in London the British government found itself under intense diplomatic pressure from the governments of neighbouring South Africa and Southern Rhodesia to intervene. South Africa had just introduced its new policy of apartheid or separate development under which marriage between the races was illegal. Although the British did not condone this policy, the South Africans held a trump card as the supplier of uranium that Britain needed for its nuclear weapons programme. The British, fearing that South Africa under its newly elected National Party prime minister Dr Malan, might leave the Commonwealth and pursue an independent foreign policy including development of its own atomic bomb capability, bent to its will.

Early in 1950 Seretse was summoned to the Colonial Office in London, leaving his now pregnant wife behind in Serowe. Here Seretse was told that he was stripped of any entitlement to become the kgosi, or king, and he and his new wife were to be exiled in England for five years. The tribal chieftainship had, by edict of the colonial power, therefore passed back to Tshekedi. However, as a consequence of this unholy alliance between Tshekedi, the Colonial Office and the South African government, Tshekedi now found himself an outcast amongst his own people.

Although at the time Winston Churchill the opposition leader had denounced this whole episode as 'a very disreputable transaction' when the Conservatives returned to power in 1951 they extended Seretse's exile for an indefinite period.

The succession remained clouded in controversy because for most of the tribe Seretse was still their leader by birthright. It was during this period of exile that the poignant photographs of Ruth and baby Ian we had seen in the Red House museum were taken.

Ultimately, in 1956, things moved back in Seretse's favour. The tribe cabled the Queen asking for her to intercede. Seretse agreed to surrender any entitlement to the chieftainship and he, with Ruth, was allowed by the British to return to Serowe.

In the years that followed Seretse maintained a low profile. Despite all the tribal traditions of the Batswana as cattle herders he was a notoriously unsuccessful farmer and during this period was plagued with illness until he was diagnosed as diabetic in 1960. Almost miraculously he became a changed man; energised, he embarked on a political career forming the BDP, the Botswana Democratic Party. In 1965 his centrist party overcame the more nationalistic but divided opposition in the country's first election and a year later he was to lead his country to independence as prime minister and later president of the first BDP-led government – the party that has continued to rule Botswana ever since.

At the end of Seretse's exile Tshekedi and Seretse were reconciled although Tshekedi was to die only three years later in 1959, leaving Leapeetswe, his eldest son, as the chief. Clearly in light of circumstances his legitimacy to be the chief was still questioned by many, leaving him with an uncertain and insecure position at the head of tribal affairs.

This was the situation when I met Leapeetswe for the first time. Nevertheless despite his youth and the problems of his role inherited from his father, I soon came to appreciate that Leapeetswe was well respected and popular within the Ngwato.

Later, in 1969, the tribe agreed to Leapeetswe's request for permission to return to university and he travelled to England to study land management at Wolfson College, Cambridge. Segkoma, his younger brother, temporarily in his absence assumed the chieftainship. At around this time Leapeetswe was diagnosed as suffering from a kidney complaint. Later his younger brother was to be the donor in a transplant operation but Leapeetswe's medical problems recurred and he subsequently died at the relatively young age of 50.

To complete the recent Khama family history: despite Leapeetswe's fine efforts as chief, succession remained an issue within the tribe. After Independence, Seretse's right to be the chief of the Bamangwato was at last acknowledged and the chieftainship formally restored to him, although he was by now head of state and was never to perform his duties as traditional tribal chieftain.

Then finally in 1980, shortly before his own death, Seretse resolved the whole matter of the Bamangwato chieftainship when his first son Ian was installed as paramount chief at a huge gathering at the Serowe kgotla. Sandhurst trained, Ian subsequently became head of the BDF, the Botswana Army, then vice president and in 2008 he became president.

Chapter Twelve

Life in the Bush

Life at Radisele was never routine in the sense of dreary repetition but a regular pattern developed and I quickly settled down to my new life in the bush. The Gibberds were determined to live a simple life with few concessions to comfort and their rondavel, in contrast to my own, were the genuine article with mud walls and a dirt floor. One relative luxury they enjoyed was the use of paraffin fuelled hurricane or storm lamps for purposes of illumination. Tineke did the cooking in a pot in a small area surrounded by a brush fence; although this was often over a fire as another small concession she also had use of a primus stove.

The most popular dish in the Gibberd household, judging by the frequency it was served, was a tinned fish of uncertain origin with a distinctive flavour I can recall even now, not being particularly to my taste. My guess looking back was that it was curried tuna. Fresh meat was unusual given the heat and lack of refrigeration facilities, being confined to an occasional goat stew. Goats, unlike the cattle population badly decimated by the drought, seemed capable of surviving anything that nature threw at them with robust constitutions ensuring they were capable of digesting the most unlikely things in the name of survival. Whatever they had eaten to fill their bellies did not detract from the welcome alternative they provided to the dreaded tinned fish.

Despite the cramped conditions the Gibberds' living quarters contained a large bookshelf crammed with Penguin paperbacks which were to be a great source of entertainment in the coming months given the absence of newspapers, television and with the radio reception of a quality so poor that made it difficult to listen for pleasure. We usually contented ourselves with the news bulletin from the BBC World Service before our early evening dinner. I was not at that time at all well read but casting an eye along the bookshelves the name Brendan Behan caught my attention. I would not necessarily have chosen his books but recalled reading about him and his tumultuous lifestyle when he died only a few months before. Even today I recall the pleasure of reading his *Borstal Boy* and *The Quare Fellow*.

After dinner, not wishing to overstay my welcome and to give the Gibberds some personal space, I would take a torch and tentatively make my way back down the path through the middle of the settlement. The night was always full of the sound of crickets and as I made my way past the dying embers of the fire in front of the foreman's hut my nostrils would twitch as my lungs filled with the smoke and smells of firewood. Then back into the blackness towards my own rondavel always aware from the rustling in the sparse surrounding bush that I was not entirely alone. Once inside to read or study but mainly to sleep. Be it through fatigue or boredom or a combination of the both I found I needed a regular ten hours' sleep rather than my hitherto normal seven or eight hours a night. I cannot recall with total certainty but memory suggests that despite the high daily temperatures the nights in comparison were cool and quite bearable with the dry air and low humidity.

After a few weeks came the welcome but spasmodic trickle of mail from England. This, however, was dependent upon Vernon making the occasional trip to faraway Palapye where our post office box was situated. Letters came from my long-time friends Bob and Mick with news of Colchester United, our local team, and of the table tennis team in which we all played that seemed to be faring remarkably well in my absence. Letters too from old friends from college, my old room mate Alan, and Ann, the chef's daughter. Skinny but very good-looking, I liked her a lot; it was a relationship that continued on and off during my two years at college without really going anywhere.

Then the first brown paper parcel from my mother, containing English newspapers and magazines. Although the news was out of date it didn't seem to matter. The parcels travelled by sea to South Africa where, although in transit to their eventual destination in Bechuanaland, they were subject to official government censorship. Thus by the time they reached Radisele I would often receive a six-week-old Daily Mail with a small square carefully removed by the censor's scissors. Of course I could only speculate about the missing news item but with some certainty can say that if not a critical reference to apartheid then it would have been reporting on the latest sex scandal in 'swinging sixties' England, South Africa being, at the time, a bastion of puritanism. Bizarre but true.

The peculiar effect is that from the BBC World Service, old newspapers, letters from home and other accumulated snippets, overall my knowledge of news and sport during my year in Africa remains remarkably unimpaired. For example, although I have no interest whatsoever in either team, I clearly recall that the 1966 World Cup final was won by Everton, thanks to a dreadful error by the Sheffield Wednesday centre half and two goals from an until then unknown Cornishman Mike Trebilcock. Amazing recall, many more recent cup finals have left absolutely no impression, although I learnt the result from seeing a 35 mm newsreel at Swaneng School about six weeks after the actual match.

One exception to normality in term of memories of the period is pop music. Play a couple of bars and I can still name most UK hit records of the sixties, except for those popular between September 1965 and September 1966. Even here there are some exceptions, faintly obscure hits like '1-2-3' by Len Barry and 'Yesterday Man' by Chris Andrews I do remember. This thanks to extended airplay on a radio station, the African equivalent of Radio Luxemburg, which operated out of Lourenco Marques in the Portuguese colony of Mozambique, the state controlled South African radio being far too staid and conservative to play music from the decadent UK pop scene.

Thanks to Vernon and the BDA I was given an office for the still to be formed Bamangwato cattle marketing co-operative. Furniture comprised two rickety old desks and an aged typewriter shared with the BDA. Later, courtesy of Trevor, Tshoagong and I collected a surplus filing cabinet from a government office in nearby Mahalapye. The telephone as I was to discover was an unreliable form of communication in Bechuanaland but of little matter to us at the BDA as the nearest telephone was to be found at Palapye, nearly 20 miles away, leaving Trevor to resort to other means of communication on important matters. The policeman based at nearby Radisele would regularly come to the office bearing a handwritten radio message received from Gaberones. It would of necessity have to be brief and typically cryptic and would say something like, 'Can you attend an important meeting later this week in the capital?' It was a coded message; Barbara had returned to the UK, Trevor was lonely and wanted an opponent for Scrabble. Before that, however, much of those early weeks were to be spent with Tshoagong travelling around the tribal villages and seeking support for the marketing co-operative idea.

Tshoagong and I travelled most days during my initial three months at Radisele. Invariably this involved rising at dawn and driving the Bedford truck to visit a local village. Ours was a propaganda mission with the aim of providing villagers with an understanding and getting commitment to the new cattle marketing co-operative. We were also starting up thrift and loan co-operatives, encouraging the villagers to save and then to borrow money from the co-operative to make essential purchases: typically to buy seed for the next growing season.

Most trips enabled us to return to Radisele within the day but occasionally we stayed overnight, at Swaneng if we found ourselves in the vicinity of Serowe or in the bush close to some remote village we were visiting. Occasionally the routine would be interrupted and I would be required to make a trip south to Lobatsi, Gaberones or even Mafeking, followed by the pedestrian late night return by the train, which arrived at Radisele sometime in the early hours requiring a long and hopefully moonlit walk back up the track to the BDA. The same daily train north that brought me on that first journey up from Jo'burg arrived at Mafeking in early morning and at Gaberones around dusk, eventually reaching Palapye sometime after midnight and would finally steam into Bulawayo in Rhodesia some 36 hours after starting its journey.

Trips into the bush were inevitably hot and dusty on tracks that rarely saw use by a motorised vehicle. Built onto the back of our truck was a metal frame with a tarpaulin cover. The sides were covered with a wire mesh. The tarpaulin could be rolled up at the sides creating something akin to a cage or could be unfolded and tied down totally enclosing the rear of the vehicle. Tshoagong told me the wire mesh was a way to 'keep out the venomous Black Mamba snake' that was inclined to leap through the air and become entangled with people riding on the back of the vehicle. I was never quite sure about the story but you rarely saw a vehicle not crammed with people and therefore they might be at risk from a flying snake. The ability of this creature to become airborne was more problematical but 'better safe than sorry' seemed a sound principle. Anyway, having an aversion to snakes I was content if the wire and canvass canopy added some protection particularly on those long trips when the truck provided not only our means of transport but also our overnight accommodation.

Public transport was extremely limited in those days. A rudimentary bus service operated between the main population centres; although called buses the vehicles used were actually open backed trucks like our Bedford. Typically for Africa the service was irregular and usually involved large numbers of people and their possessions travelling in great discomfort in a very confined space. The bus of course also required payment of a fare. As a consequence any vehicle on the road was regarded as 'fair game' to be pressed into service to transport people and their belongings. Being government officers in a government vehicle we were not supposed to give lifts although once away from the main north-south highway Tshoagong invariably stopped when hailed by people making their way through the bush. They would clamber into the back of the vehicle and we would proceed into the interior for miles until there was a bang on the cab. Tshoagong would stop the truck, there would be a quick exchange of words and our passengers would alight making their way purposefully off into the bush. Where they were headed and why was never apparent.

Our truck was equipped with an auxiliary petrol supply in the form of a 40-gallon drum in the style of those popular with Caribbean steel bands. It sat permanently perched on the back of the vehicle. Refuelling opportunities were few and far between, requiring a visit to a government owned pump in one of the larger population centres, like Gaberones or Mahalapye. When petrol in the tank ran low we refilled it from our petrol drum. This required insertion of one end of a rubber hose into the drum, putting our mouth over the other end and sucking hard. The trick was to stop sucking once you had produced the desired effects of a gravity feed, at which point you quickly removed the hose from your mouth and inserted the end into the fuel tank. This required split second timing otherwise you had the unpleasant sensation generated by finding yourself with a mouthful of petrol. At the very least one had to accept a lung full of petrol fumes and until the technique was mastered even worse. Not pleasant. Fortunately neither Tshoagong nor I were smokers because on many occasions we could easily have accidentally ignited ourselves.

To avoid the dangers of dehydration we carried water bottles made of canvas which we rather perversely hung on the outside of the vehicle in the blazing heat to keep cool. Water slowly seeped through the canvas but through some freak of physics, which I don't entirely understand, the water remaining inside the bottle turned from tepid to refreshingly cool. The bottles were filled at every opportunity when we found a borehole, pretty well the only source of water in a country devoid of surface water other than in the Okavango delta to the northwest, well beyond our normal territory.

Once we arrived at a village the first task was to seek out the village headman. This was the normal courtesy to tell him the nature of our business in his village. Once again a reflection of the deference to the tribal hierarchy shown by ordinary people. The headman would invariably be found at the kgotla in the centre of the village together with the other village elders where they squatted on their haunches in that particularly African, and for Europeans the very uncomfortable way, talking and swatting flies. These introductions could be a time-consuming process, invariably in Tswana, leaving me wondering what on earth they had to talk about.

In due course Tshoagong would give his customary cluck and tell me that it was time to go. In villages where we had already established a co-operative, after meeting the elders we would then find the village school and schoolmaster because invariably he would be the person appointed as secretary for the local co-operative. We would discuss with him the business of the co-operative and look at the books. Then after some simple refreshments a meeting of the co-operative members would be convened. Tshoagong would talk about the co-operative principles and of course it would provide the opportunity for us to bring into the conversation our plans for the new cattle marketing co-operative.

Chapter Thirteen

Francistown

About an hour's drive short of Francistown I picked up my mobile telephone again and called Botho, the name of the contact I had been given by Ngae before leaving Gaberone. What should have been a straightforward request to speak to Botho proved far more difficult than I had imagined. Firstly I assumed Botho was a surname when in fact it proved to be his forename, a mistake I was to make on more than one further occasion as the trip proceeded. Only later did I learn from the man himself that he is Botho Gabanamotse.

A female voice came on the line. I asked for Mr Botho. She seemed confused. Was it Botho, Both-O, Bot-O or even Bootho? Because however I said the word I got the same blank response. Even with my pronunciation surely it couldn't be that difficult? How many people could they have in a regional office? Five? Ten even? It shouldn't be difficult to identify a Botho amongst them. Eventually my man came on the line. He was expecting my call but much to my consternation claimed that he was too busy to help. No sooner had I digested this news in the next breath he said that he had arranged for me to visit co-ops at Maropong and Sowa. I thanked him for this but pressed him for more detail. Who would I see? How would I get there? What sort of co-operatives were they?

I needed a face-to-face.

'What time do you need to leave the office?'

'At around 4.30 p.m.'

I looked at the clock on the car dashboard and made a quick mental calculation.

'I can be at your office in Francistown in about an hour, which should give us plenty of time for a chat before you have to leave.'

He agreed to my idea although I could hear in his voice a begrudging acceptance that he had been outmanoeuvred and with some reluctance on his part he gave me directions to get to his office.

Francistown, as the name suggests, is a town and unlike most of the other centres of population in Botswana, that are traditional tribal villages. In fact it is a well-established town. Indeed it has a history dating back into the middle of the nineteenth century. As we make our approach from the south here we find urban sprawl, modern buildings and even road signs but this does not stop us getting lost.

After skirting the suburbs of Francistown for some time seeking the landmarks Botho has described, I have to telephone him again for further directions. Eventually, vital minutes lost, we approach the office. Botho is outside the building waiting to greet us. A short and rotund figure, physically he reminded me of the auditor Lesetswe who I had met in Gaberone, except his demeanour is more brusque and controlled. He ushered me up the stairs into a first floor office. A smell of paint hung heavy in the air for which he apologised profusely, saying that the office redecoration was the reason why he could not accompany me on my visit to the co-ops. A rather poor excuse, I thought. Putting myself in his position I felt sure I would have happily taken a couple of days out of the office to escort a foreign visitor around my patch.

Given Botho's apparent lack of interest in helping me I felt flattery might prove a sensible tactic and I thanked him with excessive zeal for sparing some of his valuable time. The impact of my words I think was overwhelming as he became visibly flustered, trying to move a huge pile of papers on his desk that left him invisible to me. Eventually he lifted the outstanding paperwork to a precarious position at the other end of the desk, dabbed his heavily perspiring forehead with a large white handkerchief and finally sat to face his clearly unwelcome guest.

Once we had settled into conversation he told me that he had worked in the Department of Co-operatives for 20 years. I assumed, guessing his age, this represented pretty well the whole of his working life. As I had already sensed from our earlier telephone conversation, his personal morale was low and he was pessimistic about the future. The co-ops here in this part of the country were doing badly with only a handful still active; many had been wound-up whilst others were in a form of hibernation, no longer trading but technically still solvent. In Francistown itself the once flourishing co-op business had suspended trading and Botho was in the process of liquidating various properties it owned to pay off its creditors and in the hope that there might be sufficient funds remaining to re-open one co-operative shop. When I pressed Botho on this state of affairs he gave the same reasons as Violet and her colleagues: competition and mismanagement.

'What do you mean by mismanagement?' I asked.

Botho said that there were typically two scenarios in a village co-operative. One was where the paid staff found themselves under pressure from their friends and extended family to make 'gifts', extend credit or to turn a blind eye to goods being taken without payment. The second typical situation was where the co-operative appointed a manager better educated than the committee members, who were usually older and often illiterate village elders totally lacking in any commercial expertise. Many of these managers found it a temptation and in practice very easy to begin to misappropriate goods and money.

At a personal level Botho revealed concerns about his own future and told me that rumours were rife that the Department of Co-operatives was to be wound up and its responsibilities transferred to local enterprise councils. I left a rather demoralised and concerned man but at least I had a piece of paper on which he had written the names of the people I was to meet and places I was to visit.

From Botho's office in the outskirts of the town we make our way to our hotel. I recall from the sixties that Francistown had all the attributes of a frontier town. First impressions confirm that it hasn't changed much in character. It is Botswana's second city and was built by Europeans when there was something of a gold rush here more than 100 years ago. Unlike the tribal villages there are proper streets with names. The main thoroughfare is Blue Jacket, named after the attire of a successful gold prospector, Sam Andersen, whose fame was achieved not here but in faraway Australia. The buildings are mainly of wooden construction and as you make your way along you expect cowboys to emerge through swing doors toting their smoking guns. There is a Doc Morgan Avenue and Haskins Street, taking its name from a farming family still influential here. Interspersed with the old town there are new modern buildings and adjacent to our hotel a small shopping mall.

Next day we set out to explore Francistown. We find the Supa-Ngwao Museum. It is housed within a residential area in the old administrative enclave of the town. Started 20 years ago by enthusiast Stella Rundle it is contained within some rooms, part of a domestic property. Stella greets us but then retires into the main part of the house and an enthusiastic young man who speaks excellent English shows us around. The museum has some interesting exhibits but it all looks rather tired and forlorn. In one tiny room there is a small gift shop and we enquire about purchasing a wall chart. Our guide goes to consult Stella and returns saying we can have it for free. We feel a little uncomfortable as we haven't made any financial contribution and the museum is clearly not self-sufficient.

There is not much else to see in the town and for the first time, aware of the overbearing heat, we decide to retreat to our hotel to cool off with a sundowner by the pool.

Chapter Fourteen

Matsiloje, Maropong and Sowa

Most of the initiatives to start a co-operative came from the people themselves, by letter, arriving at the Department of Co-operatives in Gaberone or maybe by message from the local district commissioner. Thus we acted not to any master plan but by responding to those who had heard about co-operatives and were interested in bringing the co-operative idea to their own community. A classic example occurred on that first evening at Swaneng School prior to our meeting in Serowe when Trevor passed to me a hand written letter that he had just received from the schoolteacher in a village called Matsiloje. It was written at some length in childlike writing. In essence it explained why Matsiloje needed a co-operative and requested help from the Department in achieving this aim.

Trevor, using one of his favourite phrases, said, 'Be a good fellow, you and Tshoagong get yourselves up there as soon as you can.'

I of course had never heard of Matsiloje but interestingly neither had Tshoagong. 'Where is it, Trevor?' we asked in unison.

'I'm not sure chaps but someone in Home Affairs told me it was somewhere beyond Francistown so I have sent a message to the DC there that you will be coming to see him.'

A few days later we set out on our journey. As instructed we first travelled north to Francistown, already well outside the Bamangwato, our normal territory. Here our business was to visit the office of the district commissioner and seek his advice. He of course knew of Matsiloje and pointed to a spot on a large map on his office wall. He described it as 'small and remote' and it was located way to the east of Francistown, very close to the border with Rhodesia. The DC was not aware of the locals' desire to establish a co-operative but he told us that he understood why, as the village did not have a store or shop.

Taking our leave we headed off. We did not have a map and were left to recall the general direction from the DC's wall map. Around Radisele driving conditions were difficult but this was to prove an experience unlike anything we had previously encountered. The problem was that this was a track and not in any sense a road. Over the years people may have made their way through the bush on foot and so paths of sorts developed, but they went around every bush or tree, never ever in a straight line. There are higher levels of rainfall in the north and as a consequence the bush is denser, with more trees and bushes to negotiate our way around. Making even the shortest journey in this terrain seemed endless. Progress was slow and tortuous, travelling miles through the bush in first or second gear, and frequently finding ourselves up to the axles in deep fine sand and having to dig out until we could get some traction. Being a long and arduous journey we shared the driving. Although I had now passed my driving test, with my limited experience in these conditions I found the driving a real struggle, keeping to engine revs low enough to maintain forward movement whilst wrestling with the steering wheel as the track wound its way through the bush. The truck of course did not enjoy the modern technologies of a synchromesh gearbox or power steering.

This was to be the first occasion that we'd spent overnight using the back of the truck as our sleeping quarters. As the sun set in early evening we established camp and, thanks to Tshoagong, built a fire and opened a can of beans. Soon after dawn we awoke and were soon once again on our way. Eventually, midway through the following morning we spotted smoke in the distance and realised that we had almost reached our destination.

On arriving at the edge of the village we almost immediately came upon the school – a simple building made from mud bricks and rectangular in shape, comprising a single classroom. The school-teacher you may recall had been the author of the letter sent on behalf of the villagers to Trevor. So instead of our customary first stop at the kgotla to find the headman, on this occasion Tshoagong said that we would first seek out the schoolteacher. He stopped the truck outside the school and we climbed down. Obviously drawn by hearing the unusual sound of a motor vehicle, a figure immediately emerged from the school to greet us. It was pure chance, it being a Saturday morning and not a school day for the children, that we had found our man so easily. I remember him as being remarkably thin and, oddly, given this was his day off and with the weather being extremely hot, he was dressed in an old suit that hung from his shoulders like a suit on a wire coat hanger. He was around 30 years of age. He later attended one of my training courses and proved a very committed student but intense and serious and never attuned to my humour. In the absence of any telecommunications he of course was unaware of our impending arrival or indeed if his letter had even been received by Trevor in far-off Gaberone.

The schoolteacher had a clear sense of his place in that society and once the initial introductions had been made he insisted that, before we got down to discussion about establishing a co-operative, he would take us to meet the village headman.

When we drove the short distance into the centre of the village people emerged from their huts – women and children as well as the men – to offer us a warm welcome. Judging by our reception in those days Matsiloje rarely had visitors of any description.

The warmth of our reception was replicated at the kgotla where we were introduced to the headman and the village elders. As we began talking with them it was soon apparent that the co-operative idea provided the perfect solution for this small and remote community. The village was too small and inaccessible for any trader driven by the profit motive to be interested in setting up a shop or store in the village. As a consequence the villagers had to get their supplies by travelling on the once-a-week truck service the not inconsiderable distance into Francistown to buy their much-needed supplies. The truck started in Francistown and returned thereafter calling at Matsiloje and other villages on the way. The complication was obvious. Once in Francistown villagers were left there for a week before being able to return home. The co-operative would provide the opportunity for some form of centralised buying and the setting up of a store in the village at the very least for a range of staples like maize meal and sugar.

We spent time with the people explaining the co-operative principles and what they needed to do to establish their own village co-op. Before we left, a secretary, the schoolteacher of course, and a committee of management were appointed.

We were to make this journey twice more in the coming weeks. Firstly to set up the books and to instruct the schoolteacher how to keep accounts and then in December to return to officially recognise the new co-operative by presenting its registration documents.

On our third visit we travelled north the day before the presentation and once again slept in our truck overnight. Being so ill-prepared on our first visit, on this occasion Tshoagong had brought with him a cooking pot enabling us to enjoy a large breakfast in the bush anticipating what was to be a long journey back home later in the day. The week before I had travelled down to Gaberones to persuade Trevor to register the co-operative at Matsiloje. This was extraordinarily quick. We had not spent the normal amount of time explaining to the members how the co-operative worked nor had we time to properly train the secretary how to keep the books. However, given the remote location and the desperate need for a co-op it was agreed that the Matsiloje Consumer Co-operative Society could be given special dispensation and registered. The certificate of registration was prepared and entrusted to my safekeeping. This was extraordinary in itself given that Trevor had personally attended the inauguration ceremony of every other co-operative so far registered in the country.

We arrived in Matsiloje at around nine in the morning. It was immediately obvious that this was to be a big occasion for the village. Matsiloje was a poor village even by Botswana standards. It comprised perhaps 70 or 80 simple rondavels scattered through the bush. Yet from somewhere trestle tables had been found and these, covered by white tablecloths, were laid out in front of the head-man's hut. There were chairs for the headman and important guests, the co-operative committee but most important, Tshoagong and myself. As we sat down for the ceremony Tshoagong whispered, 'Bernie, you will have to give a speech.' By now the whole village had gathered, some 200 people including the women and children, most sat cross-legged or squatting in rows in front of the tables.

I had never made a speech in my life so this was a daunting prospect and I quickly tried to marshal my thoughts. Thank God that Tshoagong had given me such short notice. If I had more time to dwell on the prospect I fear it would have been even more nerve-wracking. The headman made some introductory remarks of welcome and then it was my turn.

'Chief, members of the co-operative committee, villagers of Matsiloje, this is indeed a momentous day for your village. Only two months ago the registrar of co-operatives Mr Bottomley received your letter requesting that you be allowed to establish a consumer co-operative in your village. Since that time Co-operative Officer Tshoagong and myself have twice visited Matsiloje to meet your people and to explain the co-operative principles and how the co-operative can be used to encourage thrift and to make best use of your resources to enable you to buy the necessities of life at a reasonable cost. We have been greatly impressed by your enthusiasm and endeavours to establish your co-operative on firm foundations and we have reported on our visits to the registrar of co-operatives. As a result he has agreed that the co-operative is ready to become officially recognised and I am delighted to say that today I am able to present to your chairman the registration document, which makes the Matsiloje Consumer Co-operative only the 11th co-operative society to be registered here in Bechuanaland. You are to be congratulated on your commitment to the co-operative ideal and it is my very great pleasure to be here today to present this certificate and I wish your co-operative a long and successful future.'

I sat down, mightily relieved and frankly pretty pleased with my first public speaking engagement. I had the advantage of stopping after every sentence to allow Tshoagong to translate, but I had spoken slowly and clearly and said what I thought were words appropriate for the occasion. Tshoagong leant over and hissed, 'Is that all you are going to say?' When I nodded in the affirmative he quickly rose and began speaking. His first comment in Tswana raised a laugh, which I guessed was some quip about being short-changed by the young Englishmen before beginning a speech that lasted fully an hour. This seemed to be well received and was warmly applauded despite the fact we were all sat under a cloudless sky and at the mercy of the powerful African sun. For my part the sun, a sleepless night and a large breakfast all contributed to a feeling of wellbeing but whether or not I managed to stay awake throughout Tshoagong's marathon I cannot be certain.

I guess I had encountered an important cultural difference. In a society where time is of no consequence why use one word when ten will do. On reflection it is obvious: how else would the Tswana men fill their time every day sitting at the kgotla and chewing the proverbial cud? There they would sit day after day, hour after hour. What was their world, what could they find to talk about? They knew nothing of the world beyond their village and their cattle. They didn't even have the facility of commenting on a story in the morning newspaper or last night's television programmes. African life: it was all beginning to make sense.

By the time Tshoagong finished his speech it was still only about 11 a.m. The women of the village began bustling around and shortly from nearby rondavels appeared sets of china crockery and plates of food. A hot drink was served; I still can recall the distinctive and unaccustomed taste of weak tea made with condensed milk. Then a dinner plate was placed in front of me onto which was piled a substantial portion of mealie meal and this was then topped with a slice of corned beef. It was barely two hours since Tshoagong and I had eaten a hearty breakfast in the bush and sadly I was unable to do justice to the large plate set before me. I was only too acutely aware that this represented a real sacrifice to these proud people living in extreme poverty and having to survive on the very edge of starvation as their only source of income; their cattle were literally dying before their eyes. Like so many situations I was to face in Africa this provided a touching, yet deeply humbling learning experience that I pondered over long and hard as we made our tortuous journey back through the bush.

Matsiloje proved to be a long way from our normal centre of operations and was an exception. In contrast another co-operative we established was in Tshoagong's home village of Pilikwe, the closest village to my base at Radisele, perhaps ten miles distant along the road where baboons lay in ambush. At Pilikwe we established a thrift and loan co-operative encouraging the twin ideas of saving and banking. We registered the co-operative soon after my arrival at Radisele and thereafter on the last day of every month we visited the village to collect the members' savings. Tshoagong's credibility was obviously at stake, the co-operative being so close to home in his adopted village and I suspect that he did not entirely trust the secretary who, although the village schoolteacher, was I must admit rather slow and shifty. As a consequence Tshoagong wanted personally to ensure that funds were regularly collected, records properly kept and the monies subsequently deposited in the bank. In those early days funds were placed in an account with one of the major international banks, Barclays or Standard, although it was intended to create a co-operative bank eventually covering the whole country.

In time the co-operative members would be able to borrow from the co-operative to finance the purchase of seeds or cattle, maybe eventually capital equipment like a tractor but in the short term we were simply getting them into the habit of regular saving to which would be added interest. These ideas of mutuality are of course second nature in our own society, with banks and building societies having been commonplace for well over a century, but they were radical new ideas in the economy of such a small and underdeveloped country like Botswana and we would need to put ourselves in the context of Victorian Britain to properly understand their importance and significance.

Today we are to visit our first village co-operative. OK so Matsiloje was off the itinerary for the very good reason that there is no longer a co-operative in the village. Instead Botho has arranged two visits for us, today to visit Maropong and tomorrow Sowa. I hadn't heard of either but he said they were west of Francistown and therefore towards Nata, the place I had decided would be the furthest point on my journey from Gaberone.

Up until this point I thought we had in our possession a quite detailed map of Botswana, certainly sufficient for our intended route. So it was of some concern that, despite poring over the portion of the map showing the area west of Francistown, I couldn't actually see the village of Maropong marked. No matter, the staff at the hotel reception have been friendly and helpful so we will elicit their guidance. After breakfast we make our way to reception and ask for directions to Maropong. They discuss the whereabouts of the village in Setswana before assuring us in English that it is easy to find. The manager is summoned to ensure we are given best advice. He is a tiny man wearing a suit two sizes too large for him. I have seen him around the hotel reception area and I have passed the time of day with him assuming he was the bellboy. Only now as he comes across to give us instructions I note the enamel badge on his lapel 'Duty Manager'. He tells us to take the Maun road for about 60 km and then turn left at the signpost. It is little more than an hour's drive on good roads. Having obtained advice from the highest authority off we set. The journey proves as easy as he said.

We soon leave the suburbs of Francistown behind. The road is good, wide and straight with a tarmacadam surface, the vistas unchanged from those seen on the road north. Sand, sand and more sand dotted with the occasional thorn bush. The odd cow grazing. To our undiscerning eye they seem distinctly fatter and healthier than those we have seen around Gaberone.

In due course we come upon the signpost, turn left as instructed and follow this still metalled road for about 5 km from the main highway until we pass a sign signifying that we have arrived in Maropong. Here, rather perversely, as proved the case in every village we visited, the road turns to a rough sand track. Botho had told me to drive into the village and ask for the co-operative. My idea of a village not large enough to rate a mention on our map and what we discovered didn't reconcile. Imagining a cluster of mud huts I was surprised by the size of the village. Strange but once again I had forgotten the very nature of the Tswana village and had become influenced by images from other parts of Africa.

We meander along, past a sign to the kgotla and then one to the tribal office. We pass a general store but it is not the co-operative. There are no less than three schools. There are of course mud huts, but in a country with so much space they are generously spread, each within its own walled yard. There are even some open areas, brown and bare, where a few cows and goats eked out their existence on goodness knows what. So from the sign indicating the boundary of the village we must have travelled for a mile before reaching a T-junction. In front of us the third of the schools we have caught sight of during our gentle wander through the village.

Rosie, inevitably, is at the wheel and although until now we have seen little signs of life she decides that it was time to ask the way. Outside the school she spots a woman sitting beneath the branches of an enormous baobob tree selling wares from a small table. Rosie stops the car and insists that I go and speak to her. Sensing that the woman will probably not understand me, I somewhat reluctantly climb from our stationary vehicle and walk across to where she is sitting.

After the customary greeting in Setswana I enquire, 'The co-operative?' As I had anticipated I receive a blank response and a shake of the head. Perhaps she doesn't understand English, maybe it is my accent or perhaps she simply doesn't know the location of the co-operative.

Then the woman turns away and calls across through the fence where, in the adjacent schoolyard, a man is tending the gardens.

From a distance I address him, 'The co-operative?' repeating my enquiry. Bemused expression. The man comes closer to the fence and I respond by moving towards him so that our contact is more intimate. At close quarters I can see that he is a man of about 40. Surely he would have learnt English at school. He is smartly dressed for a gardener, in khakis, his balding head perspiring profusely from his endeavours in the late morning sun. Again I intone my question, 'The co-op?' Slight variation on a theme.

More slowly perhaps, 'The co-operative shop.' Blank.

Then suddenly the penny drops. 'Do you mean the co-opera-tive?' Heavy emphasis on the *op* and the *rat*.

'Yes,' I reply. Laughter all round.

'The co-operative,' the man repeats to the woman. Ha, ha, ha. They can hardly contain their mirth.

'Yes, the co-operative.' I am getting the hang of this. 'How do I find it?'

'You know xxxx?' asks the man, obviously referring to some local landmark.

'No,' I reply quite honestly, although he repeats the word twice more. Try as I might I cannot make any sense of the word. I think he is probably referring to one of the other schools we have passed.

He looks a little perplexed. 'You don't know the xxxx?' Even though I have presumably passed this notable sight on my drive through the village, he turns to the woman to tell her I don't know where the xxxx is. More near-hysterical laughter. Looking back at me he sees from my blank expression that I really did not know the xxxx.

He looks at me with continuing incredulity, clearly frustrated by being confronted by such a stupid stranger. Then almost as a last resort and with a hand gesture like a snake making its way through the bush he suggests that we make our way back from whence we came

'Look for the flag, at the flag is the police station. Here you should stop and ask someone the way.'

I climb back in the car commenting rather disagreeably to Rosie, 'What's wrong with these people?'

'Darling, this is Africa,' she replies, laughing rather smugly I think, being able to quote back to me my mantra for things not hap-pening as and when they should in this part of the world.

We drive back through the village and although we look hither and thither neither of us could see a flag nor a police station. We have almost reached the Maropong sign where we had first entered the village perhaps half an hour before when we spot some villagers crouching African style by the roadside.

'Better pull over and I will see if I can improve my skills in communication with the locals,' I rather grumpily remark to Rosie. Winding down the window I yell, 'The co-operative?' trying as best I can to replicate the way in which the man who had given me directions had pronounced the word.

To my amazement one man, clearly having no difficulty with my accent, speaks up, 'The white building down there,' pointing along an adjacent track to a building not 100 yards away.

The co-op is housed in a large solid rectangular construction within a sizeable yard surrounded by a high wire fence. Within this compound three smaller buildings. We park the car in the dusty yard and enter the shop. A stout wooden counter runs down the length of the room behind which shelves contain a range of products. An elderly lady behind the counter warmly welcomes us, extending her right hand supported by her left hand to shake mine in friendly greeting, revealing at the same time two rows of uneven and browning teeth. As it appears that she is expecting us I mistakenly assume that she is the manageress and say, 'Hello, are you Litiwe?' Evidently not, for without a word but with another toothy smile she points to a small office set at the far end of the building. Here we introduce ourselves to Litiwe. She, in contrast to her shop assistant, appears slightly nonplussed by our arrival and I immediately ask if we are expected. The response is, 'Yes, but not until the following day,' she having been informed by Botho that we will be arriving tomorrow.

Litiwe is not confident with her English and is a little shy with strangers. It is not surprising – there are not many visitors from England to be seen around these parts, but Rosie soon puts her at ease chatting about this and that: how we had got lost, the weather and the products she has noticed on the shelves. Women talk, which as usual manages to secure a magical effect enabling Litiwe to relax into the conversation. Her English is fine but probably she has little reason to use it here in Maropong. We discover that the co-operative is struggling with competition from other stores in the village. Litiwe buys through a wholesaler in Francistown and that means profit margins must be very small.

We ask Litiwe to show us around. The shop covers quite a substantial area as does a storage space at the rear. However, despite the generous space there is a narrow range of goods by our standards – commodities like sugar and sorghum but also other familiar products and we smile seeing old brands on the shelves like Omo soap powder and Sunlight soap. We ask why the shop is not self-service and Litiwe says this would be her preference but the management committee made up of village elders will not accept her idea for fear of pilferage.

We move from the main building next door to what proves to be a bar, but presumably a profitable activity for the co-op. Then Litiwe leads us across the yard. The third building is firmly locked and Litiwe says it contains newly purchased stock as the co-op is going to expand into the hardware business selling pots and pans and other kitchen utensils. We come to the fourth and final building. Litiwe pushes open the door and we are startled as two goats leap out. I am thinking this might be a small local abattoir but no, it is a grain store. Suddenly a young man with a pockmarked face appears on the scene. He looks about 20 and between them he and Litiwe explain that he is renting the building to run his own business buying and packaging sorghum, some of which he sells to the co-op. Basically sorghum, which is an important staple here, is delivered in large sacks, often too large a quantity or too expensive and cumbersome for one person to buy and carry home. This young entrepreneur has bought a piece of low-tech equipment that puts smaller quantities into 5 kilo bags that he in turn sells to the co-op and other local stores.

We return to the shop and take some photographs. The locals are always the same, feigning shyness but desperate to have their photo taken. An old man is at the counter and wants to be included. Litiwe says he is on the management committee and I cannot help but recall the old guys we had on the committee of the cattle marketing co-op, just the same with their old suits and trilby hats. It kind of reinforces my view that at village level little has changed.

The village elders still hold sway by virtue of their age and perceived wisdom, and despite their lack of literacy influence important elements of village life and can in their way decide the fate of projects such as a co-operative.

At this point a group of school children arrive to buy sweets. Giggly girls in their smart uniforms, all want to be in our photographs. If in many ways little has changed then in other respects of course it has. Now there are schools and pretty well all the kids will be educated, the brightest and more ambitious will soon take their leave of village life and move to the cities, Francistown or even Gaberone. Back in the village the children from the poorest families will be taken out of school at the earliest opportunity and will face a life spent looking after the livestock, for much of the year away from friends and family 'on the lands', until sometime in the distant future they too will become village elders bringing to bear their 'wisdom' on village affairs, whilst cousins and other arguably more fortunate relatives who have escaped from village to city life will live in a totally different world determined to make enough money that they never have to return. A few will of course succeed here, as in other parts of Africa, to become part of a new urban middle class but most will remain in poverty be it on the streets of Gaberone or back here in hot and dusty Maropong.

Time to take our leave. It is amazing, many years have passed but this sort of community project is what we were all about in the sixties. Sad that the business is struggling and that villagers' loyalty is limited to price rather than commitment to the co-op ideals.

The next day and once again we are headed west on the road towards Maun. Our destination is a place called Nata and thanks to Botho we will call in en route to visit the co-op at Sowa. We pray that we are expected.

Botho had told me that translation would not be a problem as Constance, one of his audit team, was at Sowa for the whole of the week. Sowa, like Maropong, lies a few miles south of the main Francistown to Maun road, but the turn-off is some 50 miles further west. Once again we are travelling on an excellent tarmac road. As we approach the village, however, we are amazed by the complete contrast with Maropong. A tall water tower dominates the skyline and the first business activity we see is a petrol station complete with shop. There are avenues of uniform houses with neatly tended gardens, and a school. No tribal village this but a small town with straight roads laid out on a clear grid pattern. Sowa, we are quickly to discover, is just that – in fact a company town.

We drive around until we come to a small parade of shops. We draw into the car park and Rosie says I should go and ask for directions but no need: Lo and behold on the wall of the adjacent building a small notice announces 'The Sowa Consumer Co-operative'. We enter the shop and immediately just inside we see a small glass fronted office – a more apt description might be a booth – has been constructed against the right-hand wall. It is tiny, containing a desk behind which, barely able to move, sit two ladies. One I assume to be Constance, the auditor, and the other Siviya, the name that Botho had scribbled on the piece of paper he had handed me as I left his office. I pop my head around the open door. 'Hello, are you Siviya?' I enquire. The larger of the two women responds. It is Siviya. She is a lady in her early thirties, stockily built, not unlike Litiwe at Maropong but she exudes more confidence and self-assurance. Her English is fine, which is a bonus as we discover that the other person in the booth is not Constance.

Siviya explains that Sowa township exists because of the BH Corporation, a Canadian company that is mining soda ash from below the surface of the Sowa Pan some ten miles away. All the inhabitants of the town either work at the mine or are related to mineworkers. The shop is contained within a generous floor space not unlike Maropong with a storeroom at the back. One significant difference is that the shop is self-service except for small items like soap that Siviya explains are both highly desirable and easy to steal and which are kept behind the till. We stroll around and take some photographs. The shop unlike Maropong is well stocked with a wide range of goods but is virtually empty of customers. Siviya explains that this is because everyone is at work and the busy time comes late in the day when the shift ends at the mine.

The shop stocks the usual commodity items one will find in Afri-

Back to the Bush

can stores – sorghum and maize, sugar and candles – but also some surprising items. There are electrical goods, like hot plates and irons, and to our amazement, some suitcases. There is also a refrigerated unit containing ice cream and an ATM machine not embedded in a wall but sitting on an upturned plastic crate. When we query the diversity of products Siviya explains that she tries to cater for customer needs and if they enquire about particular types of product she tries to respond positively and get them into stock – a policy that she willingly concedes does not always work, the suitcases being a good example. After Siviya managed to stock the shop with this item she discovered that the interested customer had already made a purchase from a store in Francistown. This elementary error in tying up valuable capital is surprising as Siviya seems to have good business brain and proves to be highly entrepreneurial.

There is a limited amount you can see and questions you can ask so we take some photos of Siviya and her shop assistant and look to exit when Siviya says that she has something else to show us. We all pile into our hire car and drive through the town and Siviya directs us towards what appears to be a playing field. Here there is a building and inside two young girls are working at a small table. One I assume is Constance, the auditor. This is one of Siviya's profit-making projects on behalf of the co-op. When the construction company that built the town finally left, their work completed, they donated to the town this a sports ground and social club. Siviya has persuaded the Town Council to rent these premises to the co-op as a bar and this is the most profitable part of the co-op. These are the bar girls counting last night's takings. The bar is well stocked and we have a chuckle when we spot a bottle of champagne. Surely not the tipple of choice in Sowa? Siviya confirms our thoughts on the subject. Another suspect stock selection perhaps? However, she does confirm that through the bar they are selling 70 cases a week of the popular local brew St Louis beer, on which the co-op is making a handsome profit.

Siviya used to manage a liquor store in a previous life so she is at home with the bar concept. She tells us that she is single and comes from a village about 50 miles away. She stays in Sowa during the working week and obviously the bar keeps her occupied in the evenings. To attract more trade she tells us about her latest promotion: if the punters buy a BBQ steak she throws in a plate of papa (mealie meal) for free.

We take some photos of the three women and move on. Following Siviya's instructions we drive to the edge of the town close to the striking water tower. Our next stop is the filling station. To our surprise this is also part of the co-op. Siviya is particularly pleased with her idea of opening a shop with the filling station. We would not see anything strange in this idea but here it is clearly something quite innovative. Finally Siviya steers us into a back room where two more young women are working. At last, the elusive Constance. She is in her twenties, smartly dressed in a business suit that would not be out of place in any City office. When we engage her in conversation she is complaining about having to work away from home on boring repetitive work. It is not difficult to see that she is a member of Botho's team.

Siviya guides us back to the store where we say our farewells. We have been surprised to find this enterprising lady in the middle of the bush. We suggest that we send her some photographs and ask her to confirm her name. She says 'Jane'. We are confused and ask her to write it down. She writes 'Jane Siviya'. Thanks Botho. We apologise profusely for the misunderstanding, having spent the whole morning calling her Siviya. We say our goodbyes and head back on the road to Nata. It has been an interesting visit.

Chapter Fifteen

Starting Business

Whilst Matsiloje was something of a diversion from our normal business and Pilikwe more of a norm, most of our time in the early weeks at Radisele was more directly related to the task of setting up the cattle marketing co-operative.

When the British had arrived in the nineteenth century, although the native population was small for a country the size of Bechuanaland, people still managed to congregate in large population centres for this was the Tswana custom, combining life in communities and on the lands. The white man called them 'villages' to distinguish them from the small towns they established with anglicised names like Francistown. Given that Bechuanaland was a protectorate and not a colony and of relatively little interest to the British, there were in fact few 'European' settlements or 'towns' but many 'villages' in Bechuanaland. This was not typical of many colonised parts of Africa like Kenya and Rhodesia where many whites settled and where European names proliferate, or did until the post-colonial era. For Tshoagong and me our work was exclusively within the traditional village structure of the Bangwato.

Apart from Serowe, the largest tribal village – some say the largest in Africa – we travelled from our base at Radisele to Mahalapye, another large village set beside the main north-south road, and to smaller villages like Seleka and Ramokgonani taking our message. The culmination of this recruitment drive had come in early December when Trevor addressed the meeting of tribal elders at the kgotla in Serowe following which we signed up our first members, Leapeetswe being ceremoniously enrolled as member number one, although in practice his herd was so large that he was one of the few indigenous people who could send their cattle direct to the abattoir without having to sell through the white traders.

At this time, due to the drought, the number of cattle being sent for slaughter to the abattoir at Lobatsi was increasing. To ensure the abattoir was not overwhelmed the government had introduced a new permit system. Under this new arrangement it was necessary to register with the abattoir and then apply one month in advance for a quota indicating how many cattle you intended to send for slaughter. If successful you would then be issued with a permit indicating how many cattle you could send for slaughter in the coming month. Although justified by the market situation, this system reinforced the position of the white traders at the expense of the indigenous farmer with a small herd who perhaps wanted to sell only one or two cows.

The government action was well timed as demand far exceeded the capacity of the abattoir, leading to a scaling down of quota applications. Unfortunately this was no consolation to the small farmers. The traders soon worked out how to play the system and applied for a high quota, far in excess of that they really required, whilst the small farmer, wanting to send one or two cattle, was immediately eliminated when quotas were allocated. The small farmer, quite unable to cope with the form-filling bureaucracy demanded by this new system, now desperate to sell before his animals died, had no recourse other than to sell to the speculators. He was caught in a vicious circle and was now even more at the mercy of the system. Quotas if nothing else helped to reinforce the need for co-operative action by the local farmers.

The cattle marketing co-operative encompassed ideas new to Botswana, but we already had radical plans beyond the simple buying and selling of cattle. For example, we wanted to find new grazing pastures and hold cattle for up to a month to add weight and therefore value before transporting them to the abattoir at Lobatsi. With the drought most animals were already sick and emaciated and would bring only the lowest prices at the abattoir. The co-operative was going to buy 'on the hoof', paying the farmer at that point a rate probably no more and maybe even less than that paid by the South African traders. Profits would be held in the co-operative and then shared amongst the members at the end of each year in the form of a dividend, as is normal co-operative practice. But before we could even contemplate introducing these ideas we had to actively involve local people by enrolling them as the co-operative members. In turn these members would elect their committee of management, what in a company we know as the board of directors.

A co-operative is a genuinely democratic and participative organisation but we were dealing with largely uneducated and poor farmers, few of whom spoke English. Could we really expect these people to embrace these new ideas and to run a business competing against experienced and at times ruthless traders whose very livelihood was being challenged? A very fundamental obstacle to progress was the Batswana view of life, status in that society being determined by the simple measure of number of cows owned; no matter that they may be barely alive from the lack of sustenance brought about by successive years of drought and in this condition be prone to disease and death, or that their value in the market would be much reduced by their condition. Our Western view that in these fraught and exceptional circumstances it was better to keep ten healthy cows and sell the rest for cash would not be something to be considered by the Batswana. Their view was it was better to own 50 cows, even if doing so was condemning many if not all the animals to slow death by starvation. Thus the co-operative had to fight a propaganda battle against the forces of conservatism that ruled tribal life.

We were seeking to challenge the established order in society as well as offering a genuine opportunity for the people to have the ability to manage the fruits of their labours for a reasonable return. Understandably there would be a reaction to these young white men coming and trying to change the old ways. In this struggle for hearts and minds Tshoagong, with his local knowledge and command of the local language together with the wisdom gained from his experience of life in South Africa, was to be the key element, although in this respect even Tshoagong was perceived as an outsider. Nevertheless despite the obstacles we were making progress; we were spreading the message and putting the formal structure in place.

The cattle marketing co-operative was to cover an enormous geographical area – the Ngwato tribal lands, perhaps the size of Wales. To keep in place some genuine sense of ownership and to meet the needs of tribal politics we had agreed that the board of management would be drawn from east and west, two separate electoral districts, with meetings convened both at Serowe and close to Radisele at which the members of the new co-operative could elect representatives to become the first board of management.

Here I was living and working in a remote location in Africa. So different from England yet I rarely felt that I was at risk from wild and dangerous creatures. This might partly be attributed to my own naivety as to the risks, although I do recall Vernon's stern advice, adopting the habit of shaking my shoes before putting them on in the morning to ensure that a stray scorpion had not decided to make a home inside.

For the most part there was little sign of any wildlife in the eastern part of the country; they had long since been hunted to extinction or with the inexorable movement of man from the south and east had moved west in search of both water and safer territory. Inevitably there were some exceptions to the general rule. An example was the colony of baboons that lived around a rocky outcrop in the Tswapong Hills between Radisele and Tshoagong's village, Pilikwe. They were highly territorial and aggressive and notable only for the accuracy with which they threw stones at our truck as we drove past. At the end of every month we would drive across to Pilikwe for me to collect the villagers' savings for the thrift and loan co-operative. It was almost as if the baboons had their own calendar for they would suddenly appear from behind the rocks, giving the appearance of having been lying in wait, to bombard us with a fusillade of stones as we drove past.

On one occasion I was driving with Tshoagong somewhere in the interior. By now we had built our second kraal – an enclosed wooden fenced area – this one at Serowe, and from here had travelled many miles west from the village to inspect the site of a possible holding ground for cattle purchased at this new location where we might pasture the cattle before slaughter. We were driving along a road that resembled a dried riverbed, with a steep banking of loose sand on either side totally blocking our peripheral vision. Suddenly there was a noise like thunder. Tshoagong stopped the vehicle and seconds later we were engulfed by huge numbers of a large bovine animal, scrambling down the bank and across the road in front and behind and in most cases quite literally leaping over the road and our truck. The procession continued for what must have been several minutes, although at the time it seemed an eternity until we were left with a few stragglers and then silence as the dust bowl they had created gently settled. This was the annual migration of wildebeest, also known as the gnu.

I don't really have any comprehension as to numbers but I have always thought it numbered tens of thousands. The wildebeest, although a member of the antelope family, is a large ox-like creature with strong shoulders and the rear not dissimilar to that of a horse. The animal would not be one that the layman could immediately identify and this led to the beast achieving a degree of fame being the subject of a song composed by the fifties' music hall duo Flanders and Swann who wrote and sang 'The Gnu Song' with the immortal lyrics 'G-no, g-no, g-no I'm a gnu. Spelt G N U' when visitors to the zoo mistook the beast for an elk or bison.

Another creature we did occasionally encounter was the ostrich, the sight of which invariably led to Tshoagong braking quickly before rummaging behind the driver's seat for his shotgun. On the first occasion this happened I was taken by utter surprise, firstly that he had a gun and secondly knew how to use it, although in the event his accuracy was somewhat debatable. He took careful aim and fired away but without any apparent success and the beasts loped away to what they obviously thought was a safe distance. I thought this was hysterically funny and fell about laughing.

Tshoagong couldn't see the joke and assured me that the ostrich was no easy target because he was aiming at the creature's long and narrow neck. He explained that although the beast was a fine catch for the dinner plate it was no use if full of shot. As ever his explanation was plausible if not entirely persuasive. On subsequent encounters with ostriches he never once did record a hit so perhaps it was his marksmanship after all.

I was very much reminded of Tshoagong and ostriches when before leaving Gaberone to go up country Sandy gave us a dire warning about driving through the bush, relating how recently four German tourists had been fortunate to escape with their lives after an encounter with this large two-legged beast. They had apparently obtained a permit allowing them to hunt certain animals and driving off the main road in search of some prey they had spotted some ostriches in the distance. Abandoning their 4 x 4 they had ventured closer to the birds and fired off a few rounds, then looking back to their dismay they saw their vehicle ablaze. Alone in the middle of the bush with night approaching they decided that the safest thing to do was to bury themselves in the sand with only their heads showing and remain there until daybreak. They were lucky enough to survive their ordeal when they managed to get themselves back to the road and flag down a passing vehicle after two days and nights in the bush. The fire, it appears, was caused by an accumulation of seeds being caught in the radiator as the vehicle drove through the bush, eventually combusting into what could have been a fateful fire.

The sudden appearance of a gun had come as something of a shock, although as Tshoagong quite reasonably argued, it was a tool of his trade as we were travelling in areas where predators, maybe not lions, but other unpleasant and potentially dangerous creatures, such as jackals and snakes, were around. More importantly, for a family man the chance to shoot and take home some small game like gemsbok, springbok or even the elusive ostrich were opportunities not to be missed. As ever with Tshoagong sweet reason tinged with an element of doubt. How did a black South African learn to shoot? I was left to idle speculation as to the nature of his life in South Africa and why he became a refugee from his own homeland.

Fortunately as I have a bit of a phobia I saw only one snake during my entire year in Africa and not the dreaded black mamba, such a popular feature of Tshoagong's tales. This brief encounter occurred as I was walking along the track from Radisele to the BDA. The snake wasn't particularly long nor did it do anything other than race across my eye line. It nevertheless was something of a shock, not least because it didn't gently glide as I had assumed but moved at a frighteningly quick speed that made me feel that it was a good thing it was travelling across my path rather than on it.

At the other extreme, my work ensured regular visits to Gaberones, and some semblance of returning to civilisation. Trevor was very understanding about the nature of life in the bush and in early December after two hectic months up country I received one of his cryptic radio messages to visit Gaberones. When I arrived, he suggested in the absence of Barbara and the kids – not yet returned for the Christmas holidays – that we take a weekend out in Johannesburg. I recall that we spent the day going from cinema to cinema catching 'Those Magnificent Men in their Flying Machines' and the latest Bond movie, frankly there not being much else to do in the city that even in those days made me feel uneasy and constantly looking over my shoulder. It was a thoughtful gesture by Trevor but I genuinely felt that life was safer in the bush.

Looking back at my diary for the period I can see why he was concerned. Apart from all the meetings and visits I have mentioned in Serowe and the trips to Matsiloje, I had also visited the abattoir in Lobatsi, travelled to meet veterinary experts still occupying offices in Mafeking, had three times taken the long trip down from Radisele to Gaberones and had attended endless village meetings with Tshoagong around the Bamangwato. Apart from Matsiloje we had also completed registration of a thrift and loan co-operative in Tshoagong's village, Pilikwe, soon to be followed by another at Ramokgonani.

With Christmas approaching I was facing the prospect of spending my first ever time away from home over the festive period and Trevor kindly invited me to join him and his family. I then received another tempting offer, from Chief Leapeetswe Khama no less, to join him together with the volunteer teachers from Swaneng School at his ranch. I decided that doing something completely different over Christmas was entirely in keeping with the spirit of my year in Africa and accepted. My memories are limited to huge roasts cooked over a spit, and of temperatures that reached 110°F on Christmas Day. The ranch was located somewhere to the west of Serowe and had one unusual feature for drought-ridden Bechuanaland at that time – a large waterhole. In the heat this became too tempting for some of the chief's guests, who quickly turned it into a swimming pool, despite the inherent risks from the waterborne disease bilharzia. A thoroughly unpleasant complaint in which tiny snails burrow beneath the skin, mate, incubate and ultimately find their way into the urinary tract. Given the choice I preferred to bear the heat.

Two days later I was back at Radisele and the next day collecting the savings from the co-op members at Pilikwe. Then on New Year's Eve I returned to Serowe. I enjoyed the New Year's celebrations with my very good friends at Swaneng School but the next morning found me performing the annual stocktake at the Swaneng co-op store, celebrating its first successful year in business. The following day was spent completing the audit. Next morning I was on the move again and Donald Curtis, who helped run the store, drove me in the school truck to Palapye to catch the morning train to Gaberones where, for the following week I was running a training course in bookkeeping. Life was extremely hectic.

By now much of the preliminary work towards establishing the cattle marketing co-operative had been completed. Just before Christmas we had held the first members' meetings at Ramokgonani and Serowe and taken further enrolments. The co-operative had been registered on 12 January under the official title of the Bamangwato Livestock Co-operative with 50 members, and the management committee was duly elected. Unfortunately before we could start trading we needed the promised funds from Oxfam in the UK to arrive and then a further delay occurred when an outbreak of foot and mouth disease stopped all movement of cattle and led to the closure of the abattoir at Lobatsi.

Coincidentally on the day we formally registered the new co-operative Frank Judd was in Gaberones on a field visit on behalf of IVS. It seemed very timely four months into my assignment we had overcome the first major hurdle – the formal creation of the co-operative. A few days later Frank made his way to Swaneng where we were able to have a briefing meeting. I had no time for reflection given the workload, but the feedback he had received from Trevor about my efforts was reassuring at this time when things seemed to be going badly as far as the cattle marketing co-op was concerned; with the lack of funds from England, the apparent 'wait and see' attitude of the locals, the imposition of the quota system and then receiving the devastating news that the abattoir was to close completely for a period due to foot and mouth disease.

By now the effects of the drought were biting ever deeper with an estimated one third of the national herd dying of starvation during the course of the year. The impact of the drought was difficult for me to assess for that is all I knew in Bechuanaland but the evidence seemed to suggest that this was something out of the ordinary. Because every day was dry I can in fact recall the day it did rain. It must have been in February or early March. The skies darkened and brooded ominously for days before eventually opening. The rain was so intense that I was confined to my rondavel for the duration. For several hours everything was awash. Golden brown torrents of water surrounded my little house, leaving me effectively trapped – perhaps 3 in. of rain in the day. Then it was over. Maybe the memory plays tricks; after all when we were kids the summer holidays were always full of bright sunny days, but that I am sure was pretty well all the rain that year. Within days the green shoots emerged but they disappeared as quickly as they had emerged. That was the rainy season – one day.

It is difficult for us to totally appreciate the significance of rain in a country where it is such a rare occurrence compared with our own climate where we ourselves use the term 'drought' despite an annual rainfall of at the very least 25 in. of rain a year. A measure of its importance in Botswana is that the country chose to call its new post-Independence currency the pula, pula in Setswana being rain.

The consequence of the drought was that as the years passed

the people had become increasingly dependent upon external aid in the form of supplies of sorghum maize provided by aid agencies like Oxfam. In most villages the sight of long queues of people waiting to receive their daily ration of this staple were already commonplace. This was of course 20 years or more before the high profile disasters like Ethiopia but drought is no newcomer to Africa.

With the quality and quantity of the national cattle herd in steep decline I was anxious for the co-operative to press ahead with our radical plans to help preserve both the numbers, but more importantly the quality, of the livestock owned by our members. Thanks to Vernon, we gathered together a group of local men at Makoro, the next railway halt north of Radisele, and they were put to work to construct a kraal, where we could buy and hold cattle prior to transporting them to the abattoir at Lobatsi. We were quickly approaching the time when business operations could commence.

With the support of Leapeetswe we wanted to develop this idea by holding stock further west where the soil, although not so fertile, was by the same token an area relatively under-populated and as a consequence not as over-grazed as down the eastern strip of the country.

This idea was simply an extension of the practice of keeping cattle around the farmers' 'lands' for part of the year. These 'lands' could be a considerable distance from the farmers' tribal village, typically 30 or more miles. It was customary for the young men to spend the dry season at the lands, bringing cattle east for sale and slaughter after the rains. With this in mind we began to make some forays into the interior. It was on one of these trips that Tshoagong and I had encountered the wildebeest. Being able to provide not only grazing but also a water source was a perennial problem. Bringing the cattle back to the east was a long and strenuous journey impacting on the condition and bodyweight of the animal at the time when these factors were most important, just before slaughter. The drought had only accentuated this inherent problem. In seeking to find good new grazing locations our thinking got a little more drastic. With the support of Trevor I visited the district commissioner in Francistown to get permission to explore the area west of the town towards Maun and the Okavango.

Despite the co-operatives' problems we received some good news: our funding had belatedly arrived from the UK enabling us to construct the second buying kraal and even more importantly, with the foot and mouth outbreak under control, the abattoir had re-opened. We were ready to start trading. However, a new quota system was now operating at the abattoir, which was faced with a large backlog. As a new business we were at the back of the queue and were not allocated any permits allowing us to send animals to slaughter. We faced the prospect of delaying the commencement of business yet again at a time many farmers wanted to sell. The alternative was to buy cattle that we would hold for an indeterminate period until we could obtain our permit to slaughter. The not inconsiderable influence of the white traders seemed to be at work in a bid to frustrate their new competitor.

Fortunately we were soon to put all these troubles behind us. February saw the timely arrival of a new volunteer, Graham Howe, who was to join me as the technical advisor in running the co-operative, being a stockman from Devon specialising in cattle. I use the word 'timely' advisedly. Here we were about to start buying cattle yet I still barely knew one end of the beast from the other. Whilst Vernon's nous was invaluable in establishing the co-operative his real job was running the Bamangwato Development Association and he was personally focussed on improving the quality of arable farming in the country. His vision was for the locals to become self-sufficient by becoming better able to grow things, albeit a by-product might be fodder to feed the national cattle herd during the dry season. So in one sense what we were trying to do with the cattle marketing co-operative was counter-intuitive to Vernon's personal mission – an odd dilemma for both parties.

Interestingly although I had a huge amount of respect for Vernon and his commitment to rural development, I was something of a sceptic with regard to the whole idea of making the Tswana self-sufficient in terms of their ability to grow crops as a staple. My own view was that they were herdsmen whose best chance of moving beyond a subsistence economy was to become better at animal husbandry, making their money in selling high quality beef to the rest of the world. This made Graham's arrival even more timely, although he was to prove a less agreeable working partner.

Where Vernon was laid-back Graham was very intense. Vernon was a bright and articulate Cambridge graduate and had an aura of self-confidence. Graham was in no sense an academic but a practical cattleman. He had come from a less privileged background; he had grown up in children's homes and with a series of foster parents. He had a definite 'chip on his shoulder' and for him everything was a battle. Having said that despite some initial misgivings he and I quickly established a good working relationship helped in no small measure by my own working class credentials. We still argued about every decision affecting the cattle marketing co-operative but Graham soon realised we had common cause and that I was merely going through the motions to satisfy his need to feel that he was winning battles against the odds. Very soon we were simply playing a game that we both clearly understood.

Suddenly things were falling into place; after all the frustrating setbacks the co-operative started operations with the first buying session at Makoro on 7 March 1966. Our system was unique in several respects. Firstly we had imported scales so that the animal could be weighed at the point of purchase and from this bodyweight an appropriate price was determined. Graham was our buyer with the right to make a judgement on quality as well as the information on weight in determining price. Secondly our pricing structure was entirely transparent insofar as the members owned the co-operative. For the first time they would know how much the abattoir had paid for their animals.

Initially business was slow. Although the co-operative had generated a lot of interest and word of this new venture had spread widely throughout the Bamangwato, the natural conservatism of the local farmers led very much to a 'wait and see' approach. At our first buying session curiosity drew many of the men, particularly the village elders, to the kraal to watch proceedings. Few brought cattle with them and on that first day we purchased only a dozen cattle, and again a week later about the same number. This reticence was understandable, if frustrating, for Graham and myself. After all the co-operative was some fancy new idea dreamed up by the white man and what made Graham and me any different in the eyes of the locals from the traders with whom they were accustomed to doing business?

Little things stick in the mind and I vividly recall at that first buying session being approached by one old man. I had seen him on visits to the nearby village of Pilikwe and I seem to recall he was a regular saver with the thrift and loan co-operative. Like many of the old men, whatever the weather – and it was invariably very hot – he wore an old suit that in better days would probably have been worn by some City gent in far-off London. Now it was torn, patched and grubby matching closely a white shirt that was now grey and frayed around the collar. To be honest in our own society he would have passed for a tramp. I was leaning on the kraal watching proceedings as Graham went into action for the first time, probably looking a little disconsolate that our efforts had attracted so little in the way of real business. He tapped me on the arm and quietly said, 'Be patient, we are very slow to change our ways but you are doing a very good thing, just give us time.' I gave a rueful nod but later that night, reflecting on the day's events, I recalled that brief encounter. I said nothing to Graham but from that point I knew we would be successful.

Following the first buying session Graham and I took the train down to Lobatsi, to the abattoir, to follow the slaughter process. The abattoir was, for such a poor Third World country 'state of the art', using an electric stunning technique and a totally automated production line technology to skin, cut and move the carcass. Despite the slow start this visit provided an important insight to enable us to begin to understand the potential of the co-operative. It was not until the animal had been slaughtered that we could determine whether it was diseased, although with the drought it was evident that badly emaciated animals were more prone to disease and in any event would achieve a low price through the grading structure used by the abattoir. On a one-to-eight scale our cattle were typically being graded at seven or eight, effectively meaning the meat was unfit for human consumption. There were exceptions. From the data provided by the abattoir we could tell who were husbanding their stock more successfully and how other members of the co-operative might benefit from this knowledge. By managing the marketing process rather than selling through traders it was already evident that huge benefits could accrue if we could only get the co-operative members to learn to use the information now available.

Chapter Sixteen

Bessie Head

Early in 1966 I became aware that I had neighbours at the BDA. After a day travelling with Tshoagong I returned to my hut and immediately realised that whilst I was away the previously empty next-door rondavel had become occupied.

A short time later Vernon knocked on my door and introduced me to my new neighbour. She was a short, plump and frankly rather unattractive coloured woman. If asked at the time my guess would have been that she was aged about 40, although I now know she was actually still in her late twenties. With her stood a young child of three or four who she in turn introduced to me as Howard.

My terminology 'coloured' is accurate, this being the term used in South Africa to describe those of mixed race, as I later discovered in this case from the unusual – and in apartheid South Africa illegal – liaison between a black man and white woman. There was a large population in South Africa designated as 'coloured' under the apartheid regime, particularly in the Cape province. They, however, unlike my new neighbour were the offspring and descendants of the early white traders and settlers and the indigenous Bantu women. As such they held a special status under apartheid even having some limited representation in parliament, something not enjoyed by the completely disenfranchised majority black population.

Whenever we met and passed the time of day my new neighbour

always appeared very agitated and unprompted she would give me a long diatribe against the bureaucrats and those in authority. If I am very polite I might describe her as highly-strung.

I had never at that time, and frankly rarely since, met someone whose emotions were so close to the surface as to be never more than barely restrained. Invariably the target for a torrent of these verbal outpourings was her own child, who she subjected to tirades of shouting and screaming despite the fact that she clearly doted on him and was ever fearful for his safety as he played in the dust outside their new home. Vernon told me that the new arrival was a refugee recently arrived from South Africa but I gleaned little more. She had no visible means of support, having neither land, livestock nor any regular work. The woman's name was Bessie Head.

It was not until many years later, reading the book reviews in an English newspaper, that I became aware that Bessie had become a novelist of note, one of the foremost African writers of her generation. I was frankly gobsmacked. Some time after this discovery I was perusing the shelves in a Charing Cross Road bookshop when my eyes were drawn to an edition of her first book *When Rain Clouds Gather*. Intrigued, I bought a copy. To my amazement I discovered that, although the storyline in the book draws heavily on Bessie's own experience as a refugee fleeing to Botswana and of her life in Radisele, the main characters in the book seemed remarkably familiar.

The first of these is an English agriculturalist, Gilbert Balfour, being very obviously based upon Vernon Gibberd, and what's more much of the story refers to a cattle marketing co-operative, clearly the Bamangwato cattle marketing co-operative. The main character in the book is a South African refugee, Makhaya, who seems to have much in common with my colleague, Tshoagong. Makhaya had a mysterious political past which is alluded to, but the true nature of which is never revealed in the novel. All those years later it got me thinking again about Tshoagong. Had Bessie Head found something of a secret past that had evaded my inquisition, or perhaps she too had met a blank leaving her, as with me, nothing else to do but speculate.

Having known Bessie in such a different context I naturally

wanted, rather belatedly I admit, to find out more about her. It appears that before her sudden appearance as my neighbour at the BDA she had been a journalist in South Africa working for the black journal, the Drum. She had left South Africa after a broken marriage, leading to a trial in which she had given evidence against her husband, to start a new life in Botswana.

After the publication of *When Rain Clouds Gather,* Bessie Head continued to write successful novels about African life. This first book had been published in 1969 and around this time she left her temporary home at Radisele and moved to Serowe where she became a well-known local character. Her second novel *Maru* was published in 1971. Sadly within weeks she had been certified insane. Not surprisingly a later work *A Question of Power*, published in 1974, is an autobiographical account of someone disturbed by paranoia. Bessie had herself been born in a mental home to which her mother had been committed after becoming pregnant by a black man. She was taken from her mother at birth and her early life involved periods living with foster parents and later in an orphanage attached to a mission school where her passion for literature was encouraged. When she left school Bessie first sought to channel this interest by becoming a teacher but realising that this was not her true vocation she left that profession to find expression, first as a journalist and of course later as a writer.

Sadly Bessie Head died of hepatitis in Botswana in 1986. She was just 48 years of age.

Poor Bessie, long gone, but thanks to her writing not totally forgotten. One of her later works *Village of the Rain Wind* is a history of Serowe and although the local people obviously thought her eccentric, if not completely mad, they also respected her work, not to mention the international recognition she brought to the village. The Red House Museum, recognising that Bessie had brought a degree of fame and attention to Serowe, has purchased for display and research many of her papers.

Chapter Seventeen

Nata

The Colonial Development Corporation had established an experimental agriculture centre in a remote area called Nata some years before, an experiment long since abandoned. In December I visited the Veterinary Department at Francistown to discuss the feasibility of using this area to hold cattle bought by the co-operative. They were helpful but non-committal. Then in January I took the old Botswana Air Dakota to fly from Serowe to Francistown to meet the district commissioner to discuss this same matter. We had of course met on a previous occasion prior to Tshoagong and I visiting Matsiloje and he must have thought I had some personal credibility because the outcome of the meeting was permission for me to visit the Nata area. Now with Graham on board and with the co-operative having taken its first tentative steps as a business it was time to check out Nata Ranch.

Early one Friday morning in April Graham and I set out from Serowe together with four of the teachers from Swaneng School for whom this was to be a rare opportunity to see something of the African bush.

The Swaneng contingent comprised two boys and two girls. John and Chris were both good fun and excellent company and when they heard of our proposed trip up country they had eagerly promoted the idea that they might join us. In keeping with the fashion amongst the volunteer teachers at Swaneng both had grown beards. As Graham was also bearded I remained the only clean-shaven, although by now, in the absence of a barber my hair had grown very long by the standards of the day. The girls were the rather quiet and intense Kirsty and the drop-dead-gorgeous Gillian. Kirsty's appearance, with mousy hair and pale complexion, always seemed totally out of place in the African bush and back in London on our orientation course I had wondered whether she was strong enough to undertake a mission to Africa. She obviously had some hidden grit and was able to take things in her stride. Gill was tall and slim with long dark shoulder-length hair, always immaculately groomed and had a haughty head girl manner, which rather than detract from, actually added to her allure. Despite the intense heat I am sure that she didn't even perspire let alone sweat profusely like the rest of us.

We anticipated the journey to Nata would take the whole day allowing us the Saturday to assess the potential of the ranch, for we had been told that an area had been fenced, albeit many years before, to conduct experiments on use of the land for grazing. We then planned to return to Swaneng on the Sunday, the teachers having to be back for classroom duties on the Monday morning.

By this time the arrival of long-awaited funds from the UK had enabled the co-operative to acquire its own transport in the form of a Land Rover truck. This was a flat bed lorry built on a stretched Land Rover chassis. Being a Land Rover it was equipped with four-wheel drive and therefore appeared to be eminently suitable for the terrain we anticipated that we would encounter; in this respect it appeared to us at the time to be a more practical option than the Bedford and was available at what seemed a remarkably cheap price. The main drawback and perhaps the reason few of these vehicles were ever made and that this one was acquired at a knockdown price, was that being built on the Land Rover chassis it was the width of a normal Land Rover. Compared with the stout and solid looking Bedford it was tall and narrow and from my perspective for a truck it looked – and once you were in the driver's seat, it felt – inherently unstable. However, having acquired our new 'toy' and tried it on the roads around Radisele we were not unhappy with our purchase. Once our trip to Nata was mooted I was beginning to have second thoughts, becoming fearful that being so high and narrow it might be prone to topple over on the little used and rough terrain that we expected to encounter. Like the good old Bedford Tshoagong and I used on government business, on the truck bed behind the driver's compartment a metal frame had been welded into place over which we could lay a tarpaulin cover, rather in the fashion of an Army truck.

At Swaneng we gathered our little party together. In rather cavalier fashion we threw the sleeping bags of the Swaneng contingent into the back of the truck. The girls had organised a supply of food and water from the school kitchens and this was packed into the back with rather more care. Some of the other teachers had gathered to say goodbye and with Graham at the wheel two of us squeezed into the cab with him; the other three perched precariously on the back of the vehicle. With a jolt we set off down the hill through the school gates and onto the main road from Serowe to Palapye. Our route was to take us initially the 20-odd miles to Palapye from where we took a left turn and headed north to Francistown. From there Nata lay to the northeast on what was then a little used route towards the Okavango Delta region.

This first part of the journey to Francistown was relatively straightforward, being one I had made on a number of occasions with Tshoagong. We had been told that the road linking Francistown to the northwest town of Maun had recently been improved and in our naivety assumed that this would be of similar quality to the main north-south road. Far from perfect but good enough to enable us to make steady progress. However, we grossly over-estimated what had been described as 'road improvements' and once beyond Francistown our progress slowed perceptibly. We were soon hours behind our planned schedule. What is more we knew that the ranch itself lay many miles to the south and we would at some stage have to leave this 'main' road and travel into the interior.

When we left Swaneng we decided to travel with the tarpaulin cover at the rear of the truck folded back to enable the three passengers in the rear to enjoy the views and the fresh air. Within a short time it was evident that this option was not very practical and if the dust didn't quickly choke the passengers travelling in the rear of the truck they would bake in the hot tropical sun. This meant stopping and after some physical effort once again pulling the tarpaulin cover over the back of the truck, thus reducing the dust problem but making for an uncomfortable ride in near blackout conditions. Undercover it was extremely hot and claustrophobic. We stopped frequently and to minimise the discomfort for those in the rear, rotated seating – three up front in the cab and three in the back under cover. As the long and arduous drive progressed morale plummeted and tempers became raised.

It was early evening and we had been driving all day when we eventually reached the point where we needed to leave the road. With dusk approaching it was clear that it would be the second day before we reached our intended destination. There was no alternative but to stop and set up camp for the night. As we were not equipped with tents, anticipating being able to use the buildings that we had been advised existed at Nata, we were left with no alternative but to stretch out, six people, head to tail in the back of the lorry.

We rose early on the Saturday morning stiff and sore and after a hurried breakfast of cold baked beans we continued our journey. We were now on tracks that had seen little recent use by motor vehicles. If progress the previous day had been slow, it now became almost pedestrian, bumpy and extremely dusty, driving in first or second gear. Being the less accomplished driver the passengers frequently thumped the driver's cab whilst I was at the wheel complaining that I was going too fast, physically throwing them from side to side in the rear of the vehicle. Having taken my turn in the rear I soon understood the discomfort, but I reasoned that after all this wasn't a pleasant Sunday afternoon drive in the English countryside. Eventually around midday Graham stopped the vehicle for what I thought must be one of our periodic driver changeovers but instead of climbing down he clambered up, hanging onto the cab roof to give himself some extra elevation. 'We've arrived,' he shouted, 'the ranch is over there.' What relief. We had reached our destination but not in the best of spirits.

After the totally miserable journey the Nata ranch was a pleasant surprise. The main building comprised a modern and well-appointed bungalow and although it had been deserted some years previously, it was remarkably free from incursion by the bush or by insects, termites or even larger forms of wildlife. Although several acres around the property had been fenced, this fencing had fared less well than the house itself and was now in a state of disrepair. The grass in this area was growing to a height of several feet and although dry, there was much more for animals to feed upon than the over-grazed scrubland to the east. Graham took samples of the grasses whilst the rest of us enjoyed a lazy afternoon in the sunshine resting from our long and arduous journey. The ranch still had in place cooking facilities and a freshwater borehole providing the opportunity for hot food and a welcome refreshing shower. A pleasant day passed into a long evening of casual conversation about all the issues in the world, from banning the bomb to successful remedies for zits.

Before retiring for the night in relative comfort, we confronted the thorny issue of how to get back to Swaneng by nightfall on the following day. We laid out our map on the floor of the large lounge, and with our only illumination from the torches that the girls had the prescience to bring, we pored over its finer detail. Graham produced a pencil and on the map drew a straight line from Nata to Serowe. The distance was but a fraction of that we had covered travelling via Francistown. The map showed that the only obstacle between Swaneng School and us was something labelled Makgadikgadi Pans. At the time none of us knew anything about these pans and the map was rather ambiguous on the subject, showing those little tufts of grass symbols that we all agreed indicated marshy land. But this was just at the end of the rainy season so was this likely to be underwater at this time of year? Lakes in drought-stricken Bechuanaland? If they existed, surely we would have heard of them. From our map we judged that water or not we would be able to negotiate a fairly direct route in our intended direction, roughly southeast towards Serowe between two of the larger pans. Despite a slower average speed than we had been able to achieve on our outward journey and accepting the inevitable discomfort, we all agreed that we would attempt to travel back by this alternative route.

It was hard to credit our ingenuousness on the very nature of the pans and only later did we discover that the Makgadikgadi are actually huge saltpans being the residue of a former lake that once covered much of what is now Northern Botswana. Climate changes less than 10,000 years ago led to the lake evaporating, leaving the lowest levels of the lake full of salt deposits. What is now the Makgadikgadi Pans cover some 12,000 km².

At daybreak we were presented with a magnificent and unforgettable spectacle: an African dawn. Waking bleary-eyed from a good night's sleep, a bright sun sat low on the horizon in a cloudless sky. Through the patio window of the bungalow we caught the sight of giraffe and zebras grazing not 100 yards away. During our journey we had seen little wildlife and almost imperceptibly the landscape had changed so we barely realised that we were now in lands not occupied by man but by animals in the wild in their natural habitat. We were now deep into the African bush and although the sight was stunning we were equally, for the first time, suddenly aware of the inherent dangers. With so many animals within our vision almost certainly lurking close by were more dangerous predators like lion. After breakfast we packed our belongings in the back of the truck and set off in high spirits. What we had seen was very much fulfilling the main reason why the Swaneng teachers had wanted to make the trip whilst for Graham and I the trip had been worthwhile from a business perspective.

We soon picked up a track running in roughly the right direction, and once again headed off into thick bush. Wildlife was now more evident with grazing animals, eland, hartebeest and wildebeest much in evidence. On the rough track progress was even slower and more uncomfortable than on our journey to Nata. Although there was a track it was little used; indeed quite possibly no motor vehicle had come this way for months, probably not in several years. Now the passengers in the cab were no longer just passive spectators enjoying the views across the African bush but navigators helping the driver trying to spot the direction of the track covered by tall grasses 6-8 ft in height.

After several hours of slow and laborious progress through this thick bush, our main concern was an overheated engine. Thankfully we eventually emerged from the bush to catch sight of our first saltpan. It was a bare and endless vista stretching as far as we could see into the distance. We began its circumnavigation. This proved just as slow and tedious as the earlier part of the journey. The edge of the pan followed an irregular pattern and with no discernable track we were tentatively making our way through virgin bush. Yet just yards away an inviting flat and even terrain stretched way into the distance in the direction in which we wanted to travel. The pan surface appeared to be of dried mud; in the distance was a shimmering haze that gave the impression of water. By now we had driven all morning but covered only a handful of miles and it was clear that progress was so slow that this route, although shorter, would take considerably longer than even the outward journey to Nata. We stopped to contemplate the alternatives.

Our guess was that the distant shimmering surface of the pan was a mirage. The short rainy season was over. Driving across the pan would save hours in journey time. It was agreed we would tentatively drive onto the pan and if it appeared safe would head straight across and give us what was our only chance of returning to Serowe that night. With the exception of Graham we all alighted whilst he slowly edged the vehicle forward onto the surface of the pan. It was completely hard, not even leaving an imprint of the tyres. In joyous mood we boarded and set off, initially with great caution and then, at increasing speed we headed towards the mirage.

I was a passenger in the rear at this time and looking backwards I could see the shoreline recede as we made our rapid progress. Unlike the rest of the journey we now moved quickly, in a straight line, and mercifully free from the bucking motion of the vehicle making its way through the almost impenetrable bush. Then quite perceptibly, even from my position in the back of the truck, I became aware that we were slowing. At first I thought we had encountered some mechanical problem then the most dreadful of all thoughts occurred. It was apparent that we were no longer skimming across the surface of the pan. My worst fear: slowly but surely we were sinking. The vehicle ground to a halt and we all leapt out onto the surface of the pan to inspect our predicament. Yes, we were up to the vehicle axles in the mud. At the wheel Graham had realised what was happening and had tried to steer a course towards the nearest shore and safety but to no avail.

Like a huge muddy rain puddle the pan had dried out, dry and firm at the edges, but towards the centre it still held water just below the surface. Here beneath the sun-dried crust of the pan was enough moisture such that once the surface was broken any heavy weight on the pan surface would cause that object to sink. How far? Could our truck actually slowly sink beneath the surface? These imponderables were hardly worth contemplating for fear of the answer. We were equipped with a spade and began feverishly digging to clear an area in front of the tyres. We then placed whatever we could find in the vehicle – the tarpaulin canopy, even spare items of our clothing – under the wheels in an effort to gain traction. Graham and I knew from our experience on the normal Botswana roads that the secret was to engage the engine at low revs in a high gear to gain traction. Sometimes we made progress only to find that we were again sinking. Gradually we reached a stage where, instead of making slow but steady progress, the more we tried the deeper the vehicle sank until it was in mud up to the axles. It was agreed that our predicament was now serious and our only hope was to find help. The source of such help was not obvious, as we had not seen signs of any form of human life for the last 48 hours. Chris and I volunteered to walk to the shore.

We set off across the surface of the pan heading towards the closest dry land. Given the size of some of the pans – they are more than 60 miles across in places – we thanked God that Graham had the presence of mind to try and make for the closest dry land and luckily we could see what seemed to be the shoreline on one, albeit distant, horizon. Trekking across the mud in temperatures of around 100°F was a taxing experience and it was about two hours before we reached land. In the event our luck held. This is a remote and thinly populated area but as we approached the shore we saw smoke from a fire obviously not very far into the bush. We headed in this direction and about a quarter of a mile from where we left the pan we came across a small village. We greeted the headman in the customary way 'Dumela rra, A o tsogile', the limit of our Tswana language skills but a necessary preliminary to our real business. We then explained: lorry (arms up and down in steering wheel motion) sinking (palms pushing down) in saltpan (arm points in direction from whence we have come). He nodded sagely. The headman looked at us with mild amusement and replied in kind with some movement of hands and arms indicating that he understood our predicament and had a ready solution. By now a small crowd of villagers had gathered and after a cursory discussion the men of the village went into action. I will not say they jumped or hurried or rushed around, for that is not the African way, but things began to happen. In due course a team of six oxen were hitched to a rudimentary yoke and we led the way back towards the pan in the direction of our beleaguered colleagues. From the reaction of the villagers we evidently were not the first to have encountered this problem, nor I am sure the last.

As we emerged from the bush to the edge of the pan with our would-be rescuers the truck was a distant speck on the horizon. Yet as we set off across the pan we realised that although it had been an arduous walk to the shore in relative terms we were fortunate to have been only three or four miles from the edge of the pan when disaster had struck. By now it was cooler, the sun beginning its progress towards the westerly horizon, and we made excellent progress. Unbeknown to us, since we had left in mid-afternoon, our four travelling companions had been debating amongst themselves whether they should spend the night on the saltpan, or, with the fear of it sinking deeper, to abandon the vehicle and make their way to the shore before nightfall. As we approached their joy was evident from the waving and shouting. However, when we arrived at the Land Rover and they saw our would-be rescuers and the intended method of recovering the vehicle, their mood changed. They were frankly sceptical about our chances of getting free. Their concerns were misplaced. The oxen were tied to the front mudguard of the vehicle with a sturdy rope. Graham jumped into the cab and started the engine, putting the truck into gear. After a little cajoling the oxen began to pull. Quite literally within seconds the truck was freed from its muddy bed. The sceptics were confounded. We thanked our rescuers profusely in English and gave them a few Rand as a reward. We quickly jumped onboard and headed for the safety of the shoreline. If we left the villagers in an unseemly haste it was for fear of sinking again into the surface of the pan and certainly through no lack of gratitude. By now dusk was falling and we were left with no alternative but to spend a third and unscheduled night in the bush.

We eventually returned our friends from Swaneng to the school almost 24 hours late but no worse for the adventure. Only now did we discover that the apparent disappearance of four teachers somewhere in the African bush had caused much consternation back at Swaneng and the authorities had been alerted. Although we eventually drove into Serowe that afternoon without having seen anybody apart from our rescuers from the pans in three days, we were told that we had been spotted some hours before making our way through the hinterland much to the relief of Patrick Van Rensburg and his staff. The 'bush telegraph' once again worked in its wondrous ways.

Our trip over, Graham and I reflected on what we had learnt. Our conclusion was that in the short term Nata was not a solution to the problems facing the farmers of Botswana who had enrolled in the new co-operative. We had seen plenty of grazing animals like giraffe, zebra, hartebeest and that almost certainly meant unseen were predators that would find domesticated cattle easy prey. Therefore holding grounds would need to be fenced and protected. More important though, any route this far away from the normal grazing areas would need to be supported by a line of boreholes every few miles to water the cattle during the movement both to and from the new grazing. The distances that we would have to drive the cattle and the dangers given the prevalence of wild animals in the area meant that for now the Nata project was on hold.

Having related the story of my visit to Nata to Rosie many times over the course of the past 25 years I was anxious that our itinerary included the opportunity for us to revisit the scene.

We check out of our hotel in Francistown. Today we are heading the 200 km or so west to Nata to re-live the little adventure I had enjoyed with Graham and the Swaneng teachers on the Makgadikgadi. That night we had been woken by a fierce wind rattling the window of our room and the morning brought the first clouds we had seen since our arrival. The rains were at least a month away and I recalled this weather pattern, with the clouds only slowly and gradually accumulating for weeks before causing any precipitation. By ten in the morning there was another totally cloudless blue sky.

The journey is uneventful; the road is wide with a metalled surface and almost traffic free. We enjoy our side trip to Sowa and by mid-afternoon we are ensconced at the Nata Lodge, a small motel located near the Makgadikgadi Pans. Here most of the guests appear to be tourists in transit between South Africa and the safari area around Maun. Rosie is convinced that I will want to drive onto the pans like I did all those years ago but her fears are unfounded. On this occasion I have decided that we will travel in a vehicle better able to cope with the conditions. I have booked for us to stay two nights including a visit to the pans with a guide. Although I had reserved a four-wheel drive vehicle from the car hire company we finished up with a small saloon car totally unsuitable for any off-road activities, so despite Rosie's concerns there is no question of our venturing out on the pans alone. The reception at the lodge has posted a sign stating 'Guests are kindly asked to note we do not recover vehicles stuck in the pans'. Even the guy who wrote my guidebook reports getting trapped up to his axles and advises against taking the pans too lightly whatever the placid nature of their appearance. As I had suspected all those years ago we were not the first and apparently by no means the last people to get stuck in the Makgadikgadi and I have no intention of there being a repeat performance.

Arriving at the motel in late afternoon we drag our bags up the steps of our cabin-style accommodation. The room is large but dark. The air here hangs heavy and is far more humid than anything we have encountered so far. A fan the size of an aeroplane prop turns aimlessly from the ceiling to no apparent purpose other than to create an uneven whirr of noise. Almost immediately Rosie freaks out at the sight of geckos scurrying around on the wall above the bed head and I have, rather sternly, to remind her that we are now indeed in the African bush. The wood framed cabin, although rather rustic is well appointed, with a large bed with huge brass bed knobs that seem a little incongruous in this setting and I notice that for the first time on this trip the bed is shrouded by a mosquito net. Like the atmosphere it hangs grey and heavy from a frame above the bed, creating in my mind the image of an elaborate four-poster.

As Rosie calms herself she tells me that she will be sure to remember my first law of Africa and shake her shoes well before putting them on the following morning to ensure that no creepie crawlies have made their way inside. It is reassuring she has re-called what I have told her about my practice at Radisele, where thankfully my rondavel had remained pretty free from unwelcome visitors. Perhaps because there was no food there to attract them, I had remained bug free apart that is from having to crunch the odd beetle or scorpion. I draw back the curtains, doubtless pulled closed in a vain effort to keep the room cool in the afternoon heat, to reveal a pleasant veranda. Taking a chance with the incumbent insect popu-lation determined to make entry to the room we decide, cold drink in hand, to sit out and enjoy the sunset.

With my sundowner, a comfortable chair and just a hint of a breeze in the early evening air and most importantly a Rosie now less agitated, I sit back taking in the scene across the unspoilt bush. I find myself reflecting back to my earlier trip to these parts and wondering what has become of the intense Graham, Miss Whiplash Gillian and the others. Only the rustle of the wind catching the branches of the adjacent palm trees that proliferate in these parts, and the occasional birdcall breaks the silence. The lodge encour-ages the local bird life by providing a feeding area. Attracted by the easy pickings are starling and stalking magpies, twice the size of those we see in Europe. A colourful array of francolin, babblers, hornbill, and the tiny and beautifully coloured lilac breasted roller and many more unidentified species come and go.

Next day we arise to the dawn chorus from a superb and even wider assortment of colourful birds, enjoy a substantial breakfast and with a free day in front of us before our evening visit to the

Makgadikgadi we decide to drive further along the main road towards Maun. On the map we have picked out Gweta, some 100 km to the west as our destination. Our guidebook describes it as a quaint village with an onomatopoeic name derived from the sound of the bullfrogs that frequent the area.

The road is still excellent and we make good progress. First, some five miles from the Nata Lodge, we pass through the village of Nata. Here are camouflage tents we assume to be occupied by the military but later discover is a camp for refugees fleeing from across the border in troubled Zimbabwe.

Gradually beyond Nata the landscape begins to change to more open savannah with palms and the mopane around which the famed worm, a local delicacy and highly nutritious, is to be found. I anticipate that we will begin to see more wildlife, but no. All we see of note are a couple ostriches and two huge vultures that unfortunately take to the air just as I am about to capture them on film. What we do see, however, are the goat dogs. I had read about this phenomenon. The dogs are brought up with the goat herd from birth and are suckled by a nanny so they think they are a goat and live a normal life with the rest of the herd. However, if any form of predatory wildlife, like lions or hyenas, endanger the herd the dog's natural instincts come to the surface, warding off the danger through their inborn aggression.

After a couple of hours' steady driving with Rosie at the wheel we approach the village of Gweta. It has been a carefree drive during which we have not only seen little of interest in the bush but only a handful of other vehicles on the road. Suddenly at the roadside a uniformed policeman waves us down. We pull over.

At first Rosie thinks he is stopping us to warn of some impending danger further down the road and winds down the window to engage him in friendly conversation. However, soon her mood changes. Unbelievably here in the middle of nowhere Rosie is being done for speeding. According to the policeman she has been caught on camera doing 70 kph in a 60 kph zone. Rosie is outraged and claims that whilst there was a 80 kph sign there was not one for 60 kph. The policeman assures her there was. Then she tries the 'I'm a tourist, surely you don't want me to leave Botswana with a bad impression?' routine but the policeman is adamant and instructs her to pull the vehicle to the side of the road where his senior colleague is waiting in their pick-up truck.

We do as instructed and climb out of our car to engage with the senior officer. His name is Sgt Makoba, and he begins to take Rosie's personal details, writing out his record sheet, resting the paperwork on the bonnet of the police vehicle. I enquire about the penalty and Sgt Makoba breaks off from his form filling to show me a schedule of fines. Ten kph over the limit equates to an on-the-spot fine of about ten pounds. I ask him what happens if we refuse to pay and he says we will have to attend court in Maun in a few weeks' time. I kid him along that we might have to pursue this course of action but eventually, paperwork complete, I have to dig deep to find 80 pula for the fine. He gives me a receipt containing details collected from my wife. Against the question 'tribe?' he has written 'not applicable'.

I manage a couple of discrete photographs of Rosie with Sgt Makoba as she continues to remonstrate with him. Then I call across, 'Come on Rosie, you are wasting your breath, let's go.' Rosie is mortified. In 30 years driving in the UK she has never had an accident and has never been stopped by the police let alone been prosecuted for a driving offence.

Still very agitated, Rosie drives on into Gweta. She is still going on about the fine when I spot an example of the painted houses illustrated in the Grants' book. Although traditional they are now apparently an unusual sight and I have no recall of seeing them before. 'Let's go over and have a look,' I suggest. In an instant she jerks the steering wheel to the left to comply with my instruction and suddenly we lose traction. I climb out to inspect the scene. The car is up to the axles in fine sand. I try the old technique, with Rosie revving the engine steadily whilst in second gear with me pushing, but to no avail. Fortunately there are some local lads close by kicking a football and I call across and ask them to help. The local shopkeeper appears from the nearby store and quickly assessing our plight manages to conjure up a spade. With the shopkeeper directing operations sand is removed from under the front wheels and then he shouts to Rosie to give it full throttle. The car lurches forward and we are free. We thank our rescuers profusely. The shopkeeper comes across to shake our hands African style and quietly says, 'Have you anything for the boys?' I reach into my pockets for the second time within 15 minutes and hand over a handful of coins. With presence of mind Rosie grabs the camera and takes a photograph. They seem suitably appreciative of this combination of cash in hand and a photograph so we head back towards Nata with Rosie still moaning about her fine.

We don't see much of Gweta and certainly don't get to inspect the painted house. There is a distinctly unhealthy sound from the front suspension so I switch on the radio to muffle the noise and tell Rosie to keep driving. We pass the policemen still awaiting further prey and drive on. At the edge of the village we pass a sign for 60 kph.

That evening we set out from Nata Lodge with George, who is to be our driver and guide, together with a couple from Johannesburg who we establish are en route home from holidaying in the Okavango. In our purpose-built safari vehicle we head to the Makgadikgadi. There are many pans, two very large, the Nwetwe and Sowa, and we are going to visit the closest and most easterly, the Sowa Pan, in the language of the San or bushmen, meaning salt. With the benefit of our map I can see that all those years ago we thought we could make our way between these two major pans to return to Serowe. Today a road is clearly marked on the map delineating what then was our intended route.

The motel lies only six miles from the entrance to the Nata Bird Sanctuary, a community project to support the tourist industry in this remote part of Botswana and to create employment opportunities for the local people. We have seen at the lodge the huge diversity of bird life in this area. Beyond the bird sanctuary lies the pan proper. We enter the park and my first impression is that the grasses are much shorter than when I had journeyed here in 1966. The road is rough and rutted but obviously now well used by tourism. There is little game to view apart from the occasional springbok.

We drive on for perhaps six or seven miles from the main road before reaching the banks of a substantial but almost dry riverbed leading onto the pan proper. George explains that the river rises far north in Zimbabwe from where for three months in every year the rains produce a fast flowing river that pours across the surface of the nearby pan covering it with shallow water just a few inches deep but full of rich nutrients that in turn attract a million flamingos from as far away as Namibia to the west and Kenya to the north. The whole of the pans turn pink. Today, standing on one foot in a puddle of water, all that remains as evidence of the last rains many months ago is one solitary pink flamingo. This lonely figure aside there is no other sign of life – birds, animals, or man – as George boldly drives the truck onto the flat, almost white surface of the pan.

We proceed for maybe a mile before George stops the vehicle and invites us to climb down onto the surface of the pan. I know from my map that from our vantage point on the northern edge of the Sowa Pan it continues in every direction for 60 miles or more, way beyond the flat horizon we can now see through 270°. The difference between this and my earlier trip I soon appreciate. I dig my heel into the surface. This is late September; with the last rains falling here months ago the pans are at their driest. Whereas all those years ago the pans had on the surface appeared both flat and firm, here the surface mud is cracking in the heat, creating mottled patterns, and as I kick at the surface all that is underneath is a crumbly dust. Any water hiding beneath has long since evaporated. It is easy to see why we, and many since, were tempted to cross the pans. When we visited Sowa village yesterday we were on the eastern edge of this very pan. With the road behind us to the north and the sun setting in the west I look to see if I can see the mine. I check with George that I am looking in the right direction. I am out by about 90°. If you find yourself in trouble in the middle of the pan this is quite a margin of error and reinforces the dangers of a place so calm, so serene in appearance.

The sun is setting. The stillness is amazing as is the speed at which the sun disappears below the horizon. We are fortunate it is full moon and already the moon is high in the totally cloudless sky. Without the aid of flash photography the light is good enough to take some incredible photographs of the moon in a powder-blue sky juxtaposed with the almost white surface of the pans.

We chat with George and our travelling companions and enjoy a drink from a chiller bag the hotel has thoughtfully provided. George, we discover, is from a local village. His ambition has always been to be a guide and he is well qualified, having attended the University of Botswana to study flora and fauna that he describes with the passion not simply of a student but of a true enthusiast for his subject.

Suddenly we all fall silent to absorb the total stillness of the scene. The temperature plummets and George suggests that it is time we head back to the motel for dinner. An afterglow from the sun, fully 30 minutes after it disappeared over the horizon, lights the whole of the western skyline. I feel Rosie's touch, she is getting cold, and I put my arm around her. 'What a beautiful place,' she whispers.

Coming here in September I knew that there would be little animal or bird life and consequently had low expectations. However, this is the essence of Africa and the reason why so many fall in love with its seductive quality without ever quite being able to articulate why. After all this is a country for the most part comprising endless bush bordering on desert where little grows and both the people and their animals eke out an existence based on no higher order drive than survival itself, yet here nature in its simplest form is a truly moving experience. Sublime tranquillity. I'm glad I came back.

Chapter Eighteen

Victoria Falls and Beyond

Although the Nata project had been put on ice, only two weeks later the co-operative received more good news. As a famine relief measure the government had persuaded the Bamangwato tribal elders to grant use of a borehole at Makoba, some 80 miles west of Serowe, where we could hold cattle that we had purchased for improving before sale to the abattoir. This was a major breakthrough embracing two of our radical ideas for improving the lot of the indigenous farmers. Firstly the idea of fenced holding ground was an anathema to the traditionalists who opposed the idea of enclosing any tribal lands. They used the same argument that had seen fierce opposition to enclosure in England in the late eighteenth century. That is, all members of the tribe own the land 'in common'. The second was the idea of holding and improving the condition of cattle in the period immediately before slaughter to enhance both their quality and value. Out of adversity we saw actions that in the fullness of time we were sure would lead to great benefits for the people of Botswana.

By the middle of April, thanks to political pressure from Trevor and members of the new government, we were beginning to get allocated sufficient quotas from the abattoir. Buying was now taking place every Monday at our kraal at Makoro and every Wednesday at Serowe. Trevor took the opportunity to attend a meeting of the members to explain the difficulties that had faced the co-operative.

His main message was clear: despite the obstacles put in its way by both the abattoir and the speculators the co-operative had succeeded in a way that the individual small farmer could not have done. The co-operative was a force to be reckoned with having powerful friends in high places in the new administration in Gaberones.

With two months' experience of trading we took stock and made a decision to change our policy. It was clear that buying cattle outright by paying cash to the farmer at point of sale brought with it a high level of risk of loss for the co-operative. If an animal was subsequently found to be diseased the co-operative had the potential for losing money. As members were generally suspicious of this method, feeling the co-operative was underpaying them and holding onto the profit, we agreed that we should offer a dual policy. Continuing to offer members the choice of selling to the co-operative or alternatively, on a commission basis. Under this arrangement the co-operative would arrange for transport to the abattoir and obtain a permit for slaughter, paying the member whatever we received for the carcass less a commission to cover the co-op's costs.

We now had firmly established the co-operative. With our policy change the confidence of our members was growing and there was a steady increase in numbers of cattle we were sending to Lobatsi. Perversely the majority still chose to sell their animals 'on the hoof' to the co-operative for a price determined by Graham based on weight and his judgement on quality. The alternative whereby the co-operative would act as an agent charging a handling fee for use of our permit and transport arrangements meant that the co-operative member would receive the full payment made by the abattoir less commission but critically they would have to wait for payment until this had been received from the abattoir. A delay of four weeks. The transparency in offering both methods had given the co-op a boost, simply because it increased the confidence of the local people that this was indeed their business.

My major task to establish the Bamangwato Livestock Co-operative was now completed and Trevor decided that we should appoint a salaried manager to run the co-operative, releasing my expertise to help him in other aspects of co-operative development in the country. One of the staff at Swaneng was Alistair MacEwen, a Rob Roy look-alike with a bushy red beard and purposeful stride. Alistair had fallen in love with and married a local girl and needed to find a regular job with a salary, his work at Swaneng having been on a voluntary basis. Trevor and I spent a lot of time discussing the merits of Alistair as a candidate. He clearly lacked expertise in running a business or in the rudiments of accounting but he was bright and energetic and committed to the new Botswana. We took some soundings; Graham, who he would be working alongside, was less than enthusiastic but Pat Van Rensburg was a firm supporter and it was agreed that Alistair be offered the job of running the Bamangwato Livestock Co-operative. He readily accepted our offer. When I met with Patrick Van Rensburg, and talking of personalities from the past, I reminded him that Alastair had succeeded me at the Bamangwato co-op. Pat said that the redheaded Scot was last heard of in the role of admiral in the Ethiopian Navy. An interesting career change.

By the end of May with the cattle marketing co-operative now properly established I formally handed over its management to Alistair and Graham and took my leave of Radisele. With the Gibberds on leave in Europe we used their rondavel for a farewell lunch – me together with Alistair, Graham and Tshoagong. The guys had bought a generous supply of Castle beers and before I knew it I was running late. My bag packed, I made a hurried exit with Tshoagong at the wheel of the trusty Bedford back down the track to the Radisele railway halt. It had been eight amazing months.

The train had already arrived and was taking on water as I shook Tshoagong warmly by the hand, in the African way of course, and boarded, heading for Gaberones where I was due to debrief Trevor and leave my possessions in his safe-keeping for the next month. I was to take what I thought was a well-earned leave before starting the final part of my assignment.

My business in Gaberones completed, Trevor was kind enough to provide a government travel warrant. This enabled me to take the train to Francistown and from there to fly Air Botswana in its rickety Dakota to Maun, a small town to the west, on the Okavango delta. The old Dakotas never flew at more than a few thousand feet above the ground and as we approached the air strip at Maun for the first time I had a view of the stereotypical 'real Africa' with the sight below of herds of animals in the wild. We landed on a bumpy landing strip cut out of the bush to be met by a couple of Land Rovers that ferried me and my fellow passengers into the nearby town. After the harsh near-desert conditions I had left behind I could only marvel at the lush vegetation as we took the short journey to the hotel. After an overnight stop I was scheduled to fly north to Livingstone in Zambia. Thereafter I was left to my own devices.

I was travelling light with a knapsack containing a change of clothes; my only map was a mental one. Plan A was to make progress by hitchhiking north. I had no specific route in mind but planned to head initially to Broken Hill in Zambia to visit former colleague from the Department of Co-operatives, Ray Pepperall and his family, who had moved from Gaberones some months before. From there I thought that maybe I might progress in a generally northerly direction, beyond Broken Hill through northern Zambia as far as Tanzania, or even Kenya, before turning south and east back through Mozambique to the capital Lourenco Marques, and from there into Swaziland where I had planned a rendezvous with my college friend Keith three weeks later. The only definite was that as a matter of principle I wanted to avoid Rhodesia and its illegal regime under Ian Smith, which a year earlier had made its unilateral declaration of independence or UDI from the government in London and had set up a white dominated regime in Salisbury.

I had little idea of distances to be travelled or how far I was likely to be able to travel in a normal day hitching lifts in countries where private transport was still a rarity, although I anticipated that the infrastructure of roads and public transport would be a tad more sophisticated than that I had so far encountered in Bechuanaland. In the event my 'take it as it comes' approach was to prove eminently sensible in the circumstances.

The following morning I was up early and soon airborne for the short hop from Maun to Livingstone. The low flying Dakota was perfect transport to take across the delta. Again like the previous evening I saw huge numbers of animals in the wild attracted by the prospect of a regular supply of water even in the driest part of the year. The Okavango was in total contrast to the Bechuanaland I had come to know, being the home of people as comfortable on water as on land and then the centre of an embryonic tourist trade unknown in the rest of Bechuanaland, where there was little to excite the interest of any visitor. We soon passed over the point where at the confluence of the Chobe and Zambesi rivers four countries – Botswana, Namibia, Zambia and Zimbabwe – meet.

Almost immediately we landed and I quickly gathered my things together and made my way down the steps onto Zambian soil sensing that my next adventure was about to start. After the immigration formalities had been completed in the makeshift hut that doubled as the terminal building, I stepped outside and cadged a lift from one of the few white people around in his ubiquitous Land Rover for the short journey into town. Here I hurried to take in the magnificent sight of the Victoria Falls from the Zambian side of the gorge. I was conscious of my time constraints and although still early morning I was soon headed out to take my first tentative steps on the road heading north.

My initial destination, the town of Broken Hill – now called Kabwe – which lies well to the north of the capital Lusaka. I set off knowing I faced a long day on the road. Ray Pepperall was one of the original members of the Department of Co-operatives. At the end of his contract in Bechuanaland Ray had taken a new job in Zambia working in the copper belt in partnership with an old friend with the hope of making a quick fortune. On leaving Gaberones at the end of 1965 Ray had insisted that I visit him and his family before my own departure from Africa. So it was that I eventually arrived at their new home in Broken Hill late that night.

The journey north, although some 300 miles distance from Livingstone and routing through the capital Lusaka, must have gone without any alarums. It's the weirdest thing, total recall of some situations and amnesia about others on the same journey. I have just the vaguest memory of walking from the falls back to the main road to seek my first lift and at some later point standing in the centre of Lusaka, a white person thumbing a lift being the centre of much attention; the rest is a blank. Anyway I do remember that when I reached the Pepperall household late that evening I received a warm and friendly reception.

Ray had a charming wife and three sons in their early teens. I had planned to stay for only two days but my hosts were insistent I stay longer to encompass a weekend when Ray had time off to show me around the area. Thus it was I spent a couple of days relaxing in the company of the boys before Ray was available. My only clear memory is that the oldest boy had been sent a Manfred Mann album from England containing a track titled 'LSD' and was anxious to know all about the teen scene as it then was in the UK, something he had clearly missed out on growing up in Africa and in particular whether the lyrics of this particular song referred to money or the hallucinogenic drug. Like many British people I met in Africa Ray couldn't see himself returning to England and being able to settle down to a life without sun and servants. Although I was a stranger in her house it didn't take long for his wife to confide in me that she had a somewhat different agenda and was desperate to return home to England. Her hope was that Ray's new job might enable the family to accumulate funds to afford the airfares.

The copper belt, as the name implies, is not the most appealing part of the world being on a par with South Wales in terms of physical attraction except the colour of the slag heaps was different. Broken Hill seemed very appropriately named. Whilst this was a pleasant interlude amongst friendly hosts I recall little of the area other than picnicking beside a large manmade lake behind a dam.

By the time I hit the road again I was already a week into my sojourn. Broken Hill is close to the border with the Congo where the transition from colonial rule to independence was proving painful. Across the border was the mineral rich province of Katanga, which had tried to split from the rest of the country leading to a bloody civil war. The Congo it seemed was a deeply troubled place and on Ray's advice I decided to return south towards the Zambian capital of Lusaka and, from there, to take the road northeast towards Malawi, my judgement being that already having used one week of my leave there was now no prospect of reaching Kenya or even Tanzania that lay still many miles to the north. So I bade my farewells to Ray and his family and retraced my steps back along the road to Lusaka.

To bring Ian Smith and his white supremacist government in Rhodesia to heel the British government had obtained UN support for trade sanctions on the regime. Most important of these was the blocking of the oil pipeline from Beira, a port to the east in the then Portuguese colony of Mozambique. However, as the pipeline also served Zambia it was this country that was suffering more from the fuel shortages than their dissident neighbours. As a consequence the British government funded alternative delivery arrangements for delivery of fuel to support the Zambian economy. This involved a fleet of petrol tankers operating from Dar es Salaam in distant Tanzania several hundreds of miles to the northeast. Logistically this was a nightmare requiring travel across difficult roads totally unsuitable for large vehicles carrying such a hazardous cargo. In the event many vehicles were wrecked and cargoes lost during this operation.

As fate would have it as I stood in the centre of Lusaka thumbing a lift the first driver to stop was at the wheel of one of these articulated monsters. As the saying goes 'beggars can't be choosers' and so it was with mixed feelings that I found myself clambering into the cab of this ten-wheeled leviathan, fortified only by the thought that at least the petrol tank was full and the tanker was empty. This had the advantages of increasing the speed at which we were able to travel and at the same time reducing the chances of being engulfed in an explosion of the volatile cargo. The journey was nevertheless hair-raising. The drivers were paid by the trip and so there were no eight-hour days or periodic rest stops.

We travelled through the rest of the day and into the night. My enduring memory is suddenly awaking from a light sleep to see in the headlights that we were at an angle of 45° and descending down a riverbank and into a fast flowing river. I held my breath not daring to speak for fear of breaking the driver's concentration. He cursed quietly under his breath as he wrestled the steering wheel avoiding the larger boulders on the far bank. We stopped momentarily but he never lost control nor stalled the engine as we finally leapt forward and recovered the road. He laughed when I expressed my concern; apparently floods had swept the bridge away some months ago and no one had got around to repairing it. The driver had subsequently driven through here many times, even with a full load, and seemed totally unconcerned about the danger. The driver's route took him close to the border with Malawi but here, unfortunately for me he began to head north, parallel with the border before he would cross into Tanzania. So it was in the early hours of the following morning that we said our goodbyes as he dropped me close to the border with Malawi at a place called Chipata. By now I had been travelling for what seemed an eternity and was feeling the fatigue in a way that I had never previously experienced.

As is common with international borders the Zambian and the Malawian posts were set about a mile apart. Having been processed by the Zambians I waited through the remaining hours of darkness in the hope of a lift. None came; I was the only traveller on this road so at first light I trudged up the road through 'no man's land' and crossed the border into Malawi at Mchinji. Looking at my old passport it says I left Zambia on the 6th and arrived in Malawi on the 7th but I am sure that this is because arriving in the early hours of the morning the immigration official at Chipata on the Zambian side of the border had forgotten to change the date on his rubber stamp.

I was tired and dispirited. The obvious thing to do was to wait at the border post for a vehicle to cross and approach the driver for a lift. However, I felt a desperate need to keep moving, to get away from the border post where I am sure the guards had decided that a white man crossing the border on foot must be quite mad. I had convinced myself that if I continued along the road from the border I would shortly come to a crossroads where the chances of getting a lift would be much higher. Two hours' walking later and with no crossroads in sight I was feeling very hot and very, very tired, for the first time beginning to wonder whether the judgement of the border guards wasn't far off the mark when, from the direction of the border, out of a billowing cloud of dust a large Mercedes appeared and drew up alongside. The window was wound down and a man in the front passenger seat asked where I was headed and whether I wanted a lift. Peering in I could see that the occupants of the car were four black men in sharp suits and an excess of flashy jewellery. They seemed distinctly out of place. To say I was apprehensive would be an understatement, in fact I was probably more than a little scared but they were heading in my direction. In the event fatigue overcame fear because I accepted their offer of a lift and was squeezed into the back seat between two of the men and we set off. Almost immediately I fell into a deep sleep. The next thing I knew I was being shaken by one of my travelling companions to tell me that we were near Zomba. I must have slept for several hours because I could see that outside dusk was gathering and Zomba, I knew, was a considerable distance from the border. The men had brought me to a small and very smart hotel outside of the town and already ensured there was a room available for me. I later realised that they had come someway from the main road to find me accommodation. Whoever they were and however doubtful their business they had performed a genuine kindness for which I was extremely grateful.

The next morning I awoke feeling refreshed and ready to resume my journey. After a hearty breakfast the hotel manager offered to drive me back to the main road. This was when I realised that the guys in the Mercedes had driven for maybe five miles up an unmade track to my accommodation. Having readily accepted his kind offer I was soon on the road travelling to Blantyre, what was then the capital of Malawi. I remember it as a somewhat quaint colonial town, quite attractive. Here my first priority was to seek out the offices of the Peace Corps. Back in Gaberone I had met Russ Schwartz who was running the Peace Corps in Southern Africa. Russ was in the throes of negotiating for Peace Corps volunteers to come to post-Independence Botswana, including a number who would be helping Trevor in the Department of Co-operatives. Russ was a friendly, amiable character who hearing of my plans to travel north had been kind enough to give me an introduction to his people who were well established in Malawi. I soon discovered the Peace Corps located in a smart suite of offices in the heart of the city. Here I introduced myself and had the good fortune to meet one of the volunteers, Rob, who without hesitation invited me to stay at his place in the nearby town of Limbe where he was teaching at a local school.

It was a generous gesture but I was no great liability as I was to soon discover. Rob's living quarters comprised a large bungalow where he had his own maid and cook and, of course, for any American, the mandatory refrigerator. The next few days provided a fascinating insight into the differences between British and American volunteer workers. The Americans certainly lived in style relative to my accommodation at Radisele. They also enjoyed what, to me, sounded like a generous salary funded by the US government. I, in contrast, received a modest allowance paid by the government in Bechuanaland. Rob told me that the initial batch of Peace Corps volunteers in Malawi had found reliance on local transport so problematical that they had complained to Russ, their full-time field officer, a salaried US government employee who had responded by providing them all with motorbikes. The IVS field support in contrast comprised a fleeting visit by Frank Judd halfway through my year in Africa. In one respect though I have to admit the Americans had got it right; namely in the commitment of the volunteers to two rather than one year in the host country.

Rob told me that in his view we Brits had style. In the event I subsequently learnt that his experience of Brits was in fact limited to one young lady who undoubtedly left an impression on him for the rest of his life. Over dinner on that first night he told me that he liked English girls because they were not such a tease as American girls who rarely allowed more than a grope in the dark at the drive-in movie on a Saturday night. Gradually his story unfolded. At the school where he was teaching there was an English volunteer, female of course, and mutual friendship as work colleagues had rapidly developed into an intimate relationship. One day the maid had entered the bedroom with the laundry and caught them in flagrante delecto; instead of being overcome with embarrassment the English girl had calmly thanked the maid and instructed her where to leave the laundry before getting back to business. He had been deeply impressed. Come to think of it so must I have been as I can still recall the story yet little else of my stay in Blantyre.

My plan was to take the train from Blantyre across the border into Mozambique and down to the port and resort city of Lourenco Marques. Quite a lively spot, I had been told, much favoured by white males from the strict apartheid regime in South Africa seeking the 'forbidden fruit' of black call girls and prostitutes. From LM, as it was popularly known, I would travel on to its next-door neighbour, Swaziland, for my rendezvous with Keith. First I would need a visa so I made my way to the Portuguese Embassy where I completed the necessary forms. I learned that it would normally take 24 hours to process my visa application. Today was Thursday, however tomorrow was a national holiday in Portugal; the Embassy was closed for the day and over the ensuing weekend. Would I please return to collect my passport with visa for entry into Mozambique the following Monday?

This left me with another three days in Malawi. I had exhausted the sights of Blantyre and Rob suggested a hike up to Lake Nyasa for the weekend on the recommendation that it was one of the most beautiful locations in Africa. I recall the lake, a boat trip and then on the Sunday morning a stiff climb up to the nearby Zomba Plateau. It was at the top of the climb that in exchanging pleasantries with a couple of fellow hikers I managed to proffer what I thought was the ultimate insult to two Dutchmen by suggesting they were Germans. Fortunately they did not seem at all offended and we fell into conversation as we descended down the steep path. As a result they invited me to stay over for the night at their place. This, it turned out, was the General Hospital in Blantyre where they both worked as doctors. An invitation too good to spurn because it meant both a lift back into the city and a guaranteed free bed and break-fast. The Dutch doctors proved excellent hosts providing me with the guests' accommodation, a pleasant bungalow set in the grounds of the hospital, where they were housed in a smart apartment block. That evening I was invited to join them at a dinner party, wine flowed and I remember being propositioned by one of the doctor's wives. How serious the proposition I will never know. In any event a combination of naivety and an excess of wine that left me without any working faculties until well into the following morning scotched any possibilities that might have developed. The likelihood is that I had offered some unaccustomed sport for a bored bunch of expatriates. Anyway whatever the motives my Dutch friends were excellent hosts and as happened so many times during my stay in Africa I was appreciative of the kindness that complete strangers were prepared to offer.

On the Monday morning I made my way to the Portuguese Embassy to collect my passport duly stamped with an entry visa for Mozambique. I was on my way again. Or was I? I spent the morning wandering around the town before going to the station in plenty of time to catch the train scheduled to leave at four o'clock. The station seemed eerily quiet and when I eventually found a uniformed employee of the railway company and enquired about the platform he told me that the train had left at two o'clock or 14.00 hours. Somehow I had fallen foul of the 24-hour clock. Unperturbed I asked the time of the next train. 'Two o'clock next Monday,' was the shocking reply. It was clearly time for Plan B.

My journey through Zambia and Malawi had been achieved entirely by hitching lifts. The only reason I had chosen the train for the next leg of my journey was the uncertain political situation in Mozambique where I had heard that local dissidents were attempting to overthrow the colonial power, Portugal. I had little comprehension as to how dangerous the road might be but nevertheless decided I would return to the roadside and hitchhike down to the coast to the port city of Beira and from there take the train to LM. I made my way to the outskirts of the town and took up position on the main road that headed towards the border with Mozambique. After three hours I had failed to make any progress along this virtually deserted road and as dusk approached it was necessary for me to return to Limbe and cadge another night of free accommodation courtesy of Rob and the Peace Corps.

I resumed my vigil early the following morning but once again there was very little traffic and not a single vehicle stopped to offer me a lift. By early afternoon I was convinced that not one vehicle I had seen was actually travelling to Mozambique. The dilemma was, if I did accept a lift just a few miles down the road I could find myself stranded somewhere in the Malawi countryside between Blantyre and the border with no way of making any further progress. My scheduled rendezvous with Keith was now only three days away so I clearly needed to consider Plan C. The road where I was attempting to hitch a lift ran along the perimeter of the airport; across the road from where I sat was a wire fence and beyond that the runway. Having failed to exit Malawi by either road or rail it seemed that flying offered the only remaining alternative way out of the country. Although not busy I had seen planes land and take off at regular intervals during my roadside vigil. Perhaps I could fly down to Lourenco Marques and from there hitchhike into Swaziland. I lifted my rucksack and with a heavy heart headed towards the airport terminal.

Apart from cost, I was, after all, a volunteer worker living off a small subsistence allowance; I was prepared to take a flight almost anywhere with the exception of the rebellious colony of Rhodesia. Sod's law. There were no flights to Mozambique. I could fly north to Nairobi the following day, take a flight today back to Lusaka, which I had left a week before or…? Yes, you've guessed it. Take the flight leaving in one hour's time down to Salisbury. I weighed up my options: in truth there was only one. I reluctantly went to the desk and purchased a one-way ticket.

Today it would not raise an eyebrow but in 1966 in ultra-conservative Rhodesia, arriving in the country by plane dressed in shorts, carrying a knapsack and sporting a 'Beatle haircut' I did not look like a typical airline passenger. Judged by appearance alone I was bound to attract the attention of the immigration officials at Salisbury Airport, and so it proved. I was asked the reason for my visit and whether I had any luggage other than the small knapsack slung over my shoulder. I replied that I was just passing through Rhodesia but could not with any certainty say in which direction I intended to travel, what mode of transport I intended to use and how long I intended to remain in the country. Confirmation that the sum total of my luggage was slung across my shoulder clearly didn't help my cause. To compound my increasing discomfort the official then began to show a considerable interest in my passport. He told me not to move, then disappeared from view.

In situations like this events develop at a pace that you barely realise what is happening. As I gathered my thoughts I realised I should have prepared a better story and, dread of dreads, what was fascinating him in my passport was all of those stamps and visas from recently visited totalitarian Eastern bloc communist states. He returned a few minutes later with a colleague, a Special Branch officer, and I was asked to join them in a small office that I might more aptly describe as the interrogation room.

As I had belatedly appreciated the subject of their interest were the Polish and Czechoslovakian visas in my passport dating from my recent student trip behind the Iron Curtain during the previous summer. I was subjected to the classic hard man, soft man routine, because they wanted to understand the purpose of my visit to those countries and how I now found myself in Rhodesia. They were ultra sensitive to anything associated with Communism and of course guerrilla groups were already being trained in other parts of Africa and in Eastern Europe for the war that was ultimately to lead to the creation of the independent Zimbabwe in 1981. After two hours they presumably felt that I was not a threat to Rhodesian security but being a young and unkempt Brit with little visible means of support they returned my passport stamped 'Prohibited Immigrant' and gave me 24 hours to leave the country.

Despite the ordeal I was in an upbeat mood. Given the jittery mood in Rhodesia following the declaration of UDI, I might have found myself locked up for a while and subject to further grilling. The Rhodesian officials were definitely sensitive to my visiting Poland and Czechoslovakia. What if they had realised that on that same trip I had also spent ten days in the Soviet Union. In those days for whatever reason the Russian visa was in the form of a separate document not a stamp in your passport. You had to show the document on entry and then return it to the Soviet authorities on leaving the country. If my Rhodesian friends had been smarter they would have realised from closer inspection of my passport that I had left Poland on one day at the border with the Soviet Union and entered Czechoslovakia ten days later at another crossing bordering the Soviet Union.

Incarceration was a valid concern, my other fear was being returned to Malawi and that had not happened either. Therefore I was free to continue my journey and had the satisfaction of being declared a PI from Rhodesia. This would have immense kudos with my fellow volunteers in Bechuanaland. Yes there was a small difficulty of finding a quick and cheap exit. My funds were much depleted by having to purchase the air flight but it was a small price to pay to get my journey underway again. With time fast running out I decided that travelling via Mozambique was no longer a realistic route for me to reach Swaziland. Reluctantly I faced what I now saw as the only feasible alternative: to catch a train south to Mafeking, even though it meant trundling down through Bechuanaland past the familiar spots, Palapye, Gaberone and Lobatsi on the way. It was cheap, ensured that I was out of Rhodesia within the prescribed time and effectively offered two free nights' accommodation. At last I could once again see the possibility of making my rendezvous with Keith.

I left the train at Mafeking on the Thursday morning. Now I was in South Africa I returned to hitchhiking, buoyed in the expectation that here I had far better prospects of getting regular lifts than in the less developed countries to the north. The only downside was that almost every lift across South Africa from Mafeking to the border with Swaziland was given to me by Afrikaaner farmers who, once they realised I was British, almost without exception would harangue me with the same diatribe, 'You people don't understand apartheid, we are trying to civilise these lazy kaffirs but they are just down from the trees.' My route took me towards Johannesburg and from there east of the city, ending up that night in the town of Bethal. The following morning I continued my journey through Piet Retief and across the border into the beautiful Kingdom of Swaziland, in stark contrast to Botswana, a country of green rolling hills.

Keith was based in the small town of Goedgegun notable only

for the impossibly tricky pronunciation that made for difficulty in communicating to prospective givers of lifts exactly where I was headed. When I eventually arrived, pretty well on time, I discovered that unlike me Keith had a pleasant apartment, personal transport in the form of a saloon car and his own operating area that he proudly spent the next day showing me around; little tribal villages set in green wooded glades: Hlatikulu, Manzini, Malkerns, Mankaiana. It was clear that Keith was doing an excellent job and had developed a good rapport with the local people. He, like me, was finding his year extremely rewarding and challenging. The thing I particularly noted was that Swaziland being a small country, his network was tighter and more intimate and we were able to tour the country meeting a lot of other volunteers in relative ease. We spent a pleasant weekend exchanging stories about our experiences and I discovered that, like me, Keith had obtained a scholarship to resume studies at the Co-operative College on completion of our year in Africa. I accused him of dubiety in not revealing his intentions to me earlier as we were in regular correspondence, but as he rightly pointed out I had acted in the same manner. Anyway it was good news that we would once again be colleagues back in the very different environment of Stanford Hall. Although neither of us knew at the time Keith was to subsequently return to Africa after completing his college studies for a second year of voluntary service, this time in Botswana.

When I eventually left Goedgegun it was to head for the administrative capital Mbabane, where Keith had effected an introduction to the Peace Corps, which I thought ensured a comfortable final day in Swaziland before I once again headed across the Transvaal, and back to Botswana. However, being perfect hosts, the Peace Corps insisted that I see more highlights of Swaziland and the chance to meet up with some more of my IVS fellow volunteers based at a place called Stegi to the west of the country up near the Mozambique border. So instead of heading back to Bechuanaland I was ferried up to the border town where a party had been laid on, eventually setting out on my homeward journey via Johannesburg and back to Gaberones at the end of a fascinating four weeks of travel through six countries of Southern Africa.

Later, back in Gaberones with time on my hands, I sent an episodic log of my journey in the form of letters to Bob and Mick back in England. On my return home I remember Bob saying it was a cliff-hanger tale and he was uncertain whether I would ever return. Today I would probably be wetting myself in some of the situations I found myself in, but then it didn't seem to matter. Even my encounter with Rhodesian Special Branch proved nothing more than an irritation on the way to my goal of getting to Swaziland even though it was the closest I have ever come to spending time behind bars.

Chapter Nineteen

Return to Radisele

I'll admit it was a rare moment of unrestrained elation as I yelled down the cell phone, 'Rosie I've found my house.' She was only a mile away but in my excitement I didn't care if to reach her my voice had to bounce off a satellite and halfway across the world and would probably cost a small fortune.

The morning following our visit to the Makgadikgadi we had once again packed our bags and loaded the car for the journey that would ultimately take us back to Gaberone. Although glad I had made the return to the pans I had no sense that this was my Holy Grail, if indeed that was the true purpose of my journey.

After a leisurely breakfast we set out on our way back from Nata. Retracing our steps travelling east, passing through Francistown where we picked up the main north-south road again, we turned south, heading for Palapye, where we intended to stay for a couple of days. Making good progress I decided to take a detour to visit some of the villages where Tshoagong and I had performed our 'missionary' work.

About 60 miles out of Francistown at Serule we left the main road and headed east following the signpost for Selebi-Pikwe. The road proved to be straight and true. About halfway to Selebi-Pikwe another signpost pointed left. It is the road to Mmadinare, in the old days a nightmare drive from Radisele, but even this road to a once remote village was tarmac. The unrelenting bush is no more than a blur and in a relatively short time we had covered 100 km and found ourselves in the middle of Selebi-Pikwe, the closest thing we were to find in Botswana to an affluent middle-class town with a main shopping thoroughfare, a mall with people enjoying al fresco dining and on its outskirts pleasant avenues with a mixture of attractive houses. Like Sowa this is a mining town, the huge copper and nickel mine laying discreetly two miles or so away from the town itself and directly employing some 5,000 out of the town's population of 70,000, making this the third largest centre of population in the country behind Gaberone and Francistown. We drove through the town centre taking a right turning south in a direction where we would skirt the edge of the Tuli Block. Occupied by white farmers, for historical reasons, having been ceded by Kgosi Khama the Third to the British in 1895 to provide a buffer between the rest of Bechuanaland and the advancing Boers across the border in the Transvaal, the land – unlike the rest of the country – is fenced into what we would view as conventional farms or ranches.

When leaving the main north-south road we had spent some time poring over our map and had decided upon a route that would keep us on what we thought would be the best roads; travelling east to Selebi-Pikwe and there turning south, taking a big loop heading towards Martin's Drift on the South African border, intending to turn back to the west again at that point. We were not disappointed: the road was good, the copper mine obviously being a major influence bringing with it not only prosperity but also a support infrastructure. Then I saw a sign for Kgagodi, another village where Tshoagong and I had worked. We stopped at the junction and I peered along this road running due west. Yet again this road looked good and wide with a tarmacadam surface so I decided on a change of plan; we would go and have a look. After about ten miles another signpost indicated that Kgagodi was off to our right and we turned onto what was now an unmade road and soon reached the outskirts of the village. We drove around what was another substantial tribal village but, rather like my return visit to Serowe, there were no memory joggers; I recognised absolutely nothing. I decided to continue our journey by returning the mile or so on the main road and travelling west until the road rejoined the main north-south highway just north of Palapye. Throughout this detour of over 100 miles we had seen perhaps a dozen other vehicles on roads that were without exception tarred and in amazingly good condition; unbelievably different from the sixties when many of the villages in this part of the country were virtually inaccessible.

Palapye today is a rather unremarkable town rather than a village although it was once the tribal capital of Khama the Great and named after the impala once found in huge numbers in this area; today a sprawling metropolis of about 30,000 people, many of who work at nearby Morupule where there is both a coalmine and power station sufficient to generate enough electricity to meet Botswana's needs. Palapye is not a particularly attractive place but we decided to stay there for a couple of days as it has one of the few hotels in this part of the country.

The following day we travelled out to Serowe returning back at our hotel in Palapye late on what was a Saturday afternoon. Outside the hotel I noticed a number of parked vehicles each bearing the name of a different co-operative. Enquiring at the desk I was told that they belonged to delegates holding a conference in the hotel. Later, seeing the delegates dispersed into breakout groups, I went to the conference room to introduce myself to the conference leader. I found him sitting alone in the room poring over his papers, no doubt preparing himself for the next session. It all seemed so familiar given my own background in personnel and development. I introduced myself and explained my interest in co-operatives as one of the pioneers from the sixties. He showed a degree of interest and told me his name. Even by Botswana standards it was unpronounceable. After I failed dismally in my attempt to repeat the name he laughed and told me he was better known as BK.

BK explained that this was a voluntary meeting of members of the savings co-operatives or SACCOS that were flourishing across the country, particularly amongst large employers. BK added that although some of the savings co-ops still existed based upon our old model of savings typically within a village community, the growth of these savings co-operatives in recent years was amongst a new and emerging class in Botswana society, namely employees of large companies and organisations earning a regular wage or salary and being based on the principle of payroll deduction. An individual would join the co-operative and agree to save so much of their earnings each month. This sum was deducted by the employer from the employee's pay and sent directly to the employee's account with the savings co-op where it would earn interest. Things were making sense; the vehicles I had seen in the car park bore the names of the mining company based in Selebi-Pikwe; the Ministry of Agriculture and the Trade Union of Railway Workers based in Mahalapye.

After all the bad news I had heard about the co-ops it was good to know that at least some were prospering. BK proved to be yet another long-serving member of the Department of Co-operatives and he told me that he normally operated from an office in Kanye, one of the larger tribal villages way to the south beyond Gaberone.

As the delegates drifted back into the room I left BK to his business. I didn't want to push the issue as BK had told me that he had a busy agenda to complete but I was a little sorry that he hadn't asked me to come and introduce myself to his group.

The conference broke up in the early evening and from our vantage point in the restaurant where we were having dinner I noticed that BK stayed around drinking with some of the delegates. We later went to our room and BK was just leaving, the journey to Kanye must have been hell on those dangerous Botswana roads late at night. There is an odd sequel to this story as we were to encounter BK again, in Gaberone a few days later.

Next morning I awake early to the sound of the dawn chorus. Although the hotel is located in the middle of the town we had noted the previous evening the proliferation of birds attracted by the small swimming pool and garden area of lawns, flower beds and mature trees formed within the quadrangle of buildings that make up the hotel.

From her breathing pattern I can tell that Rosie is still in a deep sleep. Today is going to be hectic, with a long drive back to the capital. Not wanting to disturb her I lie motionless on my back staring at the ceiling and contemplate the day ahead.

This is it. Only at this moment do I really know that this is the true purpose of my journey and I confess that I have mixed feelings. A sense of trepidation that perhaps I had come all this way after all this time to find, what? Nothing! Perhaps we wouldn't be able to find the BDA and if we did what would be there? There might even be people living on the site without any notion of what had gone on there 40 years ago. However apprehensive I feel there is no hiding a genuine tingle of excitement.

We breakfast, pack our bags once again and check out of the hotel to head back to Gaberone. Radisele lays less than an hour's drive south of Palapye and Rosie agrees to drive for this first part of our journey.

As she manoeuvres the car onto the main highway Rosie looks across to see that her exit is clear and in doing so, with the merest glance at me, she makes a throwaway remark, 'This is it, Bernie. Your big day.' I pooh-pooh the notion but of course as usual she is right. Travelling north a week earlier we had passed by the village of Radisele and sure enough off to the right there was a road across the railway line. Without doubt if the BDA is still there it should be easy to find. Now we are about to find out.

Almost before I know it we are there. Perhaps 20 miles south of Palapye with the Tswapong Hills rising gently away to our left the road climbs a small gradient before dropping away and here to my surprise is Radisele. Coming off the low hill the road turns through 90° and then flattens and straightens, and parallel now, less than 50 yards away to our left, the railway line. Rosie follows my instructions as we pass the old railway halt, 'Get ready to take a left over the railway line.' Despite my earlier confidence things are not quite as I remembered. Sure, there is a turn-off, but perhaps as a safety feature to ensure vehicles cross the railway with caution the road unlike my recollections now turns sharply through an S-bend before crossing over the railway line. Once across Rosie slows the vehicle to a stop, for here a signpost read 'To Pilikwe'. Tshoagong's old village. Of course in the old days you could get to Pilikwe this way but there were no signposts and it was a tortuous journey through the middle of the BDA and off around the hills. Things looked different but nevertheless this must be the right road.

Looking I can see that in front of us for about a mile ahead the road is dead straight; well, to be truthful there is not just one road but two. A very evidently new road with a surface of loose stones had been constructed alongside what must have been the old track with which I was so familiar. Now I am not so sure but suggest we drive on.

After her episode in Gweta where the car sank into sand, Rosie is driving with excessive caution. 'Drive any slower and we will be going in reverse,' I comment rather testily. A rather harsh observation, the insensitivity of which I only appreciate much later when I realise how stressful Rosie has found the whole African experience.

Fortunately this conversation doesn't slip into a downward spiral because at this point we spot some rondavels away to the right; adjacent to them a field, quite evidently long since abandoned but a field nevertheless that sometime in the past had been fenced and cultivated, surely by Vernon. Why am I so certain? Because here in Botswana this is tribal land and it cannot be fenced other than with special permission from the chief. The BDA had been granted such special permission to enable Vernon to conduct his experiments in arable farming.

'Let's stop here and have a look because this must have been something to do with the BDA.' Rosie obliges and stops the car and I get out to take a look, but the rondavels and field are situated on the wrong side of the road. I am convinced that we are close to the BDA site but need to travel further away from the railway line.

Given Rosie's agitated state I turn to her and say, 'Look I think we are very close so why don't you stay here with the car and I will have a look around further up the road,' a suggestion to which she readily agreed.

I set off at a purposeful pace and within a few minutes, glancing back, Rosie and the car are already little more than a speck. We exchange reassuring waves and I continue on my way.

Although the two roads are running in parallel some 20 yards apart I choose to walk down the old track with its softer sandy surface. It is easier on the soles of the feet than the gravel and in any event I know this path. I am by now utterly convinced that I am going in the right direction. I have walked this path many times before.

It is getting warm. This still being at the start of the Southern African summer the early morning had been cool and I had dressed in a pair of long trousers. Now for the first time on this trip I am experiencing that sticky feeling when your clothes seem to attach themselves to your body. I am aware of a damp patch on the back of my shirt and it feels like it is expanding by the minute. Flies drone around my face in that annoying fashion where you must appear to any passer-by to be like some wild dervish thrashing about as you seek to brush away their incessant attention. Although I remember this place as being hot it also had low humidity but today seems an exception. As I touch my brow with my forefinger it is to wipe away tiny globules of perspiration.

Quite suddenly I have this amazing sense of déjà vu, just for a moment I am transported back in time walking back from the village to the BDA. I stop for a reality check and turning once more to look back down the track I can see Rosie and the car in the middle distance but further back I can still make out the railway crossing.

It's further, I tell myself. I am conscious that I am now in a highly personal dialogue.

Now I remember: from the BDA you couldn't actually see the railway. What a bugger! I have abandoned the car and it is all coming back now; the BDA was further from the railway line than this. I need to veer left. I trudge on.

Then, sure enough away to the left, although barely visible in the grasses that now cover its surface, a track. My eyes try to pick out its direction as it arcs away into the bush. As I do so in my eye line I catch sight of some derelict buildings.

Although the track has clearly long since been abandoned by regular traffic, perhaps since the new road to Pilikwe had been built, I am able to follow its course and at a gentle canter, I am soon close to what I can now see is the collapsed circle of walls that were once two adjacent rondavel. I am trying to control a rising sense of excitement. Could this be what remained of the Gibberds' household? Approaching along the overgrown track I soon stand before the two rondavel, first examining the one on the left. Little remains, the crumbling circle of mud barely two or 3 ft high in places. I peer into what would have been the Gibberds' bedroom; disappointingly it is completely bare. I turn my attention to the rondavel on the right, albeit just a few feet away I can see that it was more intact and still has walls at, and in places even above, my waist level. On closer inspection I see within the remains of the mud brick walls some junk, including an old trunk. Crikey, could this have been what Vernon brought his worldly goods to Africa in back in the sixties? Through what would have been the doorway I find myself peering intently at the trunk, its lid firmly shut. What might I find to throw light on what had happened here? Bending over and with some effort I force open the rusty lid but to my disappointment the trunk is totally empty, devoid of any scrap of evidence to support my initial thought that I had stumbled across the remains of the Gibberds' residence. I take some photographs but remain perplexed. If this was the Gibberds' place where was my old rondavel? I look back up the track and off to the right where my rondavel would have stood. There was no sign of it or of the BDA office buildings. It doesn't quite fit.

Puzzled, I stand beside the derelict huts and look around. Then, away through the bush to my right, I catch sight of something, barely visible as it disappears into the bright African sunlight. Is it a trick of the light or could it be a thin wisp of smoke? I can't be sure but making my way through the bush towards this apparition it is soon apparent that my eyes have not deceived me, for here is another, rather larger building. A traditional mud-built structure but this one square and surrounded by the typical low wall found around most Tswana houses. Approaching, I can see that although in ramshackle condition, unlike the ruins I have just inspected, this building is still intact complete with a thatched roof.

As I get close this first impression is confirmed. A young woman sits squatting on her haunches in front of the hut. By the time I find myself standing by the outer wall I can see that she is thin and emaciated. My first thought is that she is ill and the possibility of AIDS immediately crosses my mind. As I absorb the scene I can see a young child of maybe two or three playing in the dirt around her feet. In her arms, wrapped in an incongruously elaborate crocheted shawl, she is cradling a baby. In the background a pot suspended over the ashes of a dying fire, the source of those wisps of smoke that had first drawn my attention.

Hearing me approach, the young woman lifts her head just the merest fraction and looks across in my direction. Her expression betrays no emotion, no evident sign of surprise that a white man should emerge so suddenly from the bush. Instead as I look into her face all I could see is a chilling emptiness; she looks forlorn and without hope. Such a contrast with me, so close to fulfilling my mission.

I call across to her, 'Dumela Mma. Do you speak English?'

She hesitates momentarily before responding – quite clearly not in her native tongue, but mine – 'No, I'm sorry.'

'Ah, but I can hear that you do.' Encouraged by her response I explain as briefly but clearly as I can the purpose of my visit. 'I lived here many, many years ago. I am looking for the BDA.'

Immediately she responds, for the first time showing a degree of animation. 'The BDA is over there.' She points away to the right.

Through the undergrowth I can now see there are yet more buildings and no more than 200 m away.

Already heading off in that direction without a further thought to the young woman and her plight, I shout back, 'Thank you, Mma.'

Now my pulse is racing. This is it. I am absolutely certain. I thread my way between the thorn bushes and low acacia trees.

And then, 'Oh my God, I don't believe it.' There it is, and to all intents and purposes still intact: my white rondavel. After pausing briefly to take breath I race on. In my haste I nearly stumble into a three-strand barbed wire fence encircling what I now know for certain was the old BDA site. Not here in my day, I think. I run along the fence finding a place where, after years of neglect, the supporting poles have rotted and fallen to the ground, I leap across the offending wire and run to the door of my rondavel.

My first thought is to make the call to Rosie and the cell phone is already in my hand. After telling her news that I have found my hut I shout into the telephone, 'Quick, drive along the road and I will be there to meet you.' She still sounds hesitant and I have to offer further encouragement, 'Please get up here, it's perfectly safe to drive.' Making my way up, I have realised that the old road up to the BDA is, if taken with care, quite driveable even in our VW.

I head back towards the road to rendezvous with Rosie. Now everything is falling into place. I can see that I have left the road about a quarter of a mile too soon, although I can understand why, as in the old days the road to Pilikwe simply didn't exist nor indeed did the other track and huts that I have found. This though – the site of the BDA – remains, although even from my cursory inspection obviously long since abandoned.

Now everything makes sense I want Rosie to share the moment, so instead of looking inside my old hut I am hurrying away from it and along the track to where it joins the new road, just 100 m or so.

Now standing here looking back down the road it is just as I remembered, and of course I can't see the railway; in fact I can't even see Rosie and the car. Where the bloody hell is she? I think. It couldn't have been much more than a mile or so back down the road that I had left her, so why is it taking her so long to get up here?

Perhaps my excitement was getting the better of me. It seemed an eternity but was probably only a couple of minutes later when the VW appeared.

Rosie wanted to tell me about her concerns of driving up the road but I was impatient.

'Don't worry about that. You're here now. Come quickly and see my house.'

Somewhat reluctantly she climbed out of the car. 'Will it be safe? All of our bags are in the boot.'

'Sure,' I insisted as I grabbed her arm and hurried her back up the track to show her what I had discovered.

Back at the white rondavel together we peered into what once had been the doorway of my home in the bush. Now, with time for a closer inspection, I realised that the thatched roof had collapsed in places but my first impression was confirmed: the hut itself, apart from needing a lick of paint, was pretty well as I left it all those years ago. I took a step inside as I had done all those years ago with my grey suitcase laden with textbooks, a step into what was to be my home for the following eight months. It was smaller than I remembered even though it was now devoid of the few pieces of furniture that had been there in my day.

Rosie by now had herself become quite animated, finding the hut just as I had described it to her so many times, and conscious that this was a very special moment for me had the presence of mind to take some photos: pictures of the hut, of me at the door of the hut and of me inside the hut. I am not sure what I had expected but this was weird. Almost as it was the day I left yet at the same time strange that the whole settlement appeared at first glance to have been long since abandoned.

With my initial euphoria subsiding I wanted to explore the rest of the site. Rosie's attention had turned to the toilet block located just as I remembered a few yards away. But no, this was not my carsey. 'Don't waste photos on that, it is not the original, they must have built a new one after I left.' She was not to be deterred.

I had taken in the fact that the office block was still standing but little else of what still remained. Now there was time to absorb what was actually left of the BDA. Where for instance was poor Bessie Head's place? At first sight nothing was evident but taking a closer look it was just possible to make out the circular shape where another rondavel had once stood. It seemed remarkably close to my hut, barely 10 ft away, much closer than I recalled.

Then I strode purposefully over to the offices with Rosie trailing in my wake. From a distance they looked in pretty good shape but once I got close again they proved not quite as I remembered. There were actually three offices, not two as I had recalled. The one occupied by Vernon and the BDA on the left. Then, forgotten but now remembered, a tiny office in the middle. It all came flooding back, for in here we kept a Roneo machine, used in those days for duplicating documents. On the right my old office. I first took a look in Vernon's office. It was totally and utterly bare, as was the small office in the middle. The door to my old office was ajar so I pushed hard against it. There was some resistance and looking down I was astonished to see that some old papers were jammed underneath the bottom of the door. Another firm shove and I was able to step inside. Although like the other offices completely devoid of furniture, the floor was strewn with more old papers. Bending down and randomly picking up one of the documents I saw that it was an invoice for some goods and was dated 1967. Rummaging through I could see that the papers comprised invoices, delivery notes and accounts, together with some government ordinances relating to the agricultural sector. My guess was that they were simply the contents of some old filing cabinet that had long since been removed, those responsible having no interest whatsoever in the contents, just the piece of furniture. Looking through these papers I couldn't find anything dated later than 1968.

At that point I had no idea what had happened to Vernon and the BDA after my departure, nor to my own project, the Bamangwato Livestock Co-operative. I remarked to Rosie, 'This lot has been here for the best part of 40 years. My guess is that this place was abandoned soon after I left. Judging by the droppings the only thing that has been in here since Vernon left has been the odd goat sheltering from the rains.' It was to prove an accurate prognosis.

I decided to look around for further evidence of what had happened since I left way back in 1966. Stepping outside the office I tried to recall where things had stood in those days. Away to the left my white rondavel still standing so in front of me there should be three or maybe four traditional mud-built rondavel that were occupied by the farm manager and his family, that I felt sure. Instead I found myself looking at two white-painted and rather grand looking huts still in near perfect condition: they hadn't been there. And in front of them slightly off to the right an old ox wagon: I didn't remember it. When he first arrived Vernon had trained a team of oxen for ploughing but by my time at the BDA he had acquired a tractor courtesy of some charity in the UK. Perhaps the wagon had been lying somewhere around the site and had later been moved there for one of Vernon's experiments. Away to the right should have been a path leading to the Gibberds' home. I wandered off in that direction but hard as I tried to look there was nothing to see, not even the outline of where their huts might have stood. Perhaps I should have taken longer searching through the bush but with my usual impatience I returned to the middle of the site to take a closer look at the white huts.

There were no traces of life in either, no papers, no furniture, no obvious clues to who had occupied them and when. One was quite large and actually square in shape. Inside I discovered that it contained a proper fireplace and chimney, distinctly more European than African in design. My guess was that after my departure and when they returned from Europe, Vernon from vacation and Tineke after having given birth to their first child, the Gibberds had decided to upgrade their accommodation and to build these rather more refined and sturdy houses from which to conduct family life.

And that was it. It was my Holy Grail. Rosie continued to snap away with the camera to keep a record of the scene and with one final rueful shrug I turned, took Rosie by the hand, and together we made our way back to the car.

We drove away from the BDA, back down the road towards the railway line. At first we shared an animated conversation asking each other, why hadn't local people, like the young woman I had met, living in such poverty and so close, occupied the BDA site in what even now were quite habitable houses? As we zig-zagged through the new chicane and turned south onto the main road my feelings of euphoria began to dissipate and I was overcome by a strange feeling of melancholy. It had been odd confronting one's past in that way and finding so much as I had left it.

Yet it wasn't this that was troubling me but more a sense of, was it worth it for people like me, and more pertinently Vernon, to give something of ourselves to countries like Botswana yet to leave such a small legacy? Let's face it, all the evidence we had seen that day suggested that when Vernon exited, the BDA experiment ended and that meant he and I and many others like us had failed because we didn't do enough to make the local people self-sufficient and confident or indeed committed enough to be able to carry things forward. I even questioned whether we should be trying. Why don't we leave these people in what we choose to label 'under-developed countries' to carry on with their traditional way of life without us seeking to impose our ideas?

Rosie sensed my change of mood but reassured me, applying her own logic to the situation, 'You've got nothing to reproach yourself about. You came and did your best, that's what you thought at the time and you have always believed that and nobody can take that away. Anyway you are being too hard on yourself; there is a legacy, look at the co-ops we have seen. They wouldn't be here if it wasn't for people like you and Trevor.'

Thanks, Rosie. They were comforting words at that moment of self-doubt. Reassured at last, I enjoyed a sense of 'mission accomplished'. It had been nearly five years since that telephone conversation with Trevor yet I knew from that moment that I would make this pilgrimage.

We were now backtracking on the same road on which we had embarked upon our journey north and the travelling was getting a little monotonous. The road was essentially wide and straight, the terrain flat except for slight inclines and depressions, so much so that we began to see ahead what appeared to be pools of water in the road but what are of course simply mirages. We dubbed this 'the road to nowhere' and broke the song of that title. I had the idea it was recorded by Chris Rea but Rosie said I was thinking of 'The Road to Hell', which might have been equally appropriate. Anyway after a few bars singing 'we're on the road to nowhere', as much as you would want to hear of me singing, we embarked upon a game to pass the time of song titles apposite to the road. 'We Gotta Get Out of This Place' by the Animals. 'Don't Let the Sun Go Down on Me' we thought of Elton John. And, with irony, 'Green Green Grass of Home'. One of those mysterious appearances by a local from the bush in the middle of nowhere prompted 'King of the Road' by Roger Miller and 'These Boots Are Made for Walkin'' until we noticed that he was barefoot. Mild hysteria. Anyway you get the idea, and before we knew it we were back to the outskirts of Gaberone once again.

Chapter Twenty

Vernon Gibberd

It wasn't possible to return to the BDA without recalling Vernon. Vernon was a big man; I guess around 6 ft 3 in. in height and broad shouldered with a ready smile and a genuinely handsome face. He was very much a gentle giant with a generous nature and friendly disposition. I never saw him dressed other than in khaki shorts and big hob-nailed boots that he left untied, I guess for easy removal. In today's parlance he was very laid back. He came from farming stock and was totally at one with his existence.

A century earlier he could have been a successful frontiersman. Not the archetypal colonial type who would treat the indigenous population as ignorant natives but someone genuinely motivated to want to help bring improvement to the lives of impoverished people less well educated than himself. He always showed the Batswana people respect for their traditions and ways and treated them as equals, although on occasions he showed his frustration at their reluctance to accept his new ideas as quickly and readily as he thought they deserved. Apart from these rare exceptions Vernon was always easy-going and relaxed.

His sense of destiny with Africa had come at an early age. In the year before going up to Cambridge he had spent time at Guy Clutton-Brock's famous St Faith's Mission Farm in what was then Rhodesia so going to Radisele after he had graduated was in a sense a natural development. The BDA had been founded by Clutton-

Brock sometime around 1959 under the patronage of Tshekedi Khama, uncle to the country's new prime minister, Seretse Khama. The BDA was modelled upon St Faith's Mission Farm where Clutton-Brock's perceived all-too-liberal attitudes towards the blacks had led to his detention without trial by the white-dominated colonial government of what was then Southern Rhodesia. Clutton-Brock later returned to Rhodesia but was eventually expelled in 1971 by the illegal government of Ian Smith. Although Tshekedi had died in London in 1959, not long after the start of the BDA project, Seretse Khama had succeeded him in the role as patron, giving the whole project considerable kudos within the Bamangwato. Vernon himself had arrived at the BDA in 1963 where he brought his own personal views about the development of arable farming in this society dominated by pastoral farmers.

After my foray to Radisele I began to piece together exactly what had happened to the BDA and to Vernon after I left.

Back in 1966 when I left Radisele for the final time Vernon and Tineke were in Europe. Vernon had completed his three-year contract during which time he had experimented with the growing of various crops on the BDA farm such as cotton, groundnuts and tobacco.

At this point there was no doubt about Vernon's continuing commitment to the BDA and en route on his return from England to Botswana Vernon had visited a UN-sponsored water conservation project in Sudan. It was an eye-opener for Vernon and using the methods observed there it inspired him to establish a similar project at the BDA jointly supported by Oxfam and Vernon's main financial backers throughout the period of the BDA's existence, then known as the Intermediate Technology Development Group or ITDG. This led to him spending two more years at the BDA experimenting with water conservation techniques on the Sudan model and growing vegetables rather than arable crops.

At the end of 1968, after five years at the BDA and with financial backing from the UK increasingly difficult to sustain, Vernon decided that it was time to move on. A timely decision as Pat Van Rensburg had just launched what was in many respects a similar but in terms of scale a bigger and more exciting project. So it was that in early

1969 Vernon left the BDA to join Pat at Serowe to lead his farmers' brigade. By this time, with Pat's interest in Swaneng School ebbing away as government interference in running this and his other educational ventures increased, he was turning increasingly towards developing the Brigades and their objective of bringing a range of vocational skills to the young people of Botswana. Seeking the best people he could find to head each of the specialist brigades, Vernon was the one obvious candidate when it came to farming.

Whether the BDA died there and then on the day Vernon left for Serowe or whether it continued for a time remains unclear but the site I discovered in the middle of the African bush has clearly been steadily crumbling quite undisturbed under the African sun for well over 30 years. My guess is that on the day Vernon left the BDA it was no more and the site has lain there literally untouched ever since.

Vernon was to stay at Serowe working with the Brigades through most of the seventies before moving south to run an irrigation project near Gaberone. After nearly two decades in Botswana he then moved to Zimbabwe and later worked with Eritrean refugees in the Sudan. Then, entering early middle age and perhaps realising the need to provide some financial security for his family, he took up his first proper paid employment, as an agricultural advisor for the British government. I am sure that it would have been a difficult decision requiring much soul searching.

In this new role he returned to East Africa primarily based in Kenya although other assignments took him to back to Sudan and to Ethiopia and Uganda. Then in the post-apartheid era to a land reform project in South Africa's poor East Cape province. It is here that Vernon now lives in semi-retirement and where he has returned to the sort of simple rural African lifestyle that he enjoyed at Radisele.

ABOVE: Maropong Co-op. Everyone wants to be in the picture!

RIGHT: With Lethiwe Dingane, Manageress at Marapong Co-op.

LEFT: Jane Siviya (left) and the elusive Auditor Constance (right) at Sowa Co-op.

BELOW: ATM African-style at Sowa Co-op.

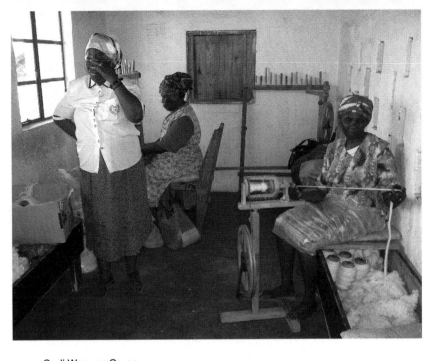

ABOVE: Oodi Weavers Co-op.
BELOW: Presenting a thank you gift to Violet Mosele, Commissioner of Co-ops.

ABOVE: Rosie in trouble with the Police.
BELOW: The offending speed sign.

B/PLACE :- ENGLAND
WARD :-
TRIBE :- N/A
MAKA :- JW
TIME :- 1119 HRS
DIRECTION :- WEST

Serial No....................
Revised Form B.P. 125 (1994)

00090072A

(MOTOR VEHICLE AND ROAD TRAFFIC OFFENCES)

TO: ROSAMARY C. LE BARGY   POLICE STATION: GWATA

RESIDENTIAL ADDRESS: NATA LODGE

PLACE: GWATA   PLACE OF WORK: ENGLAND

OCCUPATION: N/A   NATIONALITY: ENGLAND

AGE: 52 YRS   SEX: FEMALE   ID NO: 555163 AC9 MR 02

NOTICE OF INTENDED PROSECUTION

It is alleged that on 14 - 09 - 2005 in the ....
CENTRAL .... District, you owned/permitted to use/drove a motor registration

No. B 834 AKP when contravening Section/Regulation 443 ARW 45

of the Road Traffic Act Cap 69:01/Road Transport Permit Act Cap 69:03/Statutory Instrument No. ✓

Motor Vehicle Insurance Fund Act No. 30/86. (Description of the offence) OVER SPEEDING

M/V AT 70 KPH INSTEAD OF 60 KPH

You are now informed that consideration will be given to the question of prosecuting you in terms of the aforesaid Section/Regulation.
Take note that you are offered to pay P. 80-00 Admission of guilt within

days from.................... If you decline to pay admission of guilt you are

advised to report to the above Police Station on the....................day of

....................at....................hours to answer the aforesaid charge(s).

Issued by No. 5893   Rank 867   Name DICHABA A

Signature ....   Date: 16 - 09 - 05

Signature of Accused: Rosmary LeBargy   Date: 14 - 09 - 05

NB: This is not a receipt. Remember to obtain an Admission of Guilt Receipt upon payment of your fine.

DISTRIBUTION:

Original — Accused
Duplicate — Docket
Triplicate — Remains in the Book

PAID P80-00
A of GUILTY

ABOVE: The indictment. Guilty as charged. No tribe noted.

ABOVE: Bernard sets out to find the BDA.

BELOW: Bernard finds his old hut still standing in the middle of the bush after 40 years.

BELOW: The interior of Bernard's hut from the sixties.

BELOW: Bernard thinks he has found the Gibberds' hut and the trunk in which Vernon brought his worldly goods to Africa.

ABOVE: Bamangwato Livestock Co-operative office with its papers and accounts littering the floor.

Cooperatives pioneer makes 'pilgrimage'

By Kwapeng Modikwe

GABORONE - There is a group in the United States calling itself friends of Botswana. The members are former volunteers who worked in Botswana as US Peace Corps volunteers.

The club's aims include ensuring continued cordial ties between the United States of America and Botswana.

In Britain there is no such organised group, but there are individuals who worked here as volunteers and who for sentimental reasons - regardless of the distance separating the two countries - still regard Botswana as their second home.

One such person is Bernard Le Bargy, a volunteer who helped establish co-operatives in various areas around Palapye and Francistown in 1965.

Le Bargy was studying accountancy at the Co-operative College in the UK when the opportunity for interested students to spend a year helping the development of co-operatives in emerging countries presented itself. He seized the opportunity.

He had little information about a country called Bechanaland and so the temptation of traversing the Kgalagadi Desert landed him in the Central District where he became acquainted with people like Leapetswe Khama , Patrick van Rensburg and by a sheer luck, historian Sandy Grant who was a friend of a British expatriate Trevor Bottomley. Bottomley was head of the Department of Co-operatives and it was Bottomley who introduced Le Bargy to Grant. Incidentally, it was Grant who, as he usually does, 'leaked' Le Bargy's visit to me. Otherwise such an

Le Bargy with his wife Rosemary. Photo: Charles Rautenbach

When he was here last week, he was accompanied by his wife Rosemary - and for 14 days he was travelling around to see how the country has changed since he returned to his native country.

The visit was for a purpose - timed to coincide with the 40th anniversary of his first arrival in the former British protectorate.

Now 61, Le Bargy still looks fit and strong. In fact, he looks much younger than his years.

He has a recollection of a

area which was not badly hit by the 1965 drought.

Their truck got stuck in the deep and heavy sands of Nata. As they wandered around looking for someone to rescue them, they ran into a farmer's cattlepost and the man arranged a span of oxen to execute a rescue operation.

Le Bargy says being in Botswana was exciting. He says the country has made incredible changes in terms of infrastructure. His wife was particularly impressed by the

beginning to collapse. Inside what used to be his office, he was able to find documents some of which he prepared in 1965 scattered all over the floor.

He recalls that those documents used to be kept in a cabinet. The documents could have been thrown out by somebody who was only interested in the cabinet, he says.

He says he used to walk freely at midnight to catch the train at Radisele siding which was about two-and-a-half kilometres away. He

---

The Double Shock Of A Pioneer

By Gideon Nkala
Staff Writer

The year was 1965 when a 21-year-old British young man named Bernard Le Bargy ambled his way into Botswana.

When he came, he was shocked at what he saw just on the eve of independence. He left after a year. But after his recent return, 40 years later, he is experiencing a different kind of shock. One of the world's poorest countries has transformed itself beyond recognition.

"Everything seems to have changed drastically. I am impressed that there are all these good roads everywhere you go. I see all these grand tall buildings in town. There is no doubt the quality of life has changed for

the better," he says.

When he arrived his mission was simple, so he must have thought. He was sent as a volunteer with funds from the British humanitarian organisation, Oxfam, to help set-up cooperatives in then emerging state of Botswana. Used to high-rise buildings in the British metropolis, he was obviously unprepared for what he saw in Botswana.

The emerging capital city of Gaborone was a one street town with three to four blocks of buildings that formed the government enclave and a store that serviced a population of 4,000, mostly civil servants. The rest was thick, dry bush.

But even what he saw in Gaborone could not have prepared him for the cultural shock that awaited him at his duty station in

Radisele.

Then, Pilikwe was nothing more than a hamlet. The roads were very sandy. "Travelling in that Bedford; passengers had to stop so many times on the way and dig out the soil from under the wheels as the truck got stuck".

It looked like the British government had identified the cattle industry as the sector that could drive the economy of one of the poorest countries in the world.

"I was to set up livestock cooperatives in the Bangwato area and we set up our offices in the BDA roundavels somewhere between Radisele and Pilikwe. Although abandoned, I saw the rondavels the other day when I visited the area," he said.

Le Bargy added that part of his mandate

Bernard Le Bargy

was to train farmers in animal husbandry and to appreciate the quality of cattle rather than just the sheer numbers.

"We provided farmers with information on cattle grading system". If the cattle industry was to make money, the British believed that the farmers should form cooperatives so that they could do away with middlemen, whom Le Bargy reckons, were undercutting the farmers.

"Cooperatives provided self-help services and reduced people's dependence on government. It is a departure from the idea that government will solve all your problems".

In the year that he spent as volunteer, he helped set up cooperatives in places like Palapye, Mmadinare, Matsiloje and Selebi, which was

On his return to Botswana Bernard discovers he has achieved celebrity status with the local Press.

Chapter Twenty-One

Mochudi

We drive out of Gaberone once again heading in a northerly direction, by now a well-trodden route for us. This time we continue past the Oodi turn-off and leave the main road about 15 miles from the city to head into the interior. Soon we arrive in the outskirts of the Bakgatla tribal village of Mochudi. Mochudi resembles Serowe, neither being remotely as I remembered – not surprising in this case given my one visit 40 years before – nor retaining the character of an African village. Instead it is an ugly urban sprawl of untidy breezeblock buildings housing small businesses, shops and dwellings.

On our return to Gaberone I had made my promised call to Sandy to arrange to visit his Phuthadikobo Museum. He clearly instructed that I should 'take the hill up by the chief's house' but it was only with the benefit of hindsight that I appreciated I had misinterpreted this advice and in my mind was firmly convinced that he meant the hill by the kgotla, the meeting place from where the chief conducts tribal business.

So it was that we mistakenly arrived at the kgotla. We had driven up the hill with me thinking this put us exactly where we should be, but instead of finding a museum the road brought us into a large open area. In the foreground stood an enormous tree around which was a semi-circle of three white-painted, official looking single-storey buildings. The backdrop to this scene towering over the village was a steep hill with a near vertical cliff face. We were in a dead end and from my vantage point in the passenger seat of the car access to the museum was not immediately obvious. Only now did I ponder, had I correctly followed Sandy's directions, without conveying to Rosie any sense that I was having my doubts.

The area was bustling with people, some going about their business, others in small groups chattering over whatever had brought them to this place. We pulled the car over to one side and a little uncertainly climbed out to take in our situation.

Rosie said I should ask the way and looking around I saw two men stood in earnest conversation on the corner of the first building. Of middle age, both smartly dressed in white open-necked shirts and trousers, they looked like they might be able to speak English so I strolled across towards them. The first man turned in my direction as I approached and, showing no surprise at seeing a white man here at the kgotla, nodded in acknowledgement of my presence.

'Excuse me. Can you help? I am looking for the museum.'

My instinct had been correct and he replied in English, 'Do you have a car?'

'Yes, we have parked over here.' I pointed across to where Rosie stood with our car.

This seemed to present something of a problem and he turned to his companion and went into a discussion in Setswana with the other man.

Sensing a problem I said, 'We will walk if this is easier.'

The men then went into another discussion, presumably about the respective merits of driving or walking, before the first man turned back to me and said, 'Yes, walking would be better. Go here and you will find a path.' He pointed away to the right and then upwards, indicating a climb high above the kgotla seemingly up the face of the steep rocky cliff.

'Can we leave our car here?'

'Of course, it will be safe.' I thanked them and wandered back towards Rosie. 'It looks like we got ourselves a climb,' I said, pointing to the top of the hill.

We set off, picking a way through the groups of people standing and talking around the kgotla, behind the large tree, past the office buildings. At the end of the third and final building we found the start of a makeshift path. At first it meandered between some scruffy huts and breezeblock houses and then began to climb. Soon we found ourselves gazing up at a roughly hewn set of steps cut into the granite face of the rock. It was a steep climb and in the African heat we were both breathing heavily by the time we clambered up the final few steps to the top of the pathway. Here we emerged to find that on the hilltop, unseen from the kgotla below, was a plateau covering about an acre of land. Away to the right stood some quite substantial buildings. After the modest museum we had visited at Francistown and even compared with the Red House at Serowe, this was rather grander but also an infinitely less accessible location and certainly not what we expected. There was no one in sight and no sound of life from within the buildings. We stood momentarily gathering our breath and wondering what to do next before making our way across the open area to the front of the buildings where we climbed up some more steps and along a passageway with rooms either side, one with its door ajar. We poked our heads inside; it was obviously an office but there was no one to be seen. I had only just remarked to Rosie about the whole place having the feel of a sinking ship, a not entirely appropriate metaphor, when whom should we come across but Sandy, busily cleaning a brass sign on the wall. We exchanged some banter about him performing household chores when, obviously hearing our raised voices, Elinah emerged from one of the adjacent rooms. She was wearing, we felt sure in our honour, a traditional dress and matching headwear in a predominantly striking orange. On complimenting her on her appearance she said that it was a typical example dress worn by the Herero, a tribe that originates in Namibia, there being no such traditional dress amongst the Batswana women.

Having visited the museums in Gaberone, Francistown and Serowe I was intrigued by what Sandy had described as 'a special experience'. In the event I am not sure that Phuthadikobo quite met this grandiose description but its location perched on top of the hill is certainly unique.

'Sandy, why has this place got such a near unpronounceable name?' I asked.

'Phuthadikobo is the hill you have just climbed. It is one of only three hills of any size in this part of the country so you can tell that for the locals it identifies exactly the location of the museum. Come here and see the views.'

Sandy led us across the courtyard and, between the edge of the buildings and a towering pinnacle of rock that represents the very summit of Phuthadikobo, superb views across the plain below.

Sandy went on to tell us that the museum is housed in what was, from its opening in 1923 until it was abandoned in 1975 primarily due to its inaccessibility, the Bakgatla National School. From his arrival in Mochudi back in the sixties Sandy had developed a relationship with the new young chief of the Bakgatla tribe, Linchwe the Second. Once the school closed, and with the extensive buildings left empty in 1976, with the chief's support he opened this the Phuthadikobo Museum with the aim of preserving a record of the tribe's culture, traditions and recent history. Sandy told us that to coincide with the museum opening a road had been built but as it is extremely steep we had done the right thing by parking at the kgotla and making our way up the hill on foot. With that additional information it was easy to sympathise with the generations of kids who had to make their way to the top of Phuthadikobo on a daily basis in order to get an education.

Introductions and small talk over, Elinah said that before Sandy took us on a guided tour of the museum she wanted to show us how they made enough money to enable them to fund the museum and led us into the side room from which she had emerged minutes before.

As she shepherded us into the room she related that back in 1980 an enterprising German volunteer had come to work at the museum and had introduced to the museum staff a new skill that in turn led to a business venture, the profits from which had gone a long way in keeping the museum financially afloat for the past 25 years. That skill was silk screen-printing. From a modest start, over the years the staff have produced a range of goods for sale using traditional designs and patterns on wall hangings, aprons, tea towels and other items favoured by tourists combining the virtues of illustrating Botswana culture and being easy to pack. We admired the current product range combining a sense of the traditional and contemporary. Elinah introduced us to the young man responsible for the designs. Suffice to say he proved to be a Zimbabwean refugee.

This part of our visit completed, Sandy was clearly keen to take us on a guided tour around the museum and led us from the print room back into the courtyard. As we stood chatting the thing that caught our attention was a collection of old advertisements displayed on one of the exterior walls.

One was particularly amusing featuring four pictures of people using a well-known product, each with an appropriate narrative:

A doctor: 'Know its power'.

A baby: 'Makes my skin comfortable'.

A young woman: 'It makes my skin soft'.

And finally and inexplicably, the picture of a young man eating the product: 'Makes me healthy'.

The slogan: 'Always use Vaseline'!!!

It was time to move into the museum proper. Sandy is an accomplished photographer. Over the years he has gathered a collection of interesting historical artefacts to fill the showcases. As we began to wander around, at least from our perspective, a particular attraction of the museum proved to be his collection of photographs accumulated over the last 40 years offering a matchless pictorial history of the tribe during that period. The Bakgatla are uniquely blessed with records of their more recent history insofar as Sandy is the natural successor to Professor Isaac Schapera, the South African anthropologist and academic. As a graduate from Cape Town University he first arrived in what was then Bechuanaland in 1930 to research his thesis on the bogwera or initiation rites of the Bakgatla. 'Schap' as he was affectionately known continued to visit, study and write about the Bakgatla for the next 50 years. Latterly he was a trustee and contributor to the museum until his relatively recent death. This continuous study of tribal life over such a long period provides an unrivalled insight into the development of what is still a relatively young country. Although bogwera, which involved male circumcision, subsequently fell into decline in the years following Schapera's original study, some limited attempts to revive the practice took place in the seventies and were recorded on film by Sandy.

Whilst the museum is indeed interesting I was not entirely persuaded by Sandy's description of this as a unique experience but as Botswana museums go it had some fascinating exhibits tracing the history of the Bakgatla over the 130 or so years since they had settled in this area. The more typical exhibits like weapons and pottery, as I indicated, were much enhanced by the photographic records of Schapera and latterly Sandy Grant himself.

As we strolled around looking at the displays we spotted a group photograph taken in the early sixties on which Rosie correctly identified a much younger looking Sandy. This in turn triggered a conversation with Sandy about why he had come here in the first place and led to some fascinating insights. Interesting though the exhibits were, this conversation was in itself quite an eye-opener, but more of that shortly.

The tour ended, like all good museums visits, in its gift shop where we found a wide range of stock, from Sandy's books to the output from the silkscreen business. We purchased some aprons and a wall hanging. There were some baskets like those we had seen at the national exhibition in Gaberone. We commented on the 'traditional' designs with their exotic nomenclature like 'flight of the swallow' but true to form cynical old Sandy made some disparaging remark that these were a recent invention of the marketing department of the company that has cornered the export market for these products. Nevertheless we had been rather taken by the quality of the goods and made a purchase.

After my first visit to see Violet you may recall that in the car taking me back to my hotel I had asked Ngae about my former colleague and fellow college student, John Gaetsaloe. She told me that he had at some point become commissioner of co-operatives but was now retired from government service and living in Mochudi. On the morning of my visit to Sandy's museum I had telephoned John's home to signal my visit to the museum with a view to calling to see him. The telephone was answered by someone I judged to be a well-educated lady speaking beautifully articulated English who I assumed to be John's wife. 'John has gone out for some shopping but I am sure he would be delighted to meet an old colleague,' she had assured me.

Taking our leave of Elinah, at Sandy's insistence he took us in his pick-up truck on the short journey down the hill past the chief's house to where John lives. It was here that from a surprising source I was to hear a sad story concerning Tshoagong and to close another chapter on the good and the great from my earlier time in this country.

On arriving at John's house, a pleasant and by local standards large well appointed bungalow contained within a fenced yard, we were warmly welcomed by a waif of a girl who led us to an outbuilding away from the main house. Here a cold drink was poured and we were invited to await John. Left alone with time to take in our surroundings, Rosie whispered, 'Who is she?'

With a rueful smile and in hushed tones I replied, 'A sign of the times but in true colonial fashion I think she is probably the servant.'

The room was decorated in the style that made me think of an English house in the fifties, it was what we would have called the front room or parlour with comfortable armchair and settee, the walls decorated with pictures and family photographs and a tiger rug, that for Africa, seemed a little incongruous. The purpose of the room was clearly to enable guests to be received without them having to enter the main body of the house.

After a few minutes through the open door I saw a figure shuffle across the courtyard to join us. Meeting so many people again after such a long period focuses one on the ageing process. A slight stoop and a old man's gait – not, I have to say, helped by the wearing of open sandals on his feet – at first suggested someone old before their time. In this part of Africa it has to be said his age – 65 – is near double the current life expectancy. John was no longer the slim young man I remembered; he had developed a sizeable paunch only partly disguised by a loose Mandela-style overshirt. His hair, now grey and despite the Afro curls, was combed oddly straight in a manner that brought to mind James Brown and Chuck Berry. Yet the facial features were exactly as I remembered him. As John extended a hand in welcome I couldn't help but remember him as a fellow student at Stanford Hall – homesick and miserable. A misery compounded by a total inability to adjust to a particularly cold English winter.

Despite my first impressions concerning his physical wellbeing I soon appreciated that John's mental faculties had not been impaired by his age. I was of course interested in what had happened to John in the intervening years and his take on the current state of the co-operatives. However, he seemed more interested in conversing about the world political scene – the Iraq war, G8 aid to Africa and the state of the British economy – than in talking about himself.

As we sat chatting a shadow filled the still-open doorway. Looking across I could see standing there an African lady. I was immediately drawn to her fine high cheekboned features and one of those ageless faces that meant that I was genuinely uncertain whether she was John's wife or daughter. John simply introduced her as Tebago and as I stood to shake her hand at that point the only thing that was clear was that she was the lady I had spoken to on the telephone. Only as the conversation unfolded did it become clear that Tebago was indeed John's wife. Tebago comes from a wealthy local family and has travelled widely, not only as the wife of a now retired civil servant but in her own right having been educated at a South African university and with a sister living in the United States who she has visited there on a number of occasions.

By now some time had passed. I realised that I had updated John on Trevor's wellbeing, had learnt a lot about Tebago and her travels and had personally given freely on my opinions on current world events, but had learnt little about John and his career after he returned from college in England.

Turning to John I decided that a more direct approach was necessary if I were to fill any more gaps about what had happened to my former colleague in the intervening years.

'John, 40 years is a long time since we last met. Tell me what happened to you in the years since your time at Stanford Hall.'

'Well of course much has happened. When I returned home almost immediately I was posted to Francistown and that is where I met Tebago. Soon we were married and only a short time afterwards I was posted again, this time to open a new office in Palapye.'

This was interesting because of course Palapye was on Tshoagong's and my old territory. We had established an office at Radisele where we were in a sense 'guests' of the BDA primarily because of the cattle marketing co-op rather than as government officers and it made sense for the Department of Co-operatives to have a proper office somewhere in the Bamangwato.

'Unfortunately for us and for the co-operatives in Botswana, Trevor left us shortly after this, too soon. The co-ops had barely started. Not enough of us really understood the principles. When Trevor went back to England his replacement was a local. You have to understand that after Independence there was an Africanisation policy and when a senior job fell vacant it was given to one of us even when there was nobody really qualified for the role, as was the case with the co-ops. The new man was the first of many to hold the job of registrar of co-operatives, most without a great deal of success.'

'John, I have visited the Department and met the latest person to hold the role, which of course is now called commissioner of co-operatives. Where do you think the co-ops are in Botswana today?'

John paused to consider my question. 'Bernard, I will answer you by telling you a story. You will know that I was one of those people who succeeded Trevor when I was eventually promoted to the job of registrar of co-ops. I remember one day after a meeting with our minister I was pulled to one side by the permanent secretary and he said to me, "John, you must stop boring the minister with long speeches about the co-ops." He was a very experienced man, one of the few whites who had stayed on after Independence and I do think that he felt he was giving me good advice as both a colleague and a friend. But do you know that encapsulated our problems in the co-ops. The politicians were not steeped in the co-op principles. To have a co-op in your village became fashionable and to hold a position on the co-op committee became prestigious. As a result the whole process became politicised. Politicians wanted co-ops established to meet promises made to their constituents rather than for the right commercial reasons. Shortcuts were made, employees lacked training, committees were filled with political cronies of the ruling party rather than those better qualified for the role, and the ideals of democracy and accountability were ignored. As a consequence the co-ops were poorly managed, typically stock losses were excessive and subsequently a number of co-ops collapsed leaving politicians with egg on their face.'

It sounded like a situation that demanded a scapegoat and as John went on to explain he was to be 'the fall guy'. John explained that he had worked for a succession of ministers and the last of these would not countenance John's insistence that to restore credibility there must be a return to core co-op values and stricter audit controls. The minister was under political pressure and wanted John out.

Then, just as his career seemed to be in ruins, John was to be saved, by none other than Quett Masire who had been our minister back in the sixties. By then Masire had succeeded Seretse Khama as president. Facing demotion into some obscure department of government John suddenly found himself as one of the cabinet office staff reporting directly to the state president. He remained in this role until Masire retired in 1998, at which time John decided it was the right time for him to take early retirement.

With his long service as a senior civil servant and a handsome pension, John is able to enjoy a comfortable lifestyle. Nevertheless it was interesting to hear John, a retired member of the 'political elite' say that he happily spends much of his spare time tending the cattle on his lands some 35 km to the west.

The time came to take our leave and John insisted on driving us the short distance down the hill to the kgotla. In the yard where his vehicle was parked there was a fenced area containing three fierce looking dogs; an alsatian and two bull mastiffs. As a sign of changing times John said that theft and violent crime was prevalent here, not only in Gaberone but also here in Mochudi village, and at night he allows the dogs to roam freely around the yard as a deterrent to any would-be thieves. The Batswana are acknowledged as being undemonstrative and peace loving people. I always found them friendly and charming. It is a shock that crime even here in the village is rife, and violent crime at that, although on reflection one can appreciate how much this society has changed. The population explosion from half a million to more than one-and-a-half million in the relatively short period since Independence is not the result entirely of improvements in healthcare and a baby boom, but also reflects immigration from other parts of Africa, near-neighbours South Africa and Zimbabwe but also from as far away as Nigeria and also considerable numbers of incomers from the Indian sub-continent. This is now a far more complex society than it was in the sixties and at least some have come because this is a, by African standards, rich country with some easy pickings.

At the kgotla we said our farewells to John and returned to our car. Despite our earlier efforts to find a suitable parking place we readily discovered that we had in fact left our car exactly where the farmers park their truckloads of cattle whilst they obtain a permit for slaughter from the tribal office. Found: one hire car, quite safe but with one side covered in a thick layer of cow shit.

Chapter Twenty-Two

Sandy Grant

I have done my research on Sandy. I have discovered that over the years he has his fingers in a lot of pies in Botswana as historian, museum curator, author, writer and putative politician as well as an active campaigner on many local issues. He is an accomplished photographer with ample evidence of his work within the Phuthadikobo Museum and in his published works. His photographs have also appeared on Botswana postage stamps. Having met him I think that it would be fair to describe him as well intentioned and although many would see him as an irritant at least the state has recognised his efforts on behalf of his adopted country with the award of the Presidential Medal of Honour. This despite having once rejected his request for citizenship.

However, it is not until our visit to the museum that Sandy reveals exactly how he had got to Africa in the first place and why he was still here over 40 years later.

Whilst at Cambridge where he completed an MA in history Sandy became involved with the organisation later known as Amnesty International. Coincidentally around the same time, in 1963, the new paramount chief, Linchwe, of the Bakgatla, the tribe resident in the area around Mochudi, was completing his studies in England where he was introduced to the authoress Naomi Michison. Naomi subsequently introduced Linchwe to Martin Ennals, Amnesty's leading light and the man who later became its first Secretary

General. Ennals, concerned about the deteriorating political situation in Southern Africa, wanted to establish a safe haven in
Bechuanaland for 'activists' escaping from the apartheid regime in
South Africa before arranging their transit north to other friendly
African countries or to the UK. Suddenly things fell into place. From
their London base Ennals and his friends in Amnesty looked at the
map and saw that Mochudi, Linchwe's tribal village, was close to
the South African border. What better place to establish a refugee
centre given the link already established with Linchwe?

The young chief agreed, despite the dangers to his own people
brought about by building a refuge right on South Africa's doorstep.
Perils incidentally that should not be underplayed. In the years
immediately following Botswana's independence its next-door
neighbour aggressively ignored international convention with their
agents and at times even armed troops made incursions across the
border seeking out members of organisations like the ANC and PAC
who had fled to safety in Botswana. In granting permission Linchwe
was taking risks but at the same time he exacted in return a promise
from Amnesty that the centre would include facilities that could be
used by the local community as well as by refugees.

So it was that at the end of 1963 Martin Ennals persuaded the
young activist Sandy Grant to take the journey from England to this
then obscure outpost of the Commonwealth to supervise the building
and subsequently to run the rather euphemistically named Mochudi
Community Centre.

Sandy took up residence in Mochudi and the centre was built,
but Ennals and his friends in London had not done their research
properly. Although Mochudi is indeed close to the border what Ennals
had not taken into account was that it was a border area populated
by Boer farmers staunchly protective of the apartheid regime and
crossing the border here was incredibly dangerous. In practice most
political refugees crossed into Botswana further south near Lobatsi.
The reality was that the Mochudi Community Centre was never to
host more than a handful of political refugees at any one time.

Although the project was something of a debacle Sandy
nevertheless had found himself a spiritual home becoming very

involved in village life and developing a close personal friendship with the new young chief, Linchwe. As the years passed Sandy became more and more committed to the new Botswana and this in turn was to lead to his involvement in a whole raft of other community projects and various roles for himself.

I was particularly interested in Sandy's relationship with Lady Naomi Mitchison, the British authoress who had written extensively about Africa in general and specifically about Mochudi, where she was known as 'the mother of the tribe'. I recall Trevor speaking affectionately of his own relationship with her developed on her frequent visits to Africa in the sixties.

Sandy's response came as something of a bombshell. The 'mother of the tribe' sobriquet Sandy attributed to a combination of Naomi's literary imagination combined with a willing British Press only too happy to go along with the image of a member of the British aristocracy going native. Sandy said that in later years as Linchwe's career as a politician and diplomat burgeoned he largely ignored the ageing Naomi and increasingly Sandy was left chasing around trying to make her feel welcome. Lady Mitchison was born in 1897, and therefore even back in the sixties when she first travelled to Bechuanaland was already of mature years. She visited less and less frequently as the years went by and ultimately Sandy felt it necessary to actively discourage her from further visits. She died at the very considerable age of 101 in 1999.

Over the years Sandy has clearly been something of a thorn in the flesh of officialdom so the award of the country's highest civilian honour bears testament that even those in government have come to accept that his campaigns have been conducted from a genuine concern for his adopted country. Although a well-known figure in Mochudi and amongst the Bakgatla people, he famously campaigned to save the historical tribal offices in Kanye, home of the Bangwaketse. Locally he has battled the influential Dutch Reformed Church on various matters not least concerning ownership of the Mochudi hospital. He once stood for parliament but has subsequently supported the democratic process by sitting on the Independent Electoral Commission. Sandy has sat on endless committees, some quasi-governmental others purely voluntary like the Executive Committee of the Botswana Society. Although he is winding down his activities he still writes a weekly (and frequently contentious) column on cultural matters for the local independent newspaper Mmegi demonstrating no loss in his capacity to express an opinion, however controversial.

Sandy is something of a throwback to another age. Now a fully-fledged citizen of his adopted country, at heart still an English eccentric of the 'old school'. I truly hope that he will not be offended by this description.

Chapter Twenty-Three

Whither the Co-ops

Today I am due to meet Modukanele Modukanele at the offices of the Ministry of Agriculture. I am told that this is contained within one of the old pre-Independence office buildings close to the railway station so before the appointed hour I wander around to see the old Gaberone Hotel where I ate myself so many times in splendid isolation next to what was then a railway halt masquerading as a railway station. I don't recognise the area at all. Outside the station, a bustling market. I am disoriented. Later I read that the old hotel was pulled down in 1979 and re-built on a new site, as was the railway station.

The Ministry building is located within a walled compound containing one large and several smaller office blocks and covered parking for the Ministry's huge fleet of vehicles. I stroll unchallenged past the gatehouse. A young man in khakis wearing a peaked cap two sizes too big is lolling in the doorway chatting to an equally young woman. Both are too preoccupied to notice my arrival so I keep walking and head to the reception area of the main office block. Here two more uniformed security men, with the same khakis but with caps of optimum size. I ritually sign the visitor book. However, when I ask for the Department of Co-operatives they tell me that I don't need to register here as the Department of Co-operatives is not in this building, clearly the limit of their jurisdiction, but on the first floor of the adjacent building.

I make my way to the next-door building and unescorted and

unchallenged I enter; there is no security or reception area so I wander upstairs and along an empty corridor peering at names and job titles on the office doors. Eventually, at the very end of the corridor, I come to an inviting open door. I enter and find myself in an office. Quickly assimilating the scene, containing a number of workstations, I realise this area is the outer office of an executive suite. Sitting at a PC is a slim young woman in a brown dress that I assume is a secretary to one of the executives housed in the inner sanctum. I ask her for help. By pure chance this proves to be Violet's secretary, Kebonye, with who I have been in e-mail correspondence. I have found the Department of Co-operatives.

I remind Kebonye of my appointment with Modukanele Modukanele. Confusion reigns. Telephone calls are made in Setswana. Eventually Kebonye tells me that Mr Modukanele has left the office to visit another ministry but will return shortly. Mo has clearly forgotten our appointment.

Kebonye invites me to take a seat to await Mo's return. I sit waiting in this outer office. Casting around I can see that it is as I had first assumed, there are the doors to three offices. I speculate that Violet, her deputy and, when he is there, Mo occupy them.

Someone exits through one of the doors to the executive offices. He stops in front of me, looks down and says, 'You want to see me.' I am bewildered. 'You wrote to me at BOCA.' BOCA is the Co-operative Association, a body representing the marketing co-operatives and is independent of government. I sent them a fax some weeks before but like most of my correspondence I received no reply and had mentally written off the prospect of contacting this organisation. He tells me his name is Mr Kennekae and anxious not to miss this surprise opportunity to get a different perspective on the co-ops I arrange to visit him later in the day. He tells me his office is close by, within the Ministry of Agriculture compound, so I wonder how independent his organisation is in reality.

Eventually Mo returns and we go to his office for a chat. A tall man exuding a confident air, he nevertheless seems more cautious in expressing his views than Violet and her colleagues at my earlier meeting. I decide I need to find out more about him and he proves to be yet another long-serving member of the Department of Co-operatives and currently head of training. He tells me that he obtained his master's degree at the University of Strathclyde so we exchange some small talk about life in the UK. This seems to have the desired effect and when I feel that I have developed some rapport I get down to business and ask why the co-ops are doing badly. It is an open type of question and Mo chooses to answer by giving a longer historical perspective as he tells his story about the present state of the co-ops.

'I want to go back to the drought in the late seventies. It was critical because it adversely affected the cattle marketing co-ops of the type you started just as they were getting a foothold in the market. If the drought wasn't problem enough its effects were accentuated by a devastating outbreak of foot and mouth disease in Ngamiland in 1977 and later a virulent lung disease in that area all but decimating the cattle population. The Department had tried to take remedial action to save the marketing co-operatives by creating what were called multipurpose co-ops, combining shops and agricultural co-ops into one, but with limited success.'

Mo then relates the history of the Co-operative Bank, initially created for the co-operative sector but which began to see itself as a commercial bank and suffered by trying to compete with the major international banks. Although still solvent the government made a political decision in 1995 to wind it up. The effect of this and failure of the Co-operative Union, an independent association of all the co-ops, meant the co-ops have become too reliant on the government and expect the Department of Co-operatives to make important business decisions for them. Mo is hoping that with more emphasis on member training and the emergence of a non-governmental co-operative body like BOCA, things may improve.

Mo brings the conversation to a close by saying that I am to meet Violet again, for a debrief. She wants to hear about my visit to the north.

At this meeting we are joined by Mo and Violet's second-in-command, Sebius Moloi. Violet is as charming as at our previous meeting. We have a good open discussion. Violet is anxious to get my views on what I have seen. I can be positive about Maropong and Sowa because Litiwe and Jane are very committed people doing a good job but I express my disappointment that overall the co-operative sector represents such a small part of the economy and the co-ops by and large are struggling for survival. I ask Violet how she feels about the prospects for the co-operative sector. 'I am very optimistic,' she replies.

My meetings over, I make my way across to a distant corner of the site to visit BOCA. They are housed in some dilapidated old offices no longer used by the Ministry of Agriculture but still within the Ministry compound. In an outer office I find a secretary and she takes me through to see Mr Kennekae. He is smartly dressed in a light-coloured suit and has a polished demeanour that marks him out from the people I have met in the Department of Co-operatives. He proves both garrulous and engaging and without any hint of the political correctness I have sensed from my official government contacts.

Mr Kennekae tells me that before taking this job he was employed by the Department of Co-operatives and like Lesetswe, Botho, BK and Modukanele he too spent something like 20 years in the Department. However, unlike them he has moved on to become Secretary of the Botswana Co-operative Association or BOCA when it was formed in 2000 after the demise of the Co-operative Union and Co-operative Bank. Potentially BOCA has a government grant of 8 million pula for five years to be used to develop and grow the co-operative sector; however, because of the parlous state of the co-ops only 3 million pula has so far been made available and BOCA has not loaned any of the funds. BOCA is supposed to be independent of government and the co-ops have the freedom to affiliate to BOCA on payment of a small annual fee. Thirty-six co-ops are currently members.

Mr Kennekae is also less reticent than his former colleagues when we talk about the demise of the Co-operative Bank for reasons that later become apparent. His story is similar to Mo's but he goes further. He says that the winding up of the bank was a political rather than an economic decision because the organisation was not technically insolvent although its problems stemmed from trying to compete with the commercial banks rather than confining itself as banker for the co-op sector. At the time the auditors Price Waterhouse had been commissioned to report on the running of the bank and a number of other government controlled institutions. Their conclusion was that almost uniformly these organisations had political placements as board members who almost universally lacked the requisite skills and experience to act as directors. Not one director of the Co-operative Bank had any banking experience. As a consequence they simply rubber-stamped decisions of an 'autocratic top management'. There were also implications that decisions made were bordering on corruption with loans by the bank to both directors and to employees in what the report regarded as excessive amounts.

As part of my research I have been sent an article on this very subject written by Patrick Van Rensburg. As ever he pulls no punches and argues the Co-operative Bank was wound up because the general manager was a known supporter of an opposition party making him a ready scapegoat. Closing the Co-op Bank diverted attention away from the National Development Bank, in even deeper financial trouble but having key players closely associated to the BDP, which was baled out with a substantial injection of government funds.

Whatever the truth Mr Kennekae felt that winding up the Co-operative Bank had been a heavy blow for the Co-operative Movement in Botswana and he would rather that the problems identified be addressed than the more radical decision to close the bank and leave the co-ops without a source for loans. I say that not everything is bad news. What about the SACCOS? They seem to be growing. Even on this he is less optimistic than his colleagues in the Department, saying that many major employers like the mines, the railway and the abattoir are retrenching and this is bound to affect employment and therefore membership levels in the savings co-ops.

Despite all this doom and gloom Mr Kennekae is bright and entrepreneurial and when I ask him about the future prospects for the co-ops he answers my question obliquely:

'They have many problems but I believe I can help them. But let me ask for your professional advice.' It is then that Mr Kennekae reveals that he has resigned from BOCA and in a few weeks intends to start up his own management and marketing consultancy business. He hopes that the Department of Co-operatives will be his first client.

Later, as had been previously agreed, Mo arrives to collect me from the BOCA office and having said my goodbyes to Mr Kennekae together we head out of the city in a chauffeur driven car to visit the Botswana Co-operative College. The centre is at Sebele some 12 km north and is part of a complex of Ministry of Agriculture facilities including research, animal husbandry and veterinary services. The facilities, classrooms and offices set around a quadrangle are quite reasonable and the centre has two full-time tutors together with administrative staff.

Strolling around with Mo and meeting the staff I couldn't help but recall my own time at the Bechuanaland Training Centre and looking at the course syllabus I could see that if I had left my mark it was here. Unfortunately as the Department of Co-operatives has recently been transferred to the Ministry of Trade and Industry it is no longer welcome here at Sebele, although Mo says funds of 1.4 million pula have been set aside to create a new purpose built college for the co-ops. It all sounds promising but I wonder if in their current state the co-ops are going to justify such generous funding.

Before I leave the co-ops: remember BK who we encountered at the hotel in Palapye? Rosie and me were standing in the lobby of the Sun Hotel on our last night in Botswana when I overheard the receptionist declining to change some money into Pula. When I looked across, who should it be but BK. We acknowledged each other across the hotel foyer and BK comes across. We exchange pleasantries and he tells me that after we met at Palapye his delegates were fascinated when he told them about me and my journey from England to return to visit the co-ops. So it was a shame that I had missed the opportunity to address them myself. He it seems had been too polite, not wanting to disturb my trip by asking me to talk to the people from the thrift and loan co-ops and I had not been forward enough to suggest the idea. Then, changing tone, BK rather furtively and speaking in a low conspiratorial voice, presumably so the receptionist couldn't hear, asked for my help. 'My brother is leaving for England tomorrow and we are having a farewell drink but this is the only money he has.' He waved a British £20 banknote in my direction. 'Can you change it for me. They say they cannot change it as I am not a hotel resident.' I smiled a knowing smile, nodded in the affirmative, took the note from him without a word and went across to the desk. The receptionist was not amused and showed what displeasure she could but of course had no alternative but to exchange the note. I passed the pula to BK who thanked me profusely before heading off, as I had anticipated, not in the direction of the bar but towards the adjacent casino. Our friend BK was certainly a nocturnal animal.

Chapter Twenty-Four

Phalatse Tshoagong

Forty years on and I have again met with Trevor, Sandy, Patrick and John and discovered what happened to Vernon. I have, through my visits to the Department of Co-operatives and visits to Sowa and Marapong, updated myself on the progress made by the co-ops. Returning to Gaberone, Serowe and Nata and of course having found my old hut at Radisele, I am close to a sense of completeness, of closure. But what of my old friend and work companion, Tshoagong?

Just occasionally in life have I met people who from the first meeting I have sensed were fellow travellers in life, often with personalities completely different from my own but in whose company I could feel totally relaxed. People with whom I could exchange banter knowing the other person instead of being offended will counter in kind. The list of such people is short, yet the people involved all very different in character, so defining the very essence of the bond I have felt with them is difficult. My relationship with Tshoagong was like this. He could be difficult but I always knew when he was annoyed, like that first encounter with my failed driving test, but this was soon put behind us.

He did have a penchant for the women and flirted outrageously with the volunteer teachers at Swaneng. It was not crude or overtly sexual but with a certain engaging charm and flattery. Being rather shy myself, I rather admired his front yet at the same time I felt uncomfortable at the behaviour of this my colleague, a married middle-aged man who had a young wife and child in Botswana and had also left a family behind in South Africa. I could not but compare him with the Italians I had seen in action the previous year on my trip to Rimini. A Latin-like panache. On one particular occasion at Swaneng School, however, I was drawn into his web when the lovely Gillian, quite evidently furious, approached me and through clenched teeth had quietly but firmly demanded that I have a word with him as he had taken a bit of a liberty, what was called 'goosing' or a pinch on the bottom. I admit I was rather non-plussed not because of what he had done but rather more that she really thought I would actually tackle him on the matter. I rather lamely suggested that she herself was probably the best person to administer the necessary admonishment.

Yet despite this close affinity, it was not until I read Bessie Head's book *When Rain Clouds Gather* that I began to reflect on the gaps in my knowledge of Tshoagong, not least his past. Sure, I knew that he came from South Africa where he had been a school teacher. That he lived at Pilikwe where he had a young wife and child, but I could recall little more despite all the hours and days we had spent together. When I read *When Rain Clouds Gather* the character Makhaya immediately jumped out from the page. It was Tshoagong, but this character had a mysterious past. Then things that Bessie had obviously noted began to make some sense. What about the time Tshoagong had produced his gun for the first time?

By now I had met or discovered what had happened to all the main characters in my story but Tshoagong remained an enigma almost to the end. Both Sandy and Patrick had alluded to his relatively recent death and with a 'how sad' tone without actually elaborating on the exact circumstances of his demise. It was all rather unsatisfactory, and then revelation just when I least expected it.

At one point in the conversation with John Gaetsaloe he excused himself, leaving Rosie and I alone with Tebago. I am not sure what prompted my question but I said to her, 'When you and John lived in Palapye did you ever come across my old colleague, Tshoagong?'

It was an odd conversation and an unlikely source to discover what had become of my old partner.

Tebago needed no second bidding and immediately went into her story, recalling in her own words much of what John had already told us, that when John had been transferred up country from Gaberone to Francistown they met and quite soon were married. Then that John had been transferred to Palapye.

At this point the story, as related by Tebago, took on an interesting twist:

'I was this newly wed bride, in a strange town, I knew nobody. I had been working in Francistown but my family were here in Mochudi; it was a difficult and in many ways lonely time. John and Tshoagong were to become close working colleagues together in an office the Department of Co-operatives had established in Palapye and through this relationship between the two men I was introduced to Tshoagong's wife. She was about my age and, like me, a young bride, although by then she had had her first child. Soon we became close friends. Then I too became pregnant and then later, both of us young mothers; we had much in common. The years quickly passed and before long Tshoagong had a brood of four children.

All seemed well but after a number of years the two men's careers took different directions and they went their separate ways. John was promoted and we returned to live in Gaberone whilst Tshoagong left government service to work for the Peace Corps; I think with his large family he was attracted by the high salaries paid by the Americans.

Our families that had been so close of course drifted apart. Some 10 or 15 years had passed and all of Tshoagong's children were attending excellent fee paying schools when quite suddenly, out of the blue, we heard that he had left his wife and family for another woman. Tshoagong simply walked out on his family, cut all ties and disappeared from Pilikwe as suddenly as he had arrived there all those years before. The impact on his wife and eldest son was, in the truest sense of the word, traumatic. Both suffered serious mental breakdowns as a result. Fortunately for her Tshoagong's wife came from a relatively well-to-do family in Mmadinare and in due course she and the children were able to return to the family home to live with and be cared for by her parents. Then, months later, stories began to circulate that Tshoagong had reappeared in far-off Maun where he had obtained a job as a teacher, his old profession. Here he settled and in time had a fine house built for him and his new partner.'

I explained to Tebago that this story was important to me in closing another chapter in my journey of rediscovery, but what had happened to Tshoagong? Was he now dead as had been alluded to me by both Sandy and Patrick?

Tebago continued. 'It is a story with a sad ending. Many years passed and being far off in Maun we heard nothing more of Tshoagong. Then, just a few years ago, stories began to circulate that what Tshoagong had done to his wife had in turn happened to him. Tshoagong's new partner had thrown him out, presumably because of some new infidelity. We of course heard only stories but it seems that he was unable to come to terms with his predicament and he fell apart and soon lost his teaching post. Later, now destitute, he was given work by old friends in the Peace Corps but it was not to last.'

Tebego concluded by saying that she heard that Tshoagong subsequently died, albeit relatively recently, in a state of abject poverty.

It was a fascinating story but no sooner had Tebago reached the sad conclusion John returned to the room and wanted to talk only of weightier matters such as the strength of the British economy and the war in Iraq. There were questions I would have liked to ask about my old buddy and his demise but then is it not in the very nature of an enigma that some of those questions should remain unanswered?

Chapter Twenty-Five

Closing Scenes

For my final weeks in Bechuanaland I was to have a new role based in Gaberones. By now we had registered 20 co-operatives and I was to take responsibility for training the officers, the treasurers and secretaries, and for auditing their books.

Returning from my long trek around Southern Africa on a Saturday, I had to prepare to run my first course on the following Monday. I enjoyed one final night of comfort at the Bottomleys' house before Trevor ferried me together with my possessions to my new home. This accommodation proved to be almost as frugal as that at Radisele. It comprised one room attached to the Bechuanaland Training Centre or BTC, the operational base for my new job. I had become accustomed to slumming. However, these four bleak concrete walls lacked the atmosphere and sense of adventure that I had enjoyed living in a hut in the bush. The BTC, comprising a number of single storey pre-fabricated buildings with corrugated iron roofs, would have provided a feel very much akin to living in an Army barracks but for the fact that I was the only soldier on duty.

The purpose of the centre, now being run by Jon Harlow, was to provide vocational training in the form of short courses, sponsored by the various government departments. In my case I would be primarily running courses in bookkeeping. Just like setting up and running a co-operative, this was to be another new experience. I had just celebrated my 22nd birthday. Apart from those geography lessons at secondary school I had never stood in front of a class, let alone developed and delivered a training course on a technical subject like bookkeeping – another challenge that I undertook without question.

Although living in the capital might on the face of it offer more of a social life, in practice this was to prove a more lonely existence than at Radisele where I had readily accepted and embraced the isolation of the location. Indeed I think I saw the rudimentary nature of my surroundings as something of a badge of honour when comparing the relative comfort enjoyed by my fellow volunteers. Once again my accommodation was sleeping only, so Trevor had given me the facility to eat on account at the restaurant in Gaberones' one and only hotel. Looking back I note that it was at this point in my diary I started counting down the days to my return to England.

The training courses were challenging and rewarding. I was teaching groups of eight to ten students on each course, many of who I knew from setting up co-operatives at Serowe, Matsiloje and Pilikwe, and they were without exception very enthusiastic and willing to learn this totally alien concept called bookkeeping.

However, in contrast to the buzz provided by this educational work, my social life normally comprised dinner for one at the hotel in a restaurant usually deserted save for the odd loud South African businessman complaining about the service. There were the occasional invitations to someone's house. Carmel and Judy, two IVS volunteers, were nurses at the General Hospital and apart from providing the odd meal and welcome company they also performed with some relish the long overdue ceremony of cutting my hair. Then there was Bernard Palmer, a BBC man who had just arrived in Botswana to establish the new national radio station and who gave me my first and only exposure to the airwaves, although the station was so new that I guess the audience figures could be counted on the fingers of two hands.

There were regular opportunities to renew the challenge to best Trevor and Jon Harlow at Scrabble. Those apart, the evenings were long and lonely in my small room, either studying or trying to catch World Service on my radio. It was here on 30 July that, transistor radio held aloft to catch the weak signal, I heard commentary as England defeated West Germany in the World Cup final. With gut wrenching agony as the Germans scored a late equaliser, as a natural pessimist I believed England had squandered their chance of glory. Then elation as England scored not once but twice, in extra time. Sadly there was no one around to hear my joy at the final whistle.

In between running training courses there was one last trip with Tshoagong, ostensibly for me to audit the books of the co-operatives we had established at Matsiloje, Radisele, Pilikwe and Serowe, but it also provided a final chance to recapture the spirit of the times we had spent together as close colleagues.

As my period in Bechuanaland was coming to an end we were working to establish a consumer co-operative in the capital. This was seen as a prestigious project and, like my work on the Bamangwato Livestock Co-operative, funding had been obtained from a British charity to support the scheme, providing enough cash to pay for the services of a professional manager. This was Edgar Parnell, then in his late twenties. He had arrived from the UK together with his new wife, Myra, who, by one of those strange coincidences had grown up in the same area of Colchester as me. Edgar was in a desperate race against time to get the co-op shop in Gaberones open in time for the Independence ceremonies and enlisted my help. The co-op had bought a Chevrolet pick-up truck for the collection and delivery of goods and I was sent down to Johannesburg to obtain some essential fittings for the soon to be opened shop.

I drove across the South African border near Zeerust in what was then the Transvaal and headed east through this parched area where hardy Afrikaaner farmers have eked a living for generations. Gradually the landscape changes as you cross a low range of hills; here it is more scenic, judging by the properties more prosperous, and distinctly greener. With its rich soil this region provides an altogether easier living and has been termed 'the granary of South Africa'. Through here runs the Limpopo or Crocodile River. As I sped across the empty landscape, the road ahead shimmering in the hot noonday sun, I saw in the centre of the road ahead a large object. I slowed as I approached to find two enormous crocodiles basking on the metalled surface of the road. I veered off, giving them as wide a berth as I dared before rejoining the road some 50 yards beyond. I stared long and hard into my rear-view mirror to confirm what I had seen. I was in a state of some shock given that this sighting was totally unexpected but being so close to Crocodile River perhaps I shouldn't have been so surprised.

The road was wide, straight and clear for as far as you could see save for the slight undulations of the rolling hills through which I was travelling. As road conditions across the border in Bechuanaland meant we rarely got a vehicle above 30 mph I decided to give the Chevy a bit of a blast. The speed increased as I gently squeezed the accelerator. Seventy mph – 80, 90, 100. Wow! Then 105, 110, 115. Still my foot wasn't flat down. Finally 120 mph. Suddenly there was an enormous bang. My immediate reaction, demonstrating my lack of driving experience, was to lift my foot off the throttle and hit the brake as hard as I could. The vehicle slewed crazily with me struggling with the steering wheel to keep the vehicle on the tarmacadam surface. Eventually after what seemed an age the truck slowed, enabling me to pull onto the hard shoulder where it eventually ground to a halt. I slumped forward on the steering wheel staring open-eyed at the road ahead, conscious of my heart pumping away in a fashion I had never experienced before. After inhaling a few deep breaths I glanced in the rear-view mirror. Still visible was a plume of dust stretching way back down the road behind me. I gradually emerged from my state of total shock. Then, as I began to take stock of my situation, I looked around absorbing the total nothingness that surrounded me. I was in the middle of absolutely nowhere. I don't think I had seen another vehicle in the previous hour.

Eventually I climbed out of the cab and on jellylike legs went to the front of the Chevy, lifted the bonnet and looked inquisitively inside. Having absolutely no idea of the workings of the internal combustion engine this was no more than a gesture to indicate to other travellers that I was in some difficulty. Looking back down the road I saw between the parallel lines of burnt rubber a trail of oil and even with my limited knowledge of engines I guessed my problem was terminal. As for the chances of an early rescue the prospects were not good.

I had passed through a small town many miles back and given that the next little dorp might or might not be over the brow of the next hill I decided to wait by the Chevy. In the blazing mid-afternoon sun I sought shelter sitting on the shady side of the truck leaning my back against the rear wheel whilst casting my eyes up and down the deserted road. After about an hour I enjoyed some good fortune. In the distance I saw another vehicle approaching, I must admit, at a more sedate speed than I had been travelling at the time of my breakdown. As it approached I could see that it was an old pick-up truck not dissimilar to my Chevy and I moved to the middle of the road to wave down the driver. He pulled over to the roadside in front of the Chevy and by the time I had reached his vehicle he had climbed down onto the road to greet me in heavily accented English. Although inevitably for this region an Afrikaaner-speaking farmer, he must have noted the plates on the Chevy and realised I was from across the border. He took one look at the oil slick I had left down the road, shook his head ruefully and offered me a lift to the next town. I was extremely lucky; he was friendly and affable and instead of the usual diatribe about 'lazy kaffirs' he was interested about the effect of the drought across the border in Bechuanaland. More good fortune, the next town proved to be a relatively short distance, ten miles or so down the road.

When we drew up outside the local garage my rescuer told me to wait in the cab. He climbed down and went across to a very large figure dressed in overalls whose head was buried under the bonnet of a truck parked on the forecourt. The two men entered into an animated conversation. I assumed that they were speaking in Afrikaans so I was content to leave my rescuer to explain my predicament. From a distance I could see that the man who I assumed to be a mechanic was both tall and wide enough to be Springbok rugby forward. He was probably only a few years older than me but twice the size and sported a haircut that would not have looked out of place if he were a conscript in the British Army. After some deliberations the mechanic disappeared, my farmer friend came across signalling for me to get down from the truck and explained that the mechanic, Johannes, would look after me from now on. He bid me goodbye just as Johannes reappeared from somewhere at the rear of the premises at the wheel of a large and noisy heavy-duty recovery vehicle. It looked more than capable of the task; I guessed that in this farming area towing tractors and other farm implements was not that unusual. So with Johannes at the wheel I was taken back down the road to my stricken vehicle. In this case the conversation was rather stilted; Johannes did not speak much and he spoke English even less. However, in due course we reached the Chevy and an hour or so later, duly recovered, the vehicle was in the garage for repair. Despite the difficulty in communicating with Johannes by now one thing was clear: the repairs would take some days to effect. I was stranded in this small Transvaal town called Swartruggens (in English 'Black Ridge' after the low range of hills behind the town).

Unfortunately for me that very week dramatic events were happening in South Africa. Five days earlier Henrik Vervoerd, the prime minister and architect of apartheid, had been assassinated in the parliament building in Cape Town. The whole of South Africa was in shock, not least in this area, the very heartland of Afrikaanerdom. As I sped across the High Veldt without a care in the world his funeral was about to take place, the country was in mourning and I was very much stranded.

Swartruggens is a classic one-horse town in the middle of a predominantly Afrikaaner farming area. It had that frontier feeling and comparison with the American West portrayed in the genre of Western films so popular in the fifties and sixties was such that it could have been the set for any of the classics of the period. So leaving Johannes I walked down the main street, confident that I would soon come across the town hotel. I did but the doors were firmly closed. I peered through the windows but all was still. I made my way to the rear of the building and knocked on the door of what appeared to be the kitchen. Eventually, thanks only to the persistence of my banging, the proprietor emerged to tell me that the hotel was closed because of the funeral. Finally, after much pleading on my part he reluctantly agreed to give me a room for the night on the understanding that he was not able to offer any meals. I checked into the hotel and put in a telephone call to Trevor. Calls were through an operator and she told me that to make a connection could take some time. Tired and hungry I lay on the bed and dozed. I was awoken some time later by the telephone ringing. The room was now in semi-darkness with evening closing in as I lifted the receiver to hear Trevor's friendly tones. Explaining my predicament he of course promised to come to my rescue. By now it was too late for him to contemplate the journey, not least because the border crossing at Zeerust closed at dusk. It would be well into the following day before he would arrive; meantime I was confined to my hotel room.

The town was deserted, the hotel restaurant closed and me its only guest. The room had a radio but that was playing only martial music interspersed with reports on the funeral in Afrikaans. South Africa was still many years from having television. Thoroughly dejected I lay on the bed and thought of England.

Eventually the following afternoon, although it seemed like an eternity, Trevor arrived to take me back to Gaberones. I related my story in full; well ok I omitted reference to driving the Chevy at 120 mph. Interestingly the bit about the crocodiles had him falling about laughing. We were to lose contact with each other after I returned home from Africa but when we renewed our acquaintance some 30-odd years later the first thing he did was to remind me of the croc story. Even now he plainly is not convinced.

About a week later we returned to Swartruggens to recover the now repaired vehicle. Johannes told me in his broken English that he had never in his experience seen anything quite like it; the piston rod had been shot completely through the engine casing. He thought I must have been travelling at some tremendous speed to cause such an effect. I feigned surprise at this shocking news, cast a furtive eye over my shoulder to ensure Trevor was not in hearing distance, paid the bill and hurriedly left.

As a postscript to this story, Edgar eventually got his store opened on time and the Gaberones Consumer Co-operative flourished during the 20 years following Independence establishing various branches around the city. However, as Gaberones grew and the Botswana economy grew the competition from South African supermarket chains intensified. At the end of 2003 the Co-operative was close to liquidation before a takeover by Spar. The malady that seems to have affected co-ops throughout the country was true also here in the capital: competition, poor management, poor audit controls and over-borrowing. The same story I had heard already so many times.

Forty years on. After our journey to the north, Rosie and I have returned to Gaberone and our departure is imminent, although there are still things to do and people to meet. When we arrive back at the hotel Sandy has left a message suggesting that we might like to attend a lecture at the university. A Canadian economist Leith Clark is launching a book *Why Botswana Prospered* and Sandy thought it might be interesting to get another insight on modern day Botswana. We decide to go along, as the university is almost next door to our hotel. We arrive on campus early. It is large and modern and could easily pass for a UK redbrick university. Refreshments are being served in the refectory prior to the lecture and people begin to gather – some students and staff but also some older members of the small but well-established white community, members of the sponsoring Botswana Society.

We spot Sandy and he comes across and exchanges greetings and at my request points out some of the old expats. They include Quill Hermans, economic advisor to the government in the immediate post-Independence period, and an old friend of Trevor's. We fall into conversation with one of this group. I remark that he looks too young and well fed to be one of the old guard left over from the colonial times. It turns out that he is Neil Parsons, professor of history at the university so in a sense I was right. Interestingly though, whilst not a long-time expatriate he first came to Botswana before either Sandy or myself as he was one of the first VSO volunteers back in 1961. Then still a teenager he spent a year teaching at Moeng College. Neil tells us that he subsequently taught in various parts of Africa: Zambia, Swaziland and South Africa, before returning to Botswana some ten years ago. He was interested in my find at the BDA a couple of days ago and only now do I appreciate that it might have some historical significance.

I am introduced to Gideon; he is both journalist and editor of the daily newspaper Mmegi, which means 'Reporter' in Setswana, a rather radical publication as a counterpoint to the government controlled Daily News. He tells me that Pat Van Rensburg established the paper some 20 years ago but it seems apart from the occasional article is no longer actively involved in the editorial content. Sandy is another regular contributor, writing a weekly column on cultural affairs. Gideon seems interested in the purpose of my visit to Botswana and asks if he can come across to our hotel the following day, our last in Botswana, to conduct an interview.

Leith Clark proves to be a sexagenarian Canadian emeritus professor of economics and one-time advisor on economic policy to the Botswana government. I ask him about the book title and he confirms that the significance of his thesis is contained in the word 'prospered', being in the past tense.

We make our way into a large lecture theatre that could be in any university anywhere in the world. By now a reasonably large audience of 100 or so has gathered. Leith's lecture supports his proposition that Botswana's economic heyday is over by challenging the idea of 'diamonds are forever'. More precisely the mineral deposits that have helped transform the Botswana economy are running out. The De Beers mine at Orapa is running out of diamonds and the huge copper mine at Selebi-Pikwe is scheduled to close in 2011. For the first time since the immediate post-Independence years Botswana is contemplating seeking overseas aid. He goes on to argue that although the government has generally invested the income stream from mining sensibly in infrastructure projects, there has been a lack of inward investment; there is a lack of entrepreneurship amongst the Batswana and AIDS is now seriously impacting on labour as a key future resource. The lecture contains little good news but confirms all the conclusions I have reached on this my return visit.

The post lecture Questions and Answers session is enlivened by one of the students. He reminds me of Leapeetswe, a big lad and highly articulate, who accuses Leith Clark as a former advisor to the government of 'pulling his punches' before theatrically storming from the auditorium. Perhaps radical politics have not entirely died here.

Tomorrow we fly to South Africa. We plan to spend a relaxing day playing a few holes of golf at the adjacent Gaberone Golf Club. First I have to meet the Press. Sandy has arranged for the man from the government newspaper, the Daily News, to contact me. He called the previous evening and with my mid-morning appointment with Gideon I invite him over for breakfast.

His name is Kwapeng Modikwe. At the appointed hour he finds us at our breakfast table and introduces himself. He is a small man and, with his hair greying at the temples, obviously appears older than he is, as I soon discover. He says that when I came to Bechuanaland in 1965 he was still at primary school. In his subsequent article he kindly reports that I am looking 'fit and strong and much younger than my years'!! Top man.

Kwapeng has been to England and indeed has travelled widely around the world accompanying both the current president, Festus Mogae, and his predecessor, Quett Masire. He says he is usually an accredited member of the presidential entourage, which has both advantages and disadvantages insofar as you stay in the best hotels and meet interesting and important people but rarely see anything of the countries you visit.

He recalls one occasion when, due to another commitment in Botswana, he had to travel independently the day after the president. Arriving at Heathrow Airport his destination was the Botswana High Commission in central London. Following instructions he had been given he made his way to the London underground station and climbed aboard the first train. The strange station names, the dark tunnels and the people constantly coming and going caused him to become disoriented and confused and after about an hour he decides to alight. He climbs the steps and exits onto the street. He is obviously in a state of some distress and is approached by an elderly lady.

'Can I help you, dear?'

'Where am I?' he asks.

'Mile End,' she replies.

Poor Kwapeng misheard this as 'my land' and understanding the sacrosanct nature of 'lands' in his own country, thought that he had been caught trespassing. He was by now panic stricken.

Realising his anguish, the old lady said, 'Where do you want to go, luv?'

'London,' he innocently replied, not realising that he had been in London throughout his train journey and was now in the East End.

'Yes, but which part.'

'The Botswana High Commission.'

'Where's that?'

Kwapeng rummaged in his bag and from papers he was carrying was able to identify the address in the West End. The old lady hailed a cab, bundled Kwapeng inside and thrust a £20 into his hand whilst giving the cabbie instructions on Kwapeng's destination. Much to his relief he eventually reached the sanctuary of the High Commission where he related the story, only to find himself chastised for not having taken the old lady's name and address.

Kwapeng proved to be a charming man and we much enjoyed his company but as he didn't take any notes during the course of our conversation I had low expectations concerning the depth and accuracy of his article about me. A few days after I returned home a large brown envelope with the Government of Botswana insignia arrived containing a copy of the Daily News. I was to be surprised, it contained a full-page article, well crafted and factually it couldn't be faulted.

One of the lessons I recall being taught in business on the very first management training course on which I was sent as a young man was the dictum 'never make assumptions'. This was a moot point because an hour or so after I had said goodbye to Kwapeng Gideon arrived. A much younger man, seemingly on the ball, he took copious notes yet subsequently produced an altogether less interesting piece with several factual errors.

Our final afternoon. Time to relax with golf in Gaberone. It proves to be an odd experience. The clubhouse is busy and seems to attract a particular type of beer-swilling whites who, from their accents and broad girths, I judge have come from across the border to enjoy not only the golf but the gambling opportunities afforded by the nearby casino. The condition of the course is poor, I am sure due to the absence of watering given supplies in the dam are at an all-time low. We have played golf in many parts of the world and have come across all manner of creatures on courses. Here it is meerkat. I see them as I approach the fourth hole. I thought that I had hit a good shot onto the fourth green but as I approach they stand on their hind legs giving a rather quizzical look now I am not so sure.

My year in Botswana was coming to a close. When they heard my leaving date Carmel and Judy were nonplussed. 'Why don't you stay for another week and see the Independence celebrations?' they implored. I could see their point but for me it was over; whilst there might be 'a bit of a do' it really should be for the locals and not for us colonials. To be honest the final weeks had been something of an anti-climax after living in the bush and it was time for me to go.

On the final day in the office I typed out a report of my year in Africa. My final act completed, Trevor gave a nice little farewell speech in front of the assembled members of the Department. Grace, the rather buxom local girl who had joined the Department of Co-operatives about three months previously had, I suspected, a rather soft spot for me and coyly stepped forward and presented me with a glazed pottery urn which she had made herself. It was a touching moment. Like most volunteers I have met I felt that the host country had given me far more than I had been able to give it. Years of experience crammed into 12 action-filled months.

Next morning I packed my grey suitcase, donned my smart tailored double-breasted suit that had remained in mothballs for the whole of the previous year, and with Trevor acting as chauffeur I headed for the airstrip at Notwane, what now is in the heart of the city, that at the time paraded as Gaberones Airport. Here Trevor took that one and only photograph of me in Africa before I boarded the newly installed daily South African Airways flight to Johannesburg. A rather grander exit than arrival and a sign of the rapid progress this colonial backwater was already taking.

In Jo'burg I checked into a downtown hotel prior to catching the London flight the following morning. I vividly recall opening my suitcase to find the pottery urn so kindly presented to me by young Grace fractured into a thousand small pieces. Packing such a delicate article in a suitcase was of course totally crass but I was mortified; it was the one and only physical memento I had collected to remind me of my year as a volunteer – no gifts, no souvenirs, no photographs. Now I was left with just the memories.

The following morning I headed for the airport and the journey home. Thanks to fog in London I spent an unscheduled night in Rome and therefore arrived back in England on 25 September 1966, exactly a year to the day after my departure. Five days later the Bechuanaland protectorate became the independent Republic of Botswana.

Chapter Twenty-Six

Reflections

I tend not to dwell on the past so life after Bechuanaland moved onwards, and fortunately upwards, at a pace. Despite my delayed arrival by one whole day I was delighted to find a welcoming party of old chums from Colchester when I arrived at Heathrow and despite the weariness a welcome-home party took place that very night.

It was a frantic few days, visiting old colleagues at work and being interviewed by the local Press. And a week after leaving Africa I was back at college, and a new man. At the end of my first year at the Co-operative College, Bob Marshall noted in my report that I was 'reserved and not very vocal. Still young and immature, it is difficult to estimate his capacity'. On my return I discovered that I was something of a minor celebrity, was elected president of the Student Union and became editor of the college magazine. I established myself as a regular in a somewhat talentless college football team and later in the academic year, with my close friend Graham 'Muckle' Fisher, won the College Debating Society trophy. My social life improved immensely and from being very shy I was much involved in the extra-curricular activities of a group of about ten of us known as 'The Clique'. All in all it proved a great and fun year. When graduating at the end of that academic year Bob Marshall reported 'has participated fully in college life, shows considerable maturity and even scepticism'.

Soon life moved on again with a new job in a different part of the co-op and for the next two years I was a favoured guest speaker at weekend schools run by various parts of the Co-operative Movement and enjoyed regular weekend travel to a number of Britain's most obscure seaside resorts.

My experiences in Africa also led to an invitation to the House of Commons to lunch with the minister of the newly created Department for Overseas Development. The minister was Reg Prentice, who went on to have an interesting political career. An old-style Labour politician with impeccable Trade Union credentials and a safe East End seat, he shocked colleagues when he crossed the floor of the House of Commons in 1977 and later when he stood in the 1979 General Election and won Daventry for the Conservatives. His reward was a junior minister role in the first Thatcher government. He was elevated to the peerage in 1991 as Lord Prentice of Daventry and died in 2001.

As a result of that meeting with the minister out of the blue I received an invitation to the Ministry of Overseas Development in London. Bert Youngjohns had been Trevor's boss in Basutoland and was now head of the Co-operative Development section at the Ministry. To my surprise, thanks to the intervention of the minister, supported by positive reports from Trevor on my teaching abilities, he invited me to write a series of training manuals on bookkeeping for co-operatives in developing countries, for which I was paid a princely sum of £200.

One of the other odd events that followed my time in Africa is that having spent many hours behind the wheel of trucks I returned to England the holder of a Bechuanaland driving licence. Still without a pukka British driving licence I booked another driving test but disaster loomed again. After the calamitous pre-Bechuanaland driving test in Loughborough, this time I selected more familiar territory in my home town of Colchester. However my misfortunes with driving tests continued. On the tester's instruction to turn left out of the test centre I turned right. The tester told me to continue but by now I already feared the worst, and my fate was sealed by a three-point turn that took ten manoeuvres. Failed again, so I was still without a British driving licence.

I had been told, although to this day I am not sure whether from a reliable source, that my Bechuanaland licence was valid in the UK for one year after my return. It was information I relied upon when on my return to college I became the proud joint owner, with 'Muckle' Fisher, of a Standard 8, registration No. TLE 944. Purchased for the modest sum of £80 it was an unusual vehicle for its day, having a semi-automatic gearbox. To change gear you pressed a button on the gear lever avoiding the need for a clutch pedal. Frankly given my lack of co-ordination this was an unexpected boon.

All went well with our new purchase until Easter 1967. As Muckle came from far-distant Galashiels on the Scottish Borders I had driven the car home for the holidays. Driving to Clacton along a quiet country road one Saturday evening I drove straight into the back of a stationery Triumph sports car. In a bizarre scenario that followed within seconds police surrounded both cars. The driver of the sports car was escorted away. A policeman came over to my vehicle and I wound down the window. A friendly conversation followed. As is normal practice he took some details and told me that I had 48 hours to report to the local police station with my driving licence. As a parting shot he suggested that I might like to remove the dozen or so car parking tickets that decorated my windscreen as they could be affecting my vision.

The following day I made my way to the police station at Colchester. The duty officer took a cursory look at my Bechuanaland driving licence and bade me farewell. Somehow this didn't seem right. After all, I had driven into the back of another vehicle. At the very least I must be guilty of driving without due care and attention. He assured me that was all and the matter was closed. For days after I scanned the local newspapers for clues to this mysterious chain of events but nothing.

The accident damaged the Standard 8's grille and bonnet and caused me something of a dilemma. In three days' time Muckle and I, together with Willie and Clive, two other students from college, were due to take the car and ourselves on the ferry from Immingham to Malmo in Sweden and from there to Denmark. I penned a postcard to Muckle, this being long before the days of the mobile telephone.

'The car is going well, so well that yesterday evening it went straight into the back of a TR3 without stopping'.

We rendezvoused for our journey despite my concern that the car was in no fit state for a long overseas trip. The others' automotive expertise exceeded mine by some way so I left it to them to inspect the damage. A headlight had been rendered inoperative and the radiator had sprung a leak. However they were confident that with a new bulb and a magic potion you could pour into the radiator, together with the application of brute force, they could fix it. Parts duly purchased, we subsequently spent a large part of our journey across the North Sea below decks and effecting repairs to the damaged vehicle. TLE 944 survived the journey and was to give another six months of sterling service before I eventually sold it to a scrap dealer for a fiver. Muckle was not best pleased at this meagre return on our original outlay.

As I have related in that second year at Stanford Hall I was joined by John from the Co-operative Department in Botswana, and during the spring Tshoagong made a brief surprise visit en route from a course in Wisconsin in the United States. These contacts apart my links with Botswana were effectively severed.

As the years passed that time in Bechuanaland became nothing more than a faded memory as life continued as it does for most of us: career, marriage, fatherhood. Now, towards the end of a working life with more time to contemplate the 'what ifs' and 'maybes' I can review the influence of that year with the benefit of hindsight, and more so now than at the time I still believe that it was both character forming and influential on a successful career in my chosen field, even though it was not to be in accounting nor in the co-operative sector but in human resource management in large private enterprise companies.

Now 40 years on I have a new perspective. Looking at Botswana today it is easy to see that it has made 'progress' as defined from our Western perspective but this is still a 'small' country, not physically of course because it covers a huge land mass, but in terms of population size and global influence. Thanks to the income generated from mineral exports it has been able to acquire many of the trappings of a modern society yet it still exhibits many of the symptoms of under-development. I recently read someone describing Botswana as a 'village society'. I can relate to that description. This creates many paradoxes.

When I left Bechuanaland a few days before Independence, the prospects for the new country of Botswana did not appear at all promising. When I was at school in the fifties the map of the world was covered in huge swathes of pink denoting the British Empire or, as it was to become, the Commonwealth, both old and new. By the mid-sixties de-colonisation was already well advanced. All that were left were the troublesome like Rhodesia and the afterthoughts, territories so small and so remote that we hadn't got around to granting them their freedom. This ragbag comprised a mix of islands in the Caribbean and the Pacific and special cases like Bechuanaland.

Frankly in 1966 the new Botswana didn't have much going for it. It could look forward to more years of drought and living off international aid. It was not strategically important and had a small and poorly educated population of pastoral farmers. No industry, no financial expertise and few reasons why others might be inclined to invest in it. But Independence brought with it an immediate change in the fortunes of this country. In the weeks following Independence for the first time in nearly five years, and very early by local standards, the rains came. Perhaps a portent of better things to come because then they found diamonds and everything really changed. Initially deposits were found at Orapa where mining commenced in 1971, to be followed by the discovery of further significant deposits at Jwaneng where commercial activities started in 1982.

Thanks to diamonds, accounting for some 75% of total exports in the 25 years following Independence, growth in the Botswana economy averaged 7% per annum and outstripped those of Singapore and South Korea. All the statistics for this period relating to economics, health, education and literacy look brilliant but now are the wheels coming off?

They say 'diamonds are forever' but in the case of Botswana this may not be true. The deposits found at Orapa are now depleted to a level at which it is no longer economic to mine them. As we left the country at the Seretse Khama International Airport we spotted the De Beers blimp that had just arrived to help the search for new deposits of this elusive mineral. Without diamonds where will Botswana earn its foreign exchange? Further bad news is that the extensive copper deposits found at Selebi-Pikwe will run out in 2011 leading to closure of the mine there. Unless another miracle happens with the discovery of extensive mineral deposits this leaves Botswana to fall back on cattle and tourism. Both steady rather than huge earners. I read an article in a British newspaper suggesting that Botswana could become Africa's centre for the financial services industry. I suppose it is possible with the inducement of tax breaks but frankly I don't believe that the Batswana people have the skills or the drive found in the so-called Asian 'tiger' economies for this to happen. On the positive side the government is addressing these medium-term economic issues with its Vision 2016 plan that looks forward rather than back. However, despite these proactive responses President Mogae has even spoken the unthinkable and considered asking for overseas financial aid; sadly, for this is Africa, a more likely outcome.

Democracy or one-party state? The Botswana Democratic Party has ruled unchallenged for four decades since Independence. Elections may be free and fair but the BDP controls all organs of the state. Corruption scandals come and go but government nominees understandably hold most of the key jobs. Mogae is due to stand down and during our visit a number of people expressed reservations about his successor, Ian Khama, son of Seretse. His military background and apparently autocratic style are questioned.

Whilst we were in the country a parliamentary by-election was being fiercely fought in the capital. All part of the very small world that is Botswana we discover that the candidate representing the BDP, the governing party, is Elinah's brother, Robert. Elinah obviously has little time for him and describes him to us as 'a gangster'. On TV it is reported that Robert has presented a local primary school with a cooking stove. He is apparently rich but has a dubious reputation given the nature of some of his business deals. He seems a larger than life figure with his own photograph on the T-shirt he is sporting and handing out free at an election rally. I am interested in the outcome of the election and follow progress via the Internet. On polling day Robert suffers a shock and substantial defeat. For him his next priority is to defend himself in court on a rape charge. All of this poses questions. Like how arrogant is the ruling party that puts such a person up as its candidate? Or, given the outcome of the poll perhaps after 40 years in power the BDP is at last losing control. Question: after all this time will the BDP willingly give up power even if they lose an election? These political challenges lie ahead.

Life expectancy in Botswana, one of the strongest and most stable economies in Africa, is a mere 38 years and going down fast. Unbelievably, at the time of the 1991 census, it was 67 and had increased year on year since Independence. The reason is that Botswana has the unenviable record of having the highest incidence of AIDS in the world. The first case was reported there in 1988 and today nearly four out of ten of the population between the ages of 15 and 49 are HIV positive. At least the government there are not in denial and the AIDS message is everywhere. Perhaps the biggest problem is that the people are not dying in the streets. In my meetings with government officials the AIDS issue always comes up. I later learn that it is policy for AIDS to be discussed at every meeting held within government. When we checked into our hotel in Palapye, a small provincial town, there was a cookie jar on the desk. It contained condoms not biscuits. In the bedside drawers in every hotel are free packets of condoms. The message on billboards is 'love not sex'. But AIDS undoubtedly presents new challenges. The population is in steep decline. A generation will be lost.

Religion and medicine are classic examples of the mix between the traditional and the modern. In Serowe a brand new hospital is approaching completion but clearly alternative medicine still exists, and quite openly. In Francistown we came across an advertisement in a local newssheet:

> Dr Lyamba can cure the following diseases –
> > Swollen body and eyes problems
> > Misfortunes (bad luck)
> > To bring back lost lover

Remove misunderstanding in the family
Demand debts
Tuberculosis
Diabetes
Blood pressure
Education
Promotion
Protection of home or car from thieves
Weakness of the body
 Gonorrhoea, Asthma, Syphilis
Confusion in the family

We might describe these as bold claims and one wonders what are 'Doctor' Lyamba's medical qualifications, but presumably he has plenty of takers.

The advertisement concludes 'the blanket of darkness is open for you now'. This is an open example of the old ways in a modern setting but in remote villages it is easy to think that the traditional methods still hold sway.

If the good doctor's remedies should fail, on the same page an advertisement for the Ndulamo Funeral Parlour may offer solace: 'free mortuary – free food'.

Talking of food: some observations. Back in the sixties many people were virtually on the edge of starvation and international agencies were providing food relief by the sack-load usually in the form of maize. The more traditional staples up until this time were the locally grown cereals millet and sorghum. All three are made into a similar form of glutinous porridge by simply adding water. The millet version is known as mabele, sorghum becoming bogobe and maize is transformed into mielie pap or pap. It was interesting that even in large international hotels like the Sun in Gaberone with a huge and varied menu the locals invariably chose to eat a version of this dish usually with seswaa, a beef stew. Pap now seems to be by far the most common of these 'filler' dishes, suggesting that Botswana now no longer even attempts to be self-sufficient in its staple foods despite the efforts of Vernon and others like him over the years. Food certainly does not loom large in the culture, maybe because the people have a history of hunger and often people would arrive in the restaurant after us yet be gone before we had finished our starter course.

It is interesting to observe the legacy the British have left behind in its former colonies. For Botswana, three things spring to mind: driving on the left, English as the official government language and the trifle. Yes I am referring to the dessert made from jelly, fruit, custard and cream. We failed to find a hotel restaurant menu where it didn't feature.

Press and media are classic paradoxes in the Botswana 'village'. They exist but totally lack our own sophistication. We enjoyed the locally produced TV programmes only because they were so amateurish that they looked and sounded like they had been made by a bunch of primary school kids. We heard a story that a few years ago a highly paid TV executive had been hired from the BBC but his plans to professionalise the management structure and programme making at Botswana TV had been resisted; within weeks of his appointment he had been summoned to see the minister in charge of the media and was summarily dismissed. It could be argued that the reason for his quick and abrupt departure was not the usual incompetence but that he was actually too good for Botswana.

Most of the television programmes are cheap imports from the US: soap operas and drama series that have not aired in the UK, presumably because they are too awful even for our multi-channel media. In between, the occasional local programme and the News. This is equally awful – a typical report about some important conference in the capital never contains any on-site reporting and no soundtrack of the speeches, simply a voiceover with the camera scanning the audience, and always showing blank faces. In the studio an item on increased crime featuring an interview with the police chief who says, 'In 2003 there were 45 reported murders in Botswana, and the 2004 figure was 103, an increase of 56%.'!!

On the sports news a piece about netball. Interviewed about an unexpected defeat, the captain of the top team, the Moshupa Lovers, explains, 'Our goal shooter didn't turn up. She's a bitch.'

We watched the local equivalent of 'Strictly Come Dancing'

where contestants compete for a prize of 100 pula, about £10. The performance of one gawky uncoordinated teenager is so bad it looked as though he had literally been dragged off the street, into the studio and placed in front of the camera.

Star turn was always the weatherman. The script remained unchanged day after day. 'Sunshine and temperatures of 33°,' delivered deadpan and expressionless by one of the undead from some horror movie

There is a free press and more than one newspaper although it is always a concern in a democracy where the main news media is run by the government: the radio, television and the main newspaper, the Daily News. Newspapers like television have a naivety in style that readily juxtaposes boredom and hilarity. I offer recent headlines as evidence: 'Kgosi (a chief) to continue canning women' – in fairness an interesting enough story for Western eyes even without the typographical error.

'Overcrowding leads to sodomy' and 'Thirst forces residents to buy water', both amusing in themselves yet containing underlying storylines that tell us something about this society and its current stage of development.

It was my modicum of expertise in co-operatives that took me to Africa in the first place so I shouldn't close without some reflection on where they stand in modern day Botswana. Any emotional attachment to the co-operative ideals has long since passed for me. My career as it happens took me in a different direction and although I still believe in the fundamental principles underlying co-operatives I carved out a career for myself in capitalist companies driven by the profit motive. As a personnel manager I spent 30 years handling difficult people decisions or the aftermath of other people having made these decisions and twice was on the wrong end of such decisions finding myself redundant. One consequence of working for so long in people management is to know that it is not soft and fluffy as many think. It leaves you quite dispassionate about making decisions that are right for the business but highly charged emotional 'life changing' events for those on the wrong end of such decisions.

So when I look at the Botswana co-ops today I think I can be equally unemotional. Clearly the foundation was not solid enough. Maybe if Trevor had stayed longer, who knows? In any event interfering politicians and the moral laxity of the members have screwed them up. Is there anything enduring or indeed worth saving?

There is certainly a need for leadership and commitment. Violet kindly made the current strategy document for the Department of Co-operatives available to me. This at least frankly addresses past poor performance in the co-operative sector blaming weak management in the co-operatives, lack of support by co-operative members, inadequate financial resources and deficient outdated legislation under which co-operatives operate. Disappointing is the absence of questioning the contribution made by the government itself in the guise of the Department of Co-operatives, a bit of naval gazing might be appropriate.

As to my solutions. A return to the basic principles. The strength of the co-operative idea is an adherence to collectivism, not apparent in the Botswana co-ops today. I personally have always felt this a reason for the decline in the co-ops in the UK. How many shoppers at the Co-op shop know that they own the business? This actually goes back to a historical misfortune. The Rochdale pioneers made themselves shopkeepers when they should have become producers, in old-fashioned Marxist terms owners of the means of production.

Pursuing this argument the co-ops in Botswana should forget about being shopkeepers. The South African supermarket chains can snuff them out as they please as serious competition. How about the marketing co-ops we envisaged all those years ago? Well frankly the justification still seems valid but the expertise may still be lacking. Perhaps the closest things to a first level business and something that will benefit the country are the newer savings co-ops. An old idea but in a new form. The principle of saving is critical in any economy particularly one moving from a rural to a primarily urban economy. Maybe just a glimmer of hope to justify a government department of 200 people supporting what at the moment is a small and frankly unsuccessful part of the economy. Good luck to Violet and her colleagues.

Was it worth breaking that habit of a lifetime and going back?

Well 40 years on, leaving Botswana again: no regrets. I didn't go with any preconceptions. I didn't expect to find that our foundation work had led to some massive economic miracle. Africa is still Africa. I don't think the psychological make-up of the people will ever make it a boom area of the world. At a personal level it was great to share some things from my past with Rosie – to return to the Makgadikgadi and then finding my old rondavel still standing there in the middle of the bush. And hey, thanks to Pat and to John and to Sandy. Great to see you all again. And to Violet and the people in the co-ops – good luck with your endeavours, I still believe. And last but not least thanks Rosie. Sorry it was so tough for you and that I didn't realise how stressful until we were safely back in England.

Sad person that I am, I have found tucked away in a drawer at home a copy of my report, assiduously typed out in 1966 on my last day in the old Bechuanaland. Forty years on my feelings expressed then about that year are undiminished: 'I would like to say at this time that never once in the past year have I regretted my decision to volunteer. During this period I have gained a wealth of experience that I am sure will benefit me in my career, but also, and I feel this very deeply, it has given me new insight to what Africa is all about. I have lived and worked amongst the people of a country moving towards Independence; I have seen the last vestiges of colonialism; I have seen at first hand the system of apartheid in South Africa; and I have had the opportunity to briefly visit some of the newly independent countries of Africa. I return home with a host of memories and experiences and in return hope that I have provided useful service to the people of Botswana.'